Crime Online

Crime Online

Edited by

Yvonne Jewkes

WILLAN
PUBLISHING

Published by

Willan Publishing
Culmcott House
Mill Street, Uffculme
Cullompton, Devon
EX15 3AT, UK
Tel: +44(0)1884 840337
Fax: +44(0)1884 840251
e-mail: info@willanpublishing.co.uk
Website: www.willanpublishing.co.uk

Published simultaneously in the USA and Canada by

Willan Publishing
c/o ISBS, 920 NE 58th Ave, Suite 300,
Portland, Oregon 97213-3786, USA
Tel: +001(0)503 287 3093
Fax: +001(0)503 280 8832
Website: www.isbs.com

First published 2007

Hardback
ISBN 13: 978-1-84392-198-1
ISBN 10: 1-84392-198-7

Paperback
ISBN 13: 978-1-84392-197-4
ISBN 10: 1-84392-197-9

Brtish Library Cataloguing-in-Publication Data

A catalogue record for this book is available from the British Library

Project managed by Deer Park Productions, Tavistock, Devon
Typeset by TW Typesetting, Plymouth, Devon
Printed and bound by TJ International Ltd, Trecerus Industrial Estate, Padstow, Cornwall

Contents

Notes on contributors

Carol Andrews is Research Assistant at the University of Sheffield working on a Cyberprofiling project. She has previously worked as an Analyst with the Department of Internal Affairs in New Zealand profiling convicted censorship offenders. Her publications include 'Policing the Filth: The Problems of Investigating Online Child Pornography in England and Wales' in *Policing and Society* (2005) with Yvonne Jewkes, and 'Internet Traders of Child Pornography and Other Censorship Offenders in New Zealand' published by DIA in 2004.

Susan W. Brenner is NCR Distinguished Professor of Law and Technology at the University of Dayton School of Law. She has spoken at numerous events, including Interpol's Fourth and Fifth International Conferences on Cybercrimes, the Middle East IT Security Conference and the Yale Law School Conference on Cybercrime. She has published many articles and book chapters dealing with cybercrime, such as 'Cybercrime Metrics', *University of Virginia Journal of Law and Technology* (2004) and 'Toward a Criminal Law for Cyberspace: Distributed Security', *Boston University Journal of Science and Technology Law* (2004).

Rinella Cere lectures in Media and Cultural Studies at Sheffield Hallam University. She is author of articles on Italian media culture, on media representations of women, and more recently on gender and the Internet. She was one of the contributors to *Dot.cons* edited by Y. Jewkes (2003, Willan) with a chapter on 'Digital Counter-cultures and the Nature of Electronic and Social Movements'. Recent publications include a chapter on the Internet and gendered poverty: 'Bank Online for the Poor: The Internet, NGOs and Gendered Poverty', in *The Ideology of the Internet: Concepts, Policies, Uses* edited by K. Sarikakis and D. K. Thussu (2006, Hampton Press).

Stefan Fafinski is currently conducting research into the criminalisation of computer misuse at the University of Leeds. He is a Chartered Fellow of the British Computer Society and a Freeman of the Worshipful Company of Information Technologists. He recently won the BA 2006 Joseph Lister

Award for his lecture 'Computer Says No: the Social Aspects of Computer Misuse'. He is the co-author of *Identity Theft* with Emily Finch (forthcoming, Willan) as well as a regular contributor to Reading FC's premier shoddy fanzine *The Whiff*.

Emily Finch is a part-time Lecturer in Law at Brunel, Middlesex and the Open University. She has conducted research into the criminogenic potential of the Internet and other new technology and has published widely on this topic, including a chapter – 'What a Tangled Web We Weave: Identity Theft and the Internet' – in *Dot.cons* edited by Y. Jewkes (2003, Willan). Her work on identity theft was the subject of the Joseph Lister Award Lecture at the British Association Festival of Science in Dublin in 2005 and she is the co-author of *Identity Theft* with Stefan Fafinski (forthcoming, Willan)

Katja Franko Aas is Senior Researcher at the Institute of Criminology and Sociology of Law, University of Oslo. She has written extensively on the use of information and communication technologies in contemporary penal systems, including *Sentencing in the Age of Information: from Faust to Macintosh* (2005, Cavendish/Glasshouse Press). She is currently working on a project on ICTs and border controls and completing a book entitled *Globalization and Crime* (forthcoming, Sage).

Yvonne Jewkes is Reader in Criminology at the Open University. She has published several articles and chapters on the problems of policing cybercrime, as well as more generally about the relationship between new technologies, crime and deviance. Her books include *Dot.cons: Crime, Deviance and Identity on the Internet* (2003, Willan) and *Media and Crime* (2004, Sage). She is also Editor of *Crime, Media, Culture: An International Journal*.

Robert Moore is an instructor of Criminal Justice at Delta State University in Cleveland, Mississippi, USA. He has published several articles and chapters dealing with the interaction between crime and technology. His books include *Cybercrime: Investigating High-Technology Computer Crime* (2006, Anderson) and *Search and Seizure of Digital Evidence* (2005, LFB Scholarly). He is also a certified law enforcement officer who assists in the investigation of computer-assisted crime.

Russell G. Smith is Principal Criminologist at the Australian Institute of Criminology where he heads the Global, Economic and Electronic Crime Program. He has carried out research and published extensively on aspects of computer crime, fraud control, and professional regulation. His latest book *Cyber Criminals on Trial* (2004, Cambridge University Press), jointly authored with Peter Grabosky and Gregor Urbas, was awarded the

Distinguished Book Award of the American Society of Criminology's Division of International Criminology in 2005.

Maggie Wykes is Senior Lecturer in the Law School, University of Sheffield. She teaches in the areas of criminological theory, gender and Internet crime and her research focuses on issues of representation, identity, criminalisation and power. Her book publications include *News, Crime and Culture* (2001, Pluto Press) and, with Barry Gunter, *The Media and the Body* (2005, Sage).

Majid Yar is Senior Lecturer in Criminology at Keele University. He has published a number of journal articles dealing with cybercrime issues such as computer hacking and media piracy, as well as broader theoretical issues around online offending. He is the author of *Cybercrime and Society* (2006, Sage).

Chapter 1

'Killed by the Internet': cyber homicides, cyber suicides and cyber sex crimes

Yvonne Jewkes

Introduction

In recent years a number of high-profile, salaciously reported Internet offences have come to public attention, leading to calls for greater self-regulation, tougher legislation and even censorship. Anxiety about the power of the Internet to influence dangerous or vulnerable users reached an apotheosis in early 2004. The headline 'Killed by the Internet' appeared in the *Daily Mirror*, a British tabloid, on 5 February 2004. There were a number of stories in circulation at the time that this blunt and sensational headline could have referred to. Less than a week earlier, a self-confessed cannibal who killed, cooked and ate a man he had met over the Internet was sentenced to eight and a half years in prison by a German court. The relatively lenient sentence was imposed because he was found guilty, not of homicide, but of the less serious crime of manslaughter, following evidence that the victim had given his consent to being killed and eaten. According to a newspaper report, the offender's willingness to cooperate with the police had 'helped shed light on the murky world of online cannibals' estimated to number in excess of 800 participants (*Guardian*, 30 January 2004).

Another story that might have been headlined 'Killed by the Internet' reported in the British press during the first week of February 2004 was the Amnesty International report that revealed that the Chinese government was becoming increasingly heavy-handed with people using the Internet to circulate anti-government beliefs. In China all Internet Service

Providers (ISPs) have to register with the police and all Internet users must sign a declaration that they will not visit forbidden sites (among those routinely blocked are news, health and education sites, although pornography sites are virtually unregulated). The Amnesty report noted that 54 individuals had been arrested, largely either for organising online political petitions or for criticising the government for policies which, it was claimed, were contributing to the spread of AIDS and SARS. Arrestees faced sentences of up to 12 years, but Amnesty reported incidents of torture and even deaths in detention (http://web.amnesty. org/web/content.nsf/pages/gbr_china_internet; cf. *Guardian*, 7 February 2004: 'China tightens net around online dissenters').

A third possible contender for the headline 'Killed by the Internet' is a story that has emerged intermittently over the last three years. According to reports, there are dozens of 'suicide sites' which are said to be responsible for the self-inflicted deaths of hundreds of people each year. A report in the *British Medical Journal* notes that some of the suicide websites are highly graphic, with copies of suicide notes, death certificates and colour photographs. There are also electronic bulletin boards, where suicide notes or suicidal intentions are posted, and one site alone has 900 postings a month, mostly from people considering suicide (http:// bmj.bmjjournals.com). In Japan, 55 people reportedly took their own lives in 2004 after visiting suicide websites, and 91 people did so in 2005 (*Independent*, 10 February 2006). Many die in groups, often by carbon monoxide poisoning in sealed vehicles at secluded or scenic places, having met each other only hours before following initial contact via the Net. However, police in Japan have also investigated Internet sites that supply cyanide capsules to customers who – to use the phrase from the site – 'do not know how to obtain the right drug' (http://news.bbc.co.uk). Most of the individuals involved are in their teens, twenties or early thirties and many are drawn from the *hikkikomori* – social recluses who lock themselves in their rooms with just television and their computers for company, sometimes for years on end. While the *hikkikomori* is a phenomenon that appears to be unique to Japanese society, the use of Internet suicide sites to meet, share stories and impart advice on how to die is not confined to that country, and cases have been reported in the US, UK, Australia, Sweden, Germany, South Korea and Hong Kong, among others. One of the most infamous cases occurred in January 2003 when the naked body of a young American man, Brandon Russell, was found lying on his bed by his mother. The 21-year-old had died after taking marijuana and prescription drugs with alcohol. Disturbingly, he had taken the drugs, lapsed into a coma, and died while being watched by twelve 'friends' who he had met in a 'suicide chat room' and who observed and encouraged his actions via a live webcam feed over the Internet. Brandon Russell's last words, typed to the twelve witnesses to his death, were 'Told u I was hardcore' (*Telegraph*, 9 February 2003).

Thankfully, 'Killed by the Internet' did not refer to the use of Internet chat sites by a paedophile to groom children as a precursor to real-life abuse, abduction and murder, though a case that unfolded at the same time as this headline appeared was that of the trial of a 31-year-old American man, found after a high-profile police hunt for a twelve-year-old British girl whom he abducted after meeting her in an chat room. Following the child's safe return home it was reported that police in Toby Studabaker's home town found downloaded child pornography on his computer, and discovered that he had a previous criminal record for unlawful sexual conduct in the United States. In court, the prosecution detailed how the ex-marine had 'groomed' the child over a period of eleven months, during which their exchanges had developed into cyber-sex. He pleaded guilty at Manchester Crown Court to abduction and incitement of a child to commit an act of gross indecency. Further charges against him included transporting a child across international borders for the purpose of sexually exploiting her and using the Internet to entice a child to engage in criminal sexual activity (*Manchester News*, 13 February 2004).

Three months after 'Killed by the Internet' dominated the front page of the *Mirror* another disturbing case emerged in Manchester. Reported by the *Manchester News* under the headline 'Boy Planned Own Murder on Internet', the bizarre story unfolded of a 'gifted' schoolboy who 'brain-washed and groomed' an older boy he had met online (*Manchester News*, 28 May 2004). The 14-year-old instigator, 'John', created a series of fictional characters in chat rooms, one of which – a female spy called Mary – ordered his 15-year-old friend, 'Mark', to murder him. After exchanging 56,000 lines of email, they met up in June 2003 and travelled to the Trafford Centre in Manchester, where they bought a knife. The following day, they met again and Mark stabbed John twice in the chest and stomach, an assault that he survived. Mark admitted attempted murder and was served with a two-year supervision order and ordered to have no further contact with his friend; John admitted incitement to murder and perverting the course of justice and received a three-year supervision order. He was also banned from using the Internet unless accompanied by an adult. Although an offence such as this would normally carry a custodial sentence, the trial judge noted that these could not be described as 'normal circumstances' and that 'skilled writers of fiction would struggle to conjure up a plot such as that which arises here' (http://bbc.co.uk/news). Depicted as being from 'respectable homes' and doing well at school, the detective investigating the case is reported as saying, 'Neither . . . boy are geeky computer nerds living solitary lives. They are both perfectly normal children. No single event has ever more clearly shown the dangers of the Internet' (*Manchester News*, 28 May 2004).

Although any of the above stories arguably could have appeared under the grisly headline 'Killed by the Internet', in fact it was used in reference to the homicide of music teacher, Jane Longhurst, who was sexually assaulted and murdered by an acquaintance who reportedly used images downloaded from the Internet to fuel his deviant sexual desires. Graham Coutts was a frequent visitor to Internet sites which featured graphic images and accounts of necrophilia and death by asphyxiation. Having killed his victim at his home in Hove, East Sussex, Coutts hired a storage unit where he kept and visited the corpse every few days until, nearly a month later he removed and set fire to it. After he had disposed of the corpse in this way, he continued to visit sites with names such as 'Necrobabes' and 'Violent pleasure', according to detectives who examined his computer hard drive. Although these sites contravene the Obscene Publications Act of 1959, the UK authorities have no powers to close them down because they are hosted by service providers in other countries. Coutts was sentenced to mandatory life imprisonment with a tariff set at 30 years.

In the first decade of a new millennium these seven cases provide a snapshot of Internet-related crimes that have resulted in the abduction, torture or death of individuals in countries around the world. Of course, there is nothing inherently sinister in the technology itself. Most cybercrimes are reasonably common offences; computer technologies have simply provided a new means to commit 'old' crimes, and it is clearly not the case that if the Internet did not exist, neither would violent and sexual crimes. What makes the role of the Internet unique in these cases, and mitigates against the argument that criminal and anti-social activities on the Internet are analogous to similar behaviour in the physical world, is its scale and reach. As John Naughton (1999) points out, it took the World Wide Web just three years to reach its first 50 million users; a feat which eluded television for 15 years and which took radio 37 years to achieve from its point of inception. A mere decade after it became a domestic, as opposed to military, technology, the number of Internet users was estimated at around 1 billion and, in the UK, a recent study found that Internet use has overtaken television as the chief non-work activity (apart from sleeping), with the average user spending around 164 minutes online every day compared with 148 minutes watching television. While these figures are disputable (the survey was conducted on behalf of the Internet search engine, Google), there is no doubt that we are witnessing a rapidly growing trend towards the broad adoption of the Internet thanks not only to changing leisure patterns and an increase in high-speed broadband connections at home, but also to increased business connectivity which allows office workers to surf the web all day (*Guardian*, 8 March 2006).

In addition to this inexorable growth in numbers of people regularly using it, if we consider the anonymity afforded by the Net, the sensation of many cybercrimes being 'underground' activities carried out in 'clubby' atmospheres in the company of like-minded individuals, and the lower risk of detection that accompanies most cybercrimes, it is little wonder that the Internet has become a scapegoat for a series of local and global moral panics. As an editorial in the *Guardian* (6 February 2004) commented: 'for all it gives us, the Internet, it seems, cannot escape being portrayed as a terrible curse as much as a blessing'.

Of course, a link between Internet content and violent crime is difficult, if not impossible, to prove and the most that can be said with any degree of certainty is that individuals who might otherwise have been predisposed to commit suicide, murder or abduction might be drawn to the Internet to facilitate their desires, particularly if their behaviour receives support from communities of other people who are sympathetic to their thoughts, values and behaviour. Like wider debates about the effects of harmful media content, much mediated public discourse about computer-related crime is underpinned by a strong technological determinism (that is, overstating the power of the Internet and underplaying the importance of the individual actor). Where the human element *is* central to a story, it tends to be dominated by positivist notions of vulnerable offenders (frequently characterised – as the police detective in the case outlined above put it – as 'geeky computer nerds living solitary lives').

Furthermore, much of the debate about Internet regulation and censorship appears to be based on speculative notions of the anti-social and harmful impacts it may have at some point in the future. Such predictions of apocalyptic meltdown include terrorist acts intended to sabotage water, gas and electricity supplies, close all international communications, manipulate air traffic control or military systems, hack into a hospital's computer system and alter details of medical conditions and treatments, tamper with National Insurance numbers or tax codes, and paralyse financial systems. However, most commentators believe that while these kinds of possibilities are terrifying to contemplate, the likelihood of such calamitous events occurring through human or software error is far greater than the chance of malicious hackers, mercenaries or terrorists bringing down a country's infrastructure (Hamelink, 2000) and, for the time being at least, they remain hypothetical possibilities rather than perpetrated acts of aggression (Jewkes, 2003).

The book

The dual nature of the Net – its capacity to pervert and to democratise – underpinned many of the chapters in the predecessor to this volume, *Dot.cons: Crime, Deviance and Identity on the Internet* (Jewkes, 2003). *Crime Online* takes up this theme, demonstrating that, despite the Internet offering its users freedom, democracy and communication with people around the world, anxieties concerning its potential to corrupt or facilitate heinous crimes persist in the popular imagination. However, where one of the primary focuses of *Dot.cons* is gender, sexuality and notions of sexual deviance, *Crime Online* represents a more concerted attempt to explore different constructions and manifestations of cybercrime and diverse responses to its regulation. Since the publication of *Dot.cons*, cybercrime has burgeoned into an established sub-field of criminology, and this second volume brings together some of the most renowned international scholars writing about cybercrime today.

In Chapter 2, Susan W. Brenner urges us to examine how we control the incidence of cybercrime. Historically, societies have responded to the transgression of rules and norms by creating laws to proscribe certain types of conduct 'crimes' and by employing specialists to enforce those laws by apprehending violators, who are then officially sanctioned. However, as Brenner points out, this model of reactive, police-based crime control cannot protect society from criminals who use computer technologies because cybercrime does not conform to the assumptions that structured this model. For one thing, cybercrime is transnational, which makes it difficult, if not impossible, for local law enforcement to react effectively to cybercrime. For another, cyberspace lets criminals assume impenetrable anonymity and pseudonymity, which further complicates the law enforcement process. The chapter thus proposes what some might view as a controversial new model of 'distributed security' that would supplement the reactive model (which we will still need for real-world crime) and allow us to deal more effectively with cybercrime. The new model holds users of cyberspace legally responsible for taking reasonable measures to protect themselves and others who might be affected harmfully by their actions (or inactions), and holds the software industry liable if they take inadequate measures to ensure their products' reliability and security. The combination of self-policing on the part of users and voluntary compliance to new industry regulations by the 'architects' of cyberspace enforced by means of criminal sanctions (primarily fines) is, according to Brenner, the way forward if we are all to be protected from becoming victims of cybercrime.

While the notion of Internet users taking responsibility for their own protection against victimisation might appear a radical suggestion, it is a theme that runs through many of the chapters in *Crime Online*, and is certainly endorsed by Emily Finch in Chapter 3. She introduces us to two similar and much-publicised cybercrimes of recent times – identity fraud and identity theft – and explains what 'identity' is and what it means for it to be stolen. In the news media, reports regularly appear of credit card numbers and other personal information being taken from the Internet and used fraudulently. Less common but equally newsworthy are cases of individuals who adopt another (often deceased) person's identity wholesale, several examples of whom are mentioned in the chapter. Hijacking of others' identities has been facilitated by developments in information and communications technologies which enable the cheap and easy creation or manipulation of false documents such as passports, birth certificates and drivers' licences. In particular, the burgeoning ubiquity of the Internet has facilitated an unprecedented ease of access to personal information and – given the intimacy and anonymity that may characterise online relationships – has offered false promises of trust, security, invulnerability, etc. Finch discusses these shifts in social interaction, and argues that attempts to counteract identity theft which focus exclusively on the fixity of physical identity are addressing only a partial manifestation of the problem and inevitably will result in an incomplete and imperfect solution.

In Chapter 4, Russell G. Smith picks up this theme and offers an analysis of some of the solutions being developed to the problems of identity fraud and identity theft described by Finch in the previous chapter. In an attempt to combat the problem of stolen identity, Smith notes that there has been a move away from knowledge-based systems and tokens towards using biometric technologies to identify people. Biometrics appears cutting edge (there is a suggestion of James Bond-style futurism about technologies such as iris recognition), and despite the significant costs involved, these technologies are attractive to governments and political parties who electioneer on issues such as illegal immigration and terrorism. Smith's chapter examines the many considerations that arise in deciding whether or not to use biometrics for logical access control. His conclusions support the views of Finch; that is, that although biometrics will reduce some of the risks associated with fraud in cyberspace, it will not solve the fundamental issue of determining whether an individual is who they claim to be.

While the call for a greater awareness of our own role and potential complicity in cybercrime is a laudable goal, there is possibly a danger that, in protecting ourselves and our own computers, we turn a blind eye to the bigger picture of Internet-facilitated, transnational, organised crime, including the growing industries in trafficking, violation and exploitation of vulnerable people. In Chapter 5, Yvonne Jewkes and Carol Andrews examine the problem of abusive images of children being bought, sold or simply circulated around the world via the Internet. Drawing on research primarily from the UK and New Zealand (where Andrews was until recently employed at the Censorship Compliance Unit in the New Zealand government's Department of Internal Affairs), but also from Australia, Canada and the United States, they discuss the nature and content of 'child pornography' and the characteristics of offenders who download offensive material. Their analysis of content and users is set in a cultural context; they question the frequently made assertion that media reporting of those who download abusive images of children (and, indeed, child abusers generally) constitutes the moral panic of our age, given the ways in which the mainstream media and associated cultural industries fetishise youth and youthful bodies. Such cultural hypocrisy is symptomatic of a mediatised society that perpetuates notions of 'otherness' and demonises a handful of known paedophiles, while at the same time turning a blind eye to the fact that 80 per cent of child abuse occurs within the home. It might be argued, however, that the Internet has propelled the problem of sexual exploitation of children into the open and made public a crime that was previously confined to a privatised and exclusive environment. In theory, this might suggest that policing child sexual abuse has become a more straightforward endeavour, and Jewkes and Andrews discuss the role of the police in terms of both the progress that has been made in recent years and the obstacles that law enforcers still face in their battle to combat the trade in abusive images of children and in securing convictions in this area.

One of the difficulties faced by the police and other law enforcement agents is that technology moves so quickly and they seem to be playing an endless game of 'catch-up' with a computer literate criminal elite who always seems to manage to stay one step ahead. In Chapter 6 Robert Moore provides an introductory overview of computer forensics, describing what is meant by the term and how computers store data. He offers a detailed analysis which is admirably free of baffling technological jargon, and goes on to discuss the techniques investigators and law enforcers use to recover incriminating evidence from computers and the processes they have to go through in order to bring a case to trial. His analysis concludes with a discussion of the future of computer forensics investigations, in which he highlights similar problems to those discussed in the previous chapter in relation to policing child pornography, namely, recruiting, training and adequately resourcing police officers and investigators to conduct work that is often both tedious and undervalued.

The focus of the next four chapters is the extent to which new crime problems are being socially constructed in the era of the Internet. Chapter 7 by Majid Yar explores the development of 'piracy' as a contested crime problem, tracing in particular the ways in which corporate moral entrepreneurship has attempted to create a new normative consensus around cultural copying, and the ways in which this labelling process has been received and contested by those identified as 'pirates'. Yar notes that, since the development of Napster and other Internet file-sharing services, online sharing and downloading of music, film and computer software has become one of the most hotly debated forms of online crime. The copyright industries have targeted file-sharers – more often than not young people – branding them 'criminals' and 'thieves'. Advocates of cultural copying and 'borrowing' have responded by claiming that they are being unjustly criminalised, and that the real villains are not music fans but the music industries who exploit artists in the pursuit of profit.

In Chapter 8, Stefan Fafinski explores the persistent moral panics that have been whipped up throughout history around football violence. One of the most recent manifestations of media hysteria, according to Fafinski, concerns the use of the Net to mobilise football 'firms' and to orchestrate organised hooliganism. While it is not particularly surprising that the Internet (like mobile phones) is used as a primary means of communication by individuals planning disorder (it has also been used by coordinators of riots against the police in numerous towns and cities, including the violent disturbances on the streets of Paris in 2005, and has similarly been deployed by both fox hunters and hunt saboteurs in the UK), nonetheless, the importance of the Internet may have been greatly exaggerated by the popular press. Like all news stories, the perennial tales of anticipated football hooliganism that arise before, and during, every major soccer tournament rely on an element of novelty to breathe new life into them. The growth of the Internet has provided precisely that – a new angle on an old story. However, like much popular press coverage of new media, the red-top newspapers invariably fall back on technological determinism, 'blaming' the Internet for mobilising like-minded thugs and displacing violence from the CCTV-protected stadia to the streets outside the grounds. Meanwhile, as Fafinski demonstrates, the Internet has actually played a relatively minor part in football violence over the last decade – except in encouraging hate email to be sent to referees whose decisions on the pitch incite the ire of hooligans and 'ordinary' fans alike.

Yar's comments on the culpability of major media industries (at least as it is perceived by some music fans) and Fafinski's discussion of the role played by traditional media in 'creating' a social problem and scapegoating cybertechnologies are echoed in Chapter 9 where Maggie Wykes discusses the emergence of cyberstalking and the role of cyberspace in real-life stalking. She traces the processes by which stalking went from deviant behaviour or social harm to illegal act, and argues that the impetus for the criminalisation of stalking (both real and cyber) came from celebrities and from the beauty, fashion and media industries they support. Like other criminalised activities (Wykes briefly discusses 'mugging' and 'grooming'), stalking is regarded as an offence that the USA has exported to the rest of the world and one that has relied on sustained attention from traditional media to be brought to the public's attention. But also like those offences, media coverage has skewed the picture, in this case by overlooking or ignoring the mundane reality of crimes of harassment, including the everyday harassment experienced by many women in all spheres of life. At the same time, popular media routinely report cases of celebrity victims and their costly recourses to the law giving the impression that it is the young, wealthy and beautiful who are the most likely victims of cyberstalking. Wykes also links the emergence of stalking to the growing prominence of victimology in academic, political and popular discourses which, among other things, gives credence (frequently upheld in law) to celebrities' claims of feeling 'violated' when stalked by paparazzi and photographed in unflattering poses or career-damaging situations. Such actions not only threaten to spoil and devalue their most precious commodity, but also undermine the carefully managed images they post on their own websites.

Like Fafinski, Rinella Cere also looks at the use and role of the Internet in enabling individuals to orchestrate group violence, but in Chapter 10 the focus is on the 2005 riots in Paris, the ongoing conflict in Palestine and the wave of Islamophobia that has intensified in the western world since 11 September 2001. Cere's contribution is, in many ways, a development of her earlier chapter in *Dot.cons*. There, she also discussed the role of the Internet in circulating information and gathering support for radical politics and alternative social movements. However, her theme was gender and the means that information and communications technologies afford women in their political struggles against neo-liberal economic forces and structural inequalities. In *Crime Online* she applies a similar analysis in a different context, and her conclusions echo those of Stefan Fafinski and Maggie Wykes in earlier chapters and pre-empt the views of Katja Franko Aas in the following chapter, namely that technological determinism underpins much discussion of new media, especially, and somewhat ironically, in the 'old', traditional media, a tendency that leads to the criminalisation of some (sometimes quite benign) online activity and makes spurious links between online 'incitement' and 'real-life' disorder.

Finally, Chapter 11 by Katja Franko Aas explores the dynamics between offline and online aspects of governance, and discusses the dichotomy between popular perceptions of the Internet as a bastion of freedom and unregulability and the increasing importance of various kinds of regulation of the Net to thwart cybercriminals. In a sophisticated analysis that draws on the work of (among others) Baudrillard, Žižek and Lessig, Aas explores the 'real' impact that virtual harms and simulations have, and the increasing centrality of the Internet in all discursive and practical aspects of crime and punishment. Given the inextricable interweaving of offline and online crime and governance of crime, Aas also criticises academic criminology for its neglect of the cyber realm, noting that the subject tends to be consigned to specialist publications dedicated solely to the topic. Perhaps this is not surprising given the inadequate, and frequently non-existent legislation covering the virtual realm, as mentioned in earlier chapters: 'if the law fails to address cybercrime, why should criminologists?' might be an anticipated response among our academic colleagues. While *Crime Online* is arguably guilty of perpetuating the ghettoisation of cybercrime, it is – like its companion volume *Dot.cons* – intended to be read by those who are less interested in 'techy' jargon and legal statutes, and more interested in new social behaviours and the evolution of crime. As Aas observes, in a post 9/11 world, information and communication technologies have become a primary locus for the construction of 'Others' and have given new impetus to contemporary strategies of social exclusion. While *Crime Online* is undeniably a book about the virtual realm, there will be few (if any) people reading this who do not inhabit 'cyber selves' as well as terrestrial identities, and we therefore ignore cybercrime and cyber governance at our peril.

It is our hope, then, that *Crime Online* succeeds in being one of the 'meeting points between terrestrial criminology and the Internet galaxy' (Aas, this volume: 161). And while Aas is right to point out the absence of online crime from some of the major textbooks that shape criminological teaching, especially (though not exclusively) in the UK, it is noticeable that many new student-orientated introductory texts in criminology, policing, penology, etc., *are* starting to include contributions on cybercrime, and that articles on the subject are appearing with much greater frequency in mainstream criminology journals. In addition, recently published books that are dedicated to cybercrime and written in an accessible, jargon-free style (many of which, I might add, are authored by the contributors to this volume) are not only taking criminological knowledge into new realms of global significance, but are reminding criminologists that traditional distinctions between the virtual and the 'real', bounded and boundary-less, local and global, technological and social, are now redundant.

References

Hamelink, C.J. (2000) *The Ethics of Cyberspace*. London: Sage.

Jewkes, Y. (ed.) (2003) *Dot.cons: Crime, Deviance and Identity on the Internet*. Cullompton: Willan.

Naughton, J. (1999) *A Brief History of the Future: The Origins of the Internet*. London: Phoenix.

Chapter 2

Cybercrime: re-thinking crime control strategies

Susan W. Brenner

Introduction

Human societies must maintain internal order if they are to endure. 'Order' refers to the need to coordinate and allocate activities among the members of the populace in a way that ensures the performance of the functions necessary for their survival. Societies use rules to establish and maintain order. A rule is a principle that governs action and inaction; it specifies which actions are allowable and which are not. Human societies use constitutive rules to maintain internal order. Constitutive rules define the structure of a society by defining relationships among the individuals who comprise that society; they also allocate essential tasks among the members of the society and ensure that they are performed (Brenner, 2004). Societies have historically been bounded systems situated in a delimited spatial area and composed of a defined populace (e.g. 'the people of Rome'). Spatial and demographic isolation make it easier to socialise those who populate a society so that most accept and abide by its constitutive rules; they also make it easier to identify and suppress those who do not.

However, societies cannot rely solely on constitutive rules to maintain order because humans can deliberately fail to abide by applicable rules. We therefore find it necessary to implement an additional set of rules – criminal rules – to address conduct that undermines internal order. Criminal rules impose criminal liability and sanctions – such as banishment, imprisonment or death – on those who do not abide by the 'civil' constitutive rules. Criminal rules assume that sanctioning rule-violators maintains order by preventing future violations. This assumption incorporates two subordinate assumptions: first, sanctions deter violations by presenting us with a simple choice – obey rules or suffer the consequences; and second, rule violators will be identified, apprehended and sanctioned (Brenner, 2004).

For the purposes of this discussion, we will accept the validity of the first assumption and focus on the second assumption. Under that assumption, if criminal rules exist to maintain order there must be some system in place that ensures rule violators are identified, apprehended and sanctioned. There must, in other words, be a credible threat of retaliation for violating criminal rules; without such a threat, there is no discouragement of deviance or imperative to maintain order. For most of human history, societies have used citizen enforcement to maintain this threat. That began to change in 1829 when Sir Robert Peel established the London Metropolitan Police (Sklansky, 1999). This was something new: an independent agency staffed by full-time, uniformed professionals whose sole task was to maintain order by reacting to crimes and apprehending the perpetrators (Sklansky, 1999). Peel's model spread across England and, eventually, around the world. As a result, citizens in the twenty-first century assume no responsibility for maintaining order. That has become the sole province of professionalised, quasi-military police forces that ensure order by reacting to completed crimes (Brenner, 2004).

This model has been, and continues to be, effective in controlling the types of crime societies have dealt with over the past several millennia. It is not, however, effective against cybercrime.

Cybercrime

'Cybercrime' is one of the terms used to denote the use of computer technology to engage in unlawful activity. 'Computer crime', 'high-tech crime' and 'information-age crime' are also used to describe this phenomenon. Most of the 'cybercrime' we have seen so far is nothing more than the migration of real-world crimes into cyberspace (Brenner, 2001; Jewkes, 2003a). For example, fraud, theft, forgery and extortion constitute a significant proportion of cybercrime; traditional crimes like these are considered 'cybercrimes' when they are committed in non-traditional ways (Brenner, 2001). So if Jane Doe uses email instead of face-to-face conversation to defraud Mary Smith, that is a cybercrime. Generally speaking, if computer technology is used in the commission of a traditional crime, that crime will be considered a 'cybercrime' (Brenner, 2001).

The other significant portion of cybercrime consists of specifically defined cyber-offences – hacking, cracking and virus dissemination – that are online versions of real-world crimes. Hacking is gaining unauthorised access to a computer system and, as such, is conceptually analogous to real-world trespassing. Cracking, which consists of gaining unauthorised access to a computer system for the purpose of committing a crime 'inside' the system, is conceptually analogous to burglary. And we can analogise the dissemination of viruses, worms and other varieties of malicious code to vandalism (Brenner, 2001). But while we could use trespass laws to prosecute hackers and burglary laws to prosecute crackers, the conduct at issue in the online versions of these crimes takes place in an environment that is sufficiently dissimilar from the real world to justify creating new offence definitions for these activities. This same logic militates against using vandalism laws against those who distribute malware.

It seems, therefore, that the 'rule' component of the real-world crime control strategy outlined above can adequately address cybercrime; in other words, we can use existing rules to prosecute the traditional types of cybercrime, and can adopt new, cyber-specific rules for emerging varieties of cybercrime. The problem lies in the enforcement strategy.

Enforcement

To understand why our current crime control model cannot deal effectively with cybercrime, it is necessary to understand, first, how certain empirical assumptions shaped that model. It is also necessary to understand how and why these assumptions do not hold for cybercrime.

Real-world crime

Because it is situated in a physical environment, real-world crime has four characteristics that are relevant to this discussion: proximity, scale, physical constraints and patterns (Brenner, 2004). Perhaps the most fundamental characteristic of real-world crime is that the perpetrator and victim are necessarily physically proximate to each other when the offence is committed or attempted. It is, for instance, not possible to rape or realistically attempt to rape someone if the rapist and the victim are fifty miles apart, and in a non-technological world, it is physically impossible to defraud someone if the perpetrator and victim are in different cities or different countries.

The scale of real-world crime is therefore limited because it tends to be one-to-one crime, i.e. involves one perpetrator and one victim (Brenner, 2004). During the commission of the crime the perpetrator focuses his or her attention on consummating that crime. When it is complete, s/he can move onto another crime and another victim. Like proximity, the one-to-one character of real-world crime derives from the constraints physical reality imposes upon human activity: a thief cannot pick more than one pocket at a time, and prior to the rise of firearms, it was very difficult for one to cause the simultaneous deaths of more than one person. (Brenner, 2004)

Real-world crime is also subject to the physical constraints that govern activity in the physical world. Every crime, even street-level drug dealing, requires a level of preparation, planning and implementation if it is to succeed. A bank robber must visit the bank to familiarise themself with its layout, security and routine; this exposes them to public scrutiny and that can lead to them being identified and apprehended (Brenner, 2004). While in the bank, they leave trace evidence and are subject to observations that can result in being identified. As they flee after committing the robbery, they are again exposed to public view and risk being identified. Each step takes time and effort and thereby incrementally augments the exertion required to commit the crime and increases the risks involved in its commission.

Finally, over time it becomes possible to identify the general contours and incidence of the real-world crimes committed in a society. Victimisation tends to fall into demographic and geographic patterns for two reasons. One is that only a small segment of a functioning society's populace will persistently engage in criminal activity; those who fall into this category are apt to be from economically deprived backgrounds and reside in areas that share geographic and demographic characteristics. They will be inclined to focus their efforts on those with whom they share a level of physical proximity because they are convenient victims; consequently, much of a society's routine crime will be concentrated in identifiable areas.[1] The other reason is that each society has a repertoire of crimes – rules that proscribe behaviours ranging from more to less serious in terms of the 'harm' each inflicts. In a society that is successfully maintaining internal order, the more egregious crimes will occur much less often, and less predictably, than minor crimes (Brenner, 2004).

These characteristics shape the crime control strategy outlined in the Introduction to this chapter. Proximity contributes a presumed dynamic: victim–perpetrator proximity and consequent victimisation, perpetrator efforts to flee the crime scene and otherwise evade apprehension, investigation, identification and apprehension of the perpetrator. The dynamic reflects a time when crime was parochial, when victims and perpetrators tended to live in the same village or neighbourhood. If a victim and perpetrator did not know each other, they were likely to share community ties that facilitated identification and apprehension; there was a good chance a perpetrator could be identified by witnesses or reputation. If a perpetrator and a victim did not share community ties, this would likely contribute to being apprehended; they would 'stand out' as someone who did not belong (Brenner, 2004). Law enforcement dealt effectively with this type of crime because its spatial limitations meant investigations were limited in scope; the strategy still assumes that the investigation of a crime should focus on the physical scene of the offence.

The strategy also assumes one-to-one victimisation and that, along with another assumption, yields the proposition that the scale of crime will be limited in a functioning society (Brenner, 2004). The other assumption is that law-abiding conduct is the norm, and that crime is unusual. This second assumption derives not from the physical characteristics of real-world crime but from the need to maintain order. A society's constitutive and criminal rules work together to achieve this; constitutive rules define acceptable behaviours that are encouraged, while criminal rules emphasise that certain behaviours will not be tolerated (Brenner, 2004). The combined effect of these rules is that crime becomes a subset, generally a small subset, of the total behaviours in a society. The limited incidence of criminal behaviour, coupled with one-to-one victimisation as the default crime mode, means law enforcement personnel can focus their efforts on a limited segment of conduct within a given society (Brenner, 2004). The traditional crime control strategy also incorporates the concept that crime falls into patterns. It assumes crime will be limited in incidence and in the types of 'harms' it inflicts. It also assumes that an identifiable percentage of crime will occur in geographically and demographically demarcated areas (Brenner, 2004). The combined effects of localised crime and the differential frequency with which various crimes are committed gives law enforcement the ability to concentrate its resources in areas where crime is most likely to occur, which enhances its ability to react to completed crimes (Brenner, 2004).

Cybercrime

Cybercrime does not require physical proximity between victim and perpetrator for the consummation of an offence. Cybercrime is unbounded crime; the victim and perpetrator can be in different cities, in different states or in different countries. All a perpetrator needs is a computer linked to the Internet. With this, he can attack a victim's computer or obtain information he can use to assume a victim's identity and commit fraud on a grand scale.

Furthermore, one-to-one victimisation is not typical of cybercrime because, unlike real-world crime, it can be automated. This means perpetrators can commit thousands of crimes quickly and with little effort; one-to-many victimisation is the default assumption for cybercrime. Under the traditional crime control strategy outlined above, officers react to a crime by investigating and apprehending its perpetrator; the strategy assumes crime is committed on a limited scale so officers can react to discrete crimes. Cybercrime violates this assumption in two ways. First, although it is carried out by a small percentage of the population of a society (or of the world), this relatively small group can commit crimes on a scale far surpassing what they could achieve in the real world where one-to-one victimisation and serial crimes are the norm. Consequently, the number of cybercrimes will exponentially exceed real-world crimes. Second, cybercrime is added to the real-world crime with which law enforcement must continue to deal; people will still rape, rob and murder in the real world. These factors combine to create an overload; law enforcement's ability to react to cybercrime erodes because the resources that were minimally adequate to deal with real-world crime are totally inadequate to deal with cybercrime and with cybercrime-plus-real-world crime.

Cybercriminals also avoid the physical constraints that govern real-world crime; funds can be extracted from a US bank and moved into offshore accounts with little effort and less visibility (Brenner, 2004). The reactive strategy is far less effective against online crime because the reaction usually begins well after the crime has been successfully concluded; the trail, such as it is, is already cold. And since most or all of the conduct involved in committing the crime occurs in an electronic environment, the 'physical' evidence, if any, is evanescent and volatile. By the time police do react, evidence may have been destroyed. Since perpetrators need not be at the crime 'scene', assumptions about their having been observed while preparing for, committing or fleeing from the crime no longer hold. Officers may not even be able to determine from where the perpetrator carried out the crime or who they are. Even if they can identify the perpetrator, gathering evidence and apprehending them can be difficult; the country that hosts them may not regard what they did as illegal and may therefore decline to extradite them, or there may be no extradition treaty in place that governs the conduct at issue (Brenner, 2004).

Since we cannot, as yet, identify offender-offence patterns comparable to those we have for real-world crime, law enforcement cannot allocate its resources to deal effectively with cybercrime. Several factors account for our inability to identify cybercrime patterns. First, it is not well documented; agencies tend to lump online fraud with real-world fraud rather than breaking the cybercrime out into a separate category. Second, it can be difficult to parse cybercrime into discrete offences: was the 'Love Bug' virus that caused billions of dollars of damage in over 20 countries one crime or thousands of crimes (Jewkes, 2003b; Brenner, 2004)? The most important factor is that we simply do not have accurate cybercrime statistics because many cybercrimes go undetected and many detected cybercrimes go unreported (Jewkes, 2003b; Brenner, 2004; see also Jewkes and Andrews, this volume).

A new crime-control strategy

We therefore need a new crime-control strategy because our current approach is not effective against cybercrime. We have two options: first, modify our current, reactive strategy so it becomes an effective way to deal with cybercrime; second, develop a new, non-reactive strategy for cybercrime.

Improved reaction

The sections below discuss four alternatives that have been proposed as ways to improve the reactive strategy:

- the Council of Europe's Convention on Cybercrime;
- law enforcement strikeback techniques;
- civilian strikeback techniques; and
- more officers.

The final section outlines the contours of a new crime control strategy as a suggestion of what could be a fifth alternative.

Convention on Cybercrime

The Convention on Cybercrime is intended to improve law enforcement's ability to react to cybercrime (Council of Europe, 2001). It seeks to achieve this by: (1) harmonising the domestic criminal substantive law ... in the area of cyber-crime (2) providing for domestic criminal procedural law powers necessary for the investigation and prosecution of such offences ... (and) (3) setting up a fast and effective regime of international co-operation (Brenner, 2004). At the time of writing this chapter, it had been signed by 42 countries and ratified by 13.

The premise of the Convention – that an international network of consistent laws will improve national law enforcement's ability to react across borders and thereby restore the effectiveness of the current crime control strategy – is unobjectionable. The difficulty lies in its implementation. To be truly effective, the Convention must be implemented by every country. It contains 48 Articles, 33 of which require parties to adopt legislation or take other implementing measures (Council of Europe, 2001). This will be a relatively straightforward task for countries such as the United States, which already have cybercrime laws in place; it will be an onerous undertaking for those that do not. The task will be further complicated by differences in local law and culture; the Convention was drafted by Europeans with substantial input from American lawyers. Consequently, it incorporates notions of substantive and procedural law that may not be routine in other parts of the world. This does not mean it will be impossible for countries to implement the Convention; it means that implementing it will be a complicated process for many countries, and one that will take time. An additional problem may lie in this lapse of time; since the provisions of the Convention reflect the state of technology that existed when it was drafted, they may become out of date as technology continues to evolve.

So, even if the Convention ultimately proves to be a viable means of improving law enforcement's ability to react to transnational cybercrime, we are unlikely to see any marked improvement in the near future.

Law enforcement strikeback

Reidenberg (2004) proposes that countries let law enforcement officers use 'electronic sanctions' to react to cybercrime, including disseminating viruses, worms and other types of malware, along with hacking and denial-of-service attacks. Reidenberg (2004) further proposes that officers use hacking techniques to 'seize' or paralyse rule-violating web pages and launch denial-of-service attacks or viruses against those who perpetrate online fraud or other types of cybercrime. This is an 'official' response to another version of an approach that has been discussed for some time and is discussed in the next section: civilian 'strikeback'. State-sanctioned strikeback by police and other law enforcers is not an advisable strategy because it suffers from the problems outlined in the next section. More importantly, however, it adds the official imprimatur of the state to what are clearly illegal acts (Brenner, 2004).

Civilian strikeback

The premise here is that victims can react when they become the targets of cybercrime and their efforts will supplement the reactive capabilities of law enforcement officers. Like the law enforcement version discussed above, civilian strikeback raises difficult legal questions (Karnow, 2003). But it ultimately founders on the practical risks involved in authorising victim self-help: victims whose computer skills are limited may not be able to trace an attack back to the perpetrator's computer, so they may 'retaliate' against the wrong computer system (Karnow, 2003). Furthermore, their retaliation could shut down a legitimate system operated by, say, a hospital, a government agency or a telecommunications company; as Karnow notes, the remedy would be 'worse than the disease' because the strikeback would injure not only the computer system that was attacked, but also those who relied upon it for vital services (Karnow, 2003). Finally, civilian strikeback is a type of vigilantism and, as such is subject to the objections that have been raised to real-world vigilantism (Schneier, 2002).

More officers

This seems an obvious solution: increase the number of officers who can react. There are two problems, however, with this alternative. One is that societies already find it difficult to allocate the resources needed to support existing law enforcement agencies; it is highly improbable that they could summon the resources needed to recruit, train and equip enough officers to make the reactive strategy a viable approach to cybercrime (see Moore, this volume). The other problem is that since cybercrime is increasingly automated, there is no guarantee that raising the number of officers will improve the efficacy with which law enforcement agencies can react to cybercrime.

Non-reactive strategy

There are two ways to deal with crime: react to it and prevent it. The reactive strategy incorporates prevention in so far as it seeks to incapacitate and deter offenders but this is not its primary concern. Prevention is the focus of another model. Community policing emphasises cooperation between police and civilians to create a climate in which crime is not tolerated. However, community policing is not a viable option for cybercrime: it would involve assigning officers to 'patrol' cyberspace, and that would require resources which are not available. Also, cyberspace does not contain the kind of communities this approach needs to succeed (Brenner, 2004). However, a variation of community policing *can* be applied to cyberspace. Unlike community policing, which relies primarily on an active police presence and only secondarily on citizen efforts, this model relies primarily on active citizen efforts and only secondarily on police support of those efforts. It is a *distributed* policing strategy, not a *community* policing strategy.

Postulating such a strategy raises two questions. Why should we, as civilians, assume responsibility for preventing cybercrimes? And, supposing we are to assume such responsibility, how can this to be achieved?

Why?

The answer to the 'why' question lies in certain differences between cybercrime and real-world crime. Assume I go to work leaving my front door unlocked and a rear window wide open; if a burglar takes advantage of the situation and steals my laptop, I call the police who will make some effort to find the burglar and recover my property. They may make my burglary a lesser priority than other crimes out of frustration at my irresponsibility. But I will never know this is the case, and it may not be; the officers may make a sincere effort to recover my laptop and apprehend the perpetrator. My irresponsibility is legally irrelevant. A crime is an offence against the authority of the state and must be addressed without regard to the circumstances that contributed to its commission (Brenner, 2004).

So why should my obligations be different for cybercrime? The primary reason is that if I leave my front door unlocked and a rear window open and a burglar takes advantage of my carelessness, the only one harmed is me, the architect of my own victimisation. This is not necessarily true for cybercrime. Assume that instead of leaving my front door unlocked and a rear window open, I access the Internet using an always-on broadband connection without using any security to prevent my laptop being hijacked by a hacker. I have created a situation analogous to the burglary discussed above: I have carelessly exposed myself to 'harm'. But I have also created the potential for 'harm' to others; my carelessness has created a situation in which a hacker can use my laptop to victimise others. This results in the infliction of 'harms' exceeding those I would suffer from a personal attack (Brenner, 2004). The most compelling answer to the 'why' question, therefore, is that responsibility for preventing cybercrimes should be imposed upon civilians because their failure to secure their systems can result in the infliction of 'harm' upon others and can threaten the security of the entire system. Another reason is, as explained above, that law enforcement is less effective in maintaining order in cyberspace than in real-space.

How?

A voluntary approach to achieving citizen responsibility for preventing cybercrime would require creating a norm to that effect; once the members of a society internalised this norm, they would regard preventing cybercrime as the 'right' thing to do and most would try to comply. Unfortunately, creating a norm can take a very long time. This is likely to be especially true for cybercrime prevention because the norm to be created involves cyberspace, which is still an alien environment for most people. They may see it as prudent to instal security alarms to ward off real-world threats, but most people are unlikely to appreciate that cyberspace is a source of danger. And the difficulty of establishing such a norm is exacerbated by the fact that it would have to displace a deeply embedded norm, i.e. that crime is the exclusive province of law enforcement (Brenner, 2004). A voluntary approach is, therefore, unlikely to be effective. This leaves the obligatory approach; it requires us to act or to not-act on pain of formal sanctions. 'Do' laws create an obligation to act and impose sanctions for not discharging that obligation; 'do not' laws create an obligation not to act and impose sanctions for committing the proscribed act (Brenner, 2004).

A strategy utilising 'do' laws would impose an obligation to prevent cybercrime; failing to discharge that obligation would result in a sanction. Seat belt laws provide a useful point of comparison: these 'do' laws require the occupants of a motor vehicle to use seat belts when the vehicle is in operation and impose sanctions for failure to comply. Seat belt laws have been effective in increasing seat belt use among motorists, so it might seem that a similar approach would be an effective way to impose responsibility for preventing cybercrime. But there are important differences between the two security measures. In the US, federal law requires that vehicles manufactured after 1968 have seat belts, so they were available when states began requiring their use. Furthermore, the duty imposed by seat belt laws is not an onerous one – it simply requires that motorists and passengers use a device that is available and requires no technical skill to employ. The duty imposed by the proposed cybercrime prevention laws, on the other hand, is far more complex. Civilians would have to: firstly identify and obtain the tools they need to protect their computers from cybercriminals; secondly, educate themselves about these tools so they could instal them, use them, keep them updated and replace them when necessary; and thirdly, use these tools in an effective manner. Since computer software, hardware and the threats in cyberspace are constantly evolving, these tasks would be ongoing, demanding obligations. One differentiating factor, therefore, is the relative complexity of the duty being imposed.

Another differentiating factor is the likelihood of being sanctioned. Both the seat belt laws and the hypothesised cybercrime prevention laws establish a duty and impose sanctions to deter 'dangerous' behaviour. The behaviour to be deterred is, respectively, not wearing seat belts and thereby exposing oneself to injury, and not using computer security measures and thereby exposing oneself, others and the social system to cyber-attackers. The effectiveness of sanctions in deterring behaviour is a function of the risk (or perceived risk) of being apprehended and sanctioned; the deterrent effect increases as the risk (or perceived risk) of being apprehended increases (Brenner, 2004). Since compliance with seat belt laws occurs in public, it is not difficult for officers to tell if someone is obeying the law. The risk (or perceived risk) of being apprehended is high and that, coupled with the ease with which one can comply, makes seat belt laws an effective type of 'do' law. Cybercrime prevention law, on the other hand, would primarily address conduct occurring in private places – one's home or office. It would therefore be difficult for those charged with enforcing such laws to determine compliance. The consequent low risk of being identified and apprehended, coupled with the difficulty of complying, means that these hypothesised 'do' laws would not be an effective means of securing citizen collaboration in enhancing cybersecurity.

This leaves 'do not' laws. They may seem a peculiar candidate for enlisting civilians in the fight against cybercrime because 'do not' laws generally define crimes. And we are not, after all, talking about sanctioning civilians for *committing* cybercrime; we are talking about sanctioning them for not *preventing* cybercrime. Actually, as the next section explains, 'do not' laws should serve quite nicely.

Contours of a new crime-control strategy: an alternative approach

This section briefly explains how three types of criminal rules could be used to encourage civilians to prevent cybercrime. Two of the rules focus on those who merely 'use' cyberspace (the 'users'); the third focuses on those who create cyberspace (the 'architects').

'User' rules

'Users' only control their own conduct. Their efforts are essentially defensive. 'User' rules will therefore emphasise one's responsibility not to become a victim and the consequences attendant upon defaulting on that obligation.

Assumption of risk

In the United States, in a civil tort action, if one is found to have assumed the risk of the danger that caused a personal injury, one is barred from obtaining redress for that injury. We cannot literally import this principle into criminal law as part of our effort to prevent cybercrime because it would mean that criminals would in effect be given a 'Get out of jail free card' for victims who did not or could not protect themselves; we would effectively declare open season on the vulnerable. We need to impose a level of assumed risk but retain the capacity to prosecute even when a victim's precautions were less than adequate. We could do this with a modified assumption of risk principle containing two elements: first, a proposition negating the expectation of a law enforcement reaction to victimisation; and second, a statement that the negation of such an expectation does not bar the investigation and prosecution of cyber-criminals. The rule might look something like this:

1. One who accesses cyberspace without having taken all reasonable measures to protect him or herself from being victimised during that activity shall be deemed to have assumed the risk of victimisation resulting from that activity. Law enforcement agencies are under no obligation to take action with regard to those who assumed the risk of becoming a victim online, though they may do so.

2. The fact that one assumed the risk of being victimised pursuant to paragraph (1) creates no enforceable rights in person(s) who contributed to that victimisation.

Complicity

The doctrine of complicity states that one who facilitates the commission of a crime can be held liable for that crime as if he or she committed it. Complicitous liability is usually based on performing an affirmative act, but it can be based on not acting. One who has a legal duty to prevent a crime is an accomplice if he or she fails to do so.

Our goal is to hold civilians responsible for preventing cybercrime. The assumption of risk principle outlined above negates an expectation of redress for one's own victimisation. But what if by allowing myself to be victimised I contribute to another's victimisation? I have in effect facilitated the commission of a crime. Should we use complicity-by-omission liability to hold me liable for this consequent victimisation? This would appear to be unacceptable because it (a) imposes omission liability in the absence of a legal duty to act; and (b) seems to impose criminal liability without requiring *mens rea*, or intent. Actually, with some modifications complicity-by-omission liability can be used for this purpose.

The first step is to impose a duty to avoid becoming the victim of a cybercrime. The duty should be limited to preventing one's own victimisation; letting myself be attacked is, after all, how I contribute to the victimisation of others. If I protect my computer, I prevent its being used to attack others; if I do not protect my computer, I create the possibility it can be used to attack others. If a cybercriminal takes advantage of the opportunity I supplied, it is reasonable to hold me liable for the resulting cybercrimes. As to *mens rea*, the most reasonable approach is to use a negligence standard. Liability would be imposed for not taking the precautions a reasonable person would have known were necessary to protect the system(s) at issue (Brenner, 2004).

Imposing such a duty is in a sense implementing a 'do' rule; it imposes an obligation to fend off attacks by cybercriminals and liability for not discharging the obligation. This duty differs from a 'do' rule, however, in that liability is not imposed for the mere failure to discharge the duty. If I become the victim of a cybercrime, I will not be held liable as an accomplice to my own victimisation; the sanction for defaulting on my duty to prevent cybercrime is that I will be deemed to have assumed the risk of my victimisation. Criminal liability in the form of complicity is imposed only if I fail to discharge my duty to protect myself *and* that failure contributes to the victimisation of another.

'Architect' rules

The rationale for imposing an obligation to prevent cybercrime on 'architects' is based on the role they play in the collective experience we know as cyberspace: 'architects' supply the devices 'users' employ to participate in this experience. The efficacy with which 'users' can avoid cybercrime is a function of the reliability and technical adequacy of the tools they employ. 'Architects' therefore are in a position to enhance the overall effectiveness of the system of preventative, distributed security postulated here by enhancing the reliability and adequacy of these tools.

In other areas, the prospect of civil product liability suits creates incentives to ensure that products are safe and defect free, but this is not true for the 'architects' of cyberspace. But civil product liability has not been applied to software, which is the most critical tool 'users' have in their hypothesised efforts to prevent cybercrime. So far, the software industry has avoided product liability by arguing, among other things, that software is too complex to be treated as a simple product and that having to defend against thousands of frivolous civil product liability suits would chill innovation while raising the prices of software (Brenner, 2004).

These issues and arguments all deal with *civil* product liability. Could a doctrine of *criminal* product liability be used for this purpose? The first argument the software industry advances as to why product liability law should *not* be applied to software actually supports the converse proposition: why criminal product liability *should* be imposed on software. The software industry's arguments assume software is a 'civil' product like, say, a toaster, i.e. that it is functionally indistinguishable in an important respect from other products that are used in a purely 'private' capacity by individuals and entities. This assumption is incorrect. Because of the role it plays in creating and sustaining cyberspace, software has become an essential component of our national infrastructures; its importance will only increase as more and more activities move into cyberspace. Since software is an increasingly important component of our national infrastructure, it is, in effect, too important to be left to the vagaries of 'private' civil litigation; we must devise some system for ensuring that those who provide the software we rely upon are taking adequate measures to ensure that it is reliable and technically adequate.

Employing criminal liability for this purpose is not without precedent; it is analogous in certain respects to the imposition of liability for antitrust violations (Brenner, 2004). In a traditional criminal proceeding, the state acts to vindicate its obligation to protect a member of the social system it represents; in a criminal antitrust enforcement proceeding, it acts to vindicate its obligation to protect essential components of the system. The 'harm' caused by an antitrust crime is an erosion of the principle of competition. Criminal antitrust proceedings therefore target 'systemic' crimes – that is, crimes that impact on a nation's infrastructure instead of on individuals. They are in that regard precisely analogous to the type of criminal liability postulated here. Like criminal antitrust laws, criminal product liability laws would authorise the imposition of liability upon those whose conduct undermines the security of the national infrastructure.

Criminal antitrust requires affirmative criminal conduct, but the criminal product liability postulated here would be imposed for not acting: for not ensuring the reliability of software (or hardware). The imposition of such liability is not unknown in American law. In *United States* v. *Park*, 421 US 658 (1975), a corporate officer was convicted of violating 21 US Code §331, which makes it a crime to let food that is being held for sale become adulterated. Park was the president of a grocery chain that used a Baltimore warehouse to store food. Inspectors found that rodents were contaminating the food held there. Park was charged with violating section 331. Park claimed he was not responsible for the contamination; he admitted that all of the company's employees were under his control, but claimed he delegated the duty to see that the food was kept safe to a vice president in Baltimore. Park was convicted and the Supreme Court affirmed his conviction; the Court found that Park's 'responsible' position in the company's corporate structure justified holding him liable for not preventing the contamination.

The *Park* case therefore supports holding someone criminally liable for *not* preventing a systemic 'harm'. But what, if any, *mens rea* should be required? In *Park* and in other areas of real-world criminal law, strict liability suffices; the doctrine of strict liability eliminates the need to show intent, or personal fault. It suffices in cases like *Park* because the corporation or the corporate employee is being held liable not for a traditional crime but for a regulatory offence, i.e. for violating a statute that imposes a duty not to act in a way that endangers the health or safety of the public. Strict liability is used because it can be difficult if not impossible to prove personal moral fault on the part of specific corporate employees; and, the penalties associated with regulatory offences are usually small, often consisting only of a fine. The most reasonable approach to applying criminal product liability to the 'architects' of cyberspace is, therefore, to define a regulatory offence based on strict liability. The rationale is functionally indistinguishable from that used for other regulatory offences; the goal is to use criminal liability to ensure that the products or services one supplies do not harm the public directly or, here, indirectly, by eroding the security of cyberspace.

The second argument the software industry makes as to why it should not be subject to civil product liability begins with the proposition that adopting such liability would open the industry up to thousands (or thousands and thousands) of civil suits, many of which would be frivolous or would seek damages for trivial injuries. The argument concludes that these civil suits would impose significant, time, resource and incentive burdens on an industry that needs to be nimble, creative and focused it if is to design and supply the evolving tools we will need to maximise the advantages cyberspace offers for essentially every aspect of human endeavour.

Software is an admittedly complex product, far more difficult to design, maintain and upgrade than the real-world items to which product liability has been applied. Civil product liability suits would therefore be expensive, time-consuming and burdensome, and their impact on software quality is uncertain. Set against this uncertainty is the demonstrable fact that the current strategy of relying on market forces cannot ensure that software is minimally reliable, let alone secure enough to protect the national infrastructure. Clearly, some other approach is needed.

The judicious use of criminal product liability is such an approach. Unlike civil product liability suits, criminal product liability prosecutions are brought by the state, which limits the number of actions brought and tends to filter out frivolous suits. Unlike market forces, criminal product liability can be employed to create incentives to provide reliable, technically adequate software (or, perhaps more accurately, to create disincentives for producing software that is not reliable and technically adequate). We could further filter the initiation of criminal product liability actions against software companies by adapting the enforcement strategy used for environmental crimes, which can also involve complex, collaborative activity. In the States, the US Environmental Protection Agency (EPA) and the US Department of Justice cooperate in enforcing the criminal provisions of most federal environmental statutes. The EPA investigates potential violations and can request prosecution in appropriate cases; its policy is to seek criminal sanctions only if both significant environmental harm and egregious conduct are at issue.

The goal then, is to encourage self-policing and voluntary compliance. A similar approach could be used for criminal product liability. Combining criminal liability and an emphasis on self-policing has three main potential advantages. First, it resolves the 'litigation overload' objections to civil product liability; second, it resolves similar objections that would no doubt be raised to an unfiltered criminal product liability; and third, it fills the vacuum that results from relying on market forces to improve software. In the United States, prosecution authority at the federal level would reside with the Department of Justice. The authority to initiate criminal product liability prosecutions could be given to the Criminal Division or to a special enforcement unit analogous to the Antitrust or Environmental and Natural Resources Divisions. It would be necessary to decide whether local US attorney's offices could also initiate such prosecutions. However, given the technical complexity of the issues and the need for consistency in such prosecutions, it seems advisable to reserve prosecution for the Criminal Division or for a special enforcement unit created for this purpose.

Note

1 Of course, this is not to deny the 'dark figure' of hidden and unreported crime, including domestic violence, white-collar crime and corporate offences, but here we are concerned with law enforcement strategies which, unfortunately but inevitably, concentrate efforts and resources on visible offending in the public realm.

References

Brenner, S. (2001) 'Is there such a thing as virtual crime?', *California Criminal Law Review*, 4 (1).

Brenner, S. (2004) 'Toward a criminal law for cyberspace: distributed security', *Boston University Journal of Science & Technology Law*, 10 (2).

Council of Europe (2001) *Convention on Cybercrime* (ETC No. 185).

Jewkes, Y. (ed.) (2003a) *Dot.cons: Crime, Deviance and Identity on the Internet.* Cullompton: Willan.

Jewkes, Y. (2003b) 'Policing cybercrime', in T. Newburn (ed.), *Handbook of Policing.* Cullompton: Willan.

Karnow, C. (2003) 'Strike and counterstrike: the law on automated intrusions and striking back', Black Hat Windows Security (online at: http://www.blackhat.com/presentations/win-usa-03/bh-win-03-karnow-notes.pdf).

Reidenberg, J. (2004) 'States and Internet enforcement', *University of Ottawa Law and Technology Journal*, 1 (213).

Schneier, B. (2002) 'Counterattack', *Crypto-gram*, 15 December.

Sklansky, D. (1999) 'The private police', *University of California – Los Angeles Law Review*, 46 (4): 1165–287.

Chapter 3

The problem of stolen identity and the Internet

Emily Finch

Introduction

'Identity theft' and 'identity fraud' are terms which have gained currency in recent years and which have passed into common parlance as interchangeable generic terms to describe the misappropriation of personal information for nefarious ends, generally to facilitate fraudulent financial transactions. While this characterisation of identity theft is not incorrect, it is incomplete. The widespread acceptance of an imperfect understanding of the problem is potentially dangerous as it leaves individuals ill-equipped to protect themselves against victimisation. This problem is particularly pressing in relation to the Internet as the nature of social interaction differs in the virtual world; many of the safety measures that can be taken in the physical realm to protect personal information are not available in an online context. This chapter will discuss the ways in which the Internet has contributed to a recent increase in the misuse of identity, but first it is necessary to explore the nature of identity and consider what it means for identity to be stolen.

What is identity?

Identity is a complex and multi-faceted concept that is best understood by a division into three categories: personal, social and legal. Personal identity relates to the self as experienced by the individual which can be explained as 'what most of us think of when we think of the deepest and most enduring features of our unique selves that constitute who we believe ourselves to be' (Williams, 2001: 7). It is not a static self-perception but one which evolves as a result of an individual's interaction with others and their participation in the social world. Irrespective of this evolution, personal identity is characterised by a sense of continuity, an ability to remember that we were once different to how we are now and a realisation that we will change as our life progresses held with the sure knowledge that, despite this constant metamorphosis, we remain the same person (Locke, 1690: xxvii). This internalised sense of self is inherently irremovable from the individual so it cannot be the subject of identity theft.

By contrast, social identity concerns the individual as they are perceived by others; it is the external view of the self as viewed by others in society:

> Our identity therefore originates not from inside the person, but from the social realm, a realm where people swim in a sea of language and other signs, a sea that is invisible to us because it is the very medium of our existence as social beings. (Burr, 2003: 108–9)

As this constructionist perspective suggests, each individual exists amid a vast social realm in which each interaction with others creates a fresh social identity. External perceptions are multiple and some or all of them may be inaccurate in the sense that they do not match personal identity; this may be a consequence of the subjective interpretation of the observer or the deliberate adaptation of the 'face' shown to the world by the individual whose identity is at issue. Jung describes this deliberate projection of an appropriate social persona as a 'necessary convenience' to facilitate social interaction that represents 'a compromise between the individual and society' (Jung, 1988: 165). As such, the presentation of an appropriate persona is a means of negotiating everyday life and surviving complex social interactions. This, of course, raises the possibility that at least some manifestations of identity theft are merely an amplification of normalcy, as the impostor – lacking an appropriate persona to present to the world – appropriates that of another, presenting it as their own. The 'thing' that is appropriated here, however, is not social identity itself (as this is the external perception of the individual) but legal identity, which is concerned with the ability to substantiate claims to be a particular person.

Legal identity is concerned not so much with the internalised view of identity that relates to a person's sense of self or the externalised view that concerns the way that a person is viewed by others but with the way in which an accumulation of information distinguishes one individual from all others. Goffman describes this facet of identity, stating that it rests on:

[t]he assumption that the individual can be differentiated from all others and that around this means of differentiation a single continuous record of social facts can be attached, entangled like candy floss, becoming then the sticky substance to which still other biographic facts can be attached. (Goffman, 1968: 74–5)

This characterisation is more akin to identifiability than identity. Legal identity serves a pragmatic function as its purpose is to create an unbreakable association between a collection of factual information and the individual to whom this relates. For Torpey, this reflects the preoccupation of the state to impose a durable and inescapable identity on each individual in order to answer two interrelated questions: 'who is this person' and 'is this the same person' (2000: 166). In other words, this manifestation of identity serves a dual purpose; first, it enables an individual to authenticate themselves by proving who they are at any one point in time, and, second, it provides historical continuity as an individual 'here and now' is able to associate themselves with events in their past, e.g. their credit, employment or education history. This demonstrates the distinction between legal identity and the other facets of identity outlined above; personal and social identity are inclusive concepts by which an individual establishes group membership by virtue of similarity to others, while legal identity is concerned with the ability to differentiate themselves from others and thus is a means of establishing individuality and personhood. Further distinctions can be made. Personal identity and social identity tend to be reflexive concepts that evolve as an individual changes on the journey through life whereas legal identity is immutable and permanent. Social facts, once they exist, are eradicable. Legal identity has a cumulative element and this represents the only possible alteration to its nature; the facts do not change but more are added, thus an individual's legal identity becomes more detailed and comprehensive as time passes and new social facts adhere 'like candy-floss' to the existing identity information.

The primacy and tenacity of legal identity

Legal identity is established at birth with the issuing of a birth certificate that chronicles unique details about an individual such as their given name, sex, date and place of birth as well as information about their parents. Since the birth certificate is a record of historical fact, its details are unalterable, even at the behest of the individual to whom the information relates. If factual alterations need to be made due to, for example, adoption or the legitimatisation of a child due to subsequent marriage, a new birth certificate is issued to supersede the original (although this remains in its unaltered form). The progression from childhood to adulthood engenders a corresponding growth in the factual information that is gathered about the individual as medical records are linked to a particular person by their NHS number and their employment history is linked to the individual by their National Insurance number. This core of state-held information is supplemented by information gathered by private agencies, such as credit agencies, all of which contribute to the construction of a complete legal identity.

The preoccupation of the state with gathering and storing information about individuals is described by Foucault as a process which 'places individuals in a field of surveillance [and also] situates them in a network of writing; it engages them in a whole mass of documents that capture and fix them' (Foucault, 1979: 189). This conceptualisation of legal identity encapsulates the extent to which individuals are enmeshed within a documentary web of information from which escape is virtually impossible (Finch, 2003). The situations in everyday life in which an individual is required to prove some aspect of their legal identity are numerous as identification is increasingly demanded to access services that bear no relation to the information required (Steinhardt, 2004). This state of 'information richness' has created an imperative of identifiability in which an individual who is unwilling or unable to provide the information or document demanded is viewed with suspicion and generally precluded from accessing the desired service or benefit (Clarke, 1994). Without the ability to establish some or all of the various social facts that cumulatively comprise legal identity, an individual would be denied access to the most basic ingredients of everyday life; a person cannot work (legally) or claim benefit without a National Insurance number and securing a home, whether by rental or purchase, is not possible without recourse to the ability to authenticate identity and substantiate a satisfactory work and credit history.

It is clear, then, that the ability to establish one's legal identity is of paramount importance in late modern society. This raises the potential for problems if disharmony exists between the three aspects of identity; in the result of conflict, which is to prevail? The answer seems to be that legal identity has primacy over personal and social identity. For example, English courts steadfastly refuse to permit the retrospective alteration of a birth certificate to reflect the acquired gender of post-operative transsexuals despite arguments that this measure is necessary to establish concordance between the individual's personal identity (their belief that their gender was other than that recorded at birth), their social identity (their presentation of themselves to the world as a person of that gender) and their legal identity (which was their gender at birth) (*Cossey* v. *United Kingdom* [1991] 2 FLR 492; *Sheffield* v. *United Kingdom* [1998] 2 FLR 928; *Bellinger* v. *Bellinger* [2003] 2 WLR 1174). Although this conflict was rectified by the Gender Recognition Act 2004, the statute permits only the reissue of the birth certificate to reflect the individual's post-operative status with the original record remaining in existence unaltered. At the time of its enactment, the government stated that 'the original birth record is an accurate record of the facts at the time of birth' adding that the Act does not facilitate the rewriting of history. This commitment to the integrity of the birth certificate demonstrates the tenacity of legal identity and the extent to which it prevails over personal identity and social identity if conflict arises between them. The pollarding of legal identity to correspond with personal and/or social identity is not acceptable, possibly because those forms of identity, by their very nature, are changeable and diverse. It could be argued that an immutable legal identity is needed to create a single point of reference that amalgamates into a cohesive and manageable identity the historic evolution of personal identity and the fragmentation of the one into the many inherent in social identity.

The aim of legal identity is to unify the strands of personal and social identity to create a dyadic relationship between the physicality of a person and the collection of information pertaining to them: each person should correspond to a single inescapable legal identity. Paradoxically, the primacy and tenacity of legal identity may actually create the impetus for identity theft as 'the tightening of the information net . . . creates structural pressure to fabricate' (Marx, 2001: 323). The increasing requirement of identifiability that is an ineluctable aspect of modern society forces individuals with 'spoiled' identities (Goffman, 1968) to choose between perpetual disclosure of information they would rather hide from the public gaze or the denial of access that follows from the inability to provide this information. The imperative for identifiability can thus result in marginalised individuals facing further exclusion from mainstream society or, alternatively, securing participation by discarding their spoiled identities and replacing these with an acquired unspoiled legal identity. While this may be an entirely fictitious creation, these are difficult to maintain in the face of official scrutiny, hence the tendency to appropriate the existing legal identity of another individual, living or dead.

Clearly, then, an unspoiled legal identity has value and valuable commodities are always vulnerable to appropriation by those desirous yet undeserving of acquisition. In other words, the greater the need to identify, the greater the value of an unspoiled legal identity, thus the incentive to engage in identity theft increases as the benefits of possession of an unspoiled legal identity become ever more attractive. Having established that legal identity can indeed be 'stolen' in the sense that it can be taken and used by someone other than the rightful 'owner', it is necessary to consider whether such conduct will actually incur criminal liability.

Theft, fraud or something else?

The use of the terms 'identity theft' and 'identity fraud' to describe the misuse of another's identity carries two implications; firstly, that there are two distinct categories of wrongdoing and, secondly, that the conduct in question is a particular species of an existing criminal offence. Each of these issues needs to be explored in order to gain a complete understanding of the problem.

The question of terminology has been explored by several commentators who seem to concur, despite some difference in the labels used, that there is a distinction to be made between the transient use of another's identity to achieve a particular purpose (identity fraud) and the permanent appropriation of another's identity which is then 'developed' by the impostor, i.e. further elements of legal identity are added after the assumption thus leading to an amalgam of the two (identity theft) (Jones and Levi, 2001; Finch, 2003; Semmens, 2005). The key distinction between the two seems to be that identity fraud involves the impersonation of another person for a particular purpose after which the impostor reverts to their own identity while identity theft is characterised by the abandonment of one identity in favour of another, i.e. the impostor lives their life under the name of another.

Picking up on the distinction between the two forms of misuse of identity, it would be tempting to conclude that identity theft has little connection with the Internet. It is straightforward to see how the transient impersonation of another person that characterises identity fraud would be facilitated by the Internet but less clear how the wholesale acquisition of another's legal identity – effectively living life as that person – is anything other than a 'real'-world problem. However, although identity theft takes place in the physical realm, it does not follow that the Internet makes no contribution to its occurrence as it provides unparalleled opportunities for those seeking a new identity to access the necessary information. The contribution of the Internet to identity fraud is more straightforward; not only does it facilitate the information-gathering process necessary to impersonate another, but it provides a forum within which fraudulent transactions can take place that is accompanied by an illusory sense of invisibility and inviolability.

Before going on to consider the role of the Internet in facilitating the misuse of identity in any great depth, it is important to address one further implication of the language used to depict this problem. To describe identity in combination with 'theft' and 'fraud' suggests that the conduct in question falls within existing categories of the criminal law but that is not the case. Like stalking and mugging, identity theft and identity fraud are social labels that have evolved to describe a particular type of conduct. They are not legal terms; neither does the conduct that they describe necessarily amount to a criminal offence (see Wykes, this volume).

In relation to identity theft, a person will not incur criminal liability for the assumption of another's identity (living, dead or fictitious) or the abandonment of their own identity unless they do something under this assumed identity which amounts to a criminal offence as the following examples illustrate. Karl Hackett encountered difficulties in early life and decided to make a fresh start by assuming the identity of a recently deceased friend, Lee Simm, under which he lived a blameless life for 15 years. This switch of identity was discovered when 'Simm' reported 'Hackett' missing in the Paddington rail crash (Hackett was attempting to 'kill off' all vestiges of his discarded identity) but no traces of the body could be located in the train wreckage. Hackett was charged with wasting police time in relation to the time spent searching the wreckage; his conduct by assuming Simm's identity and living life under this name did not provide any basis for criminal liability (*Sunday Times*, 6 February 2000, discussed in Finch, 2003). This can be contrasted with the recent case in which a still as-yet-unidentified individual assumed the identity of a dead child, Christopher Buckingham, and adopted the title of the Earl of Buckingham (which fell into disuse in 1687) deceiving his wife, children, friends and associates into thinking he was a genuine aristocrat (*Times*, 7 November 2005). Again, the assumption of the identity of a dead person *per se* could not give rise to criminal liability but the impostor was convicted for making a false statement to obtain a passport (section 36, Criminal Justice Act 1925).

Although both of these cases would fall within the classification of identity theft as the individuals concerned discarded their own identity in favour of another, it was only a particular element of Buckingham's conduct that gave rise to criminal liability, an element which, taken in isolation, is a not uncommon instance of identity fraud in which the impostor impersonates another in order to obtain a passport. This example demonstrates the potential overlap between the two categories as many cases of identity theft will involve an accumulation of instances of identity fraud as the impostor misrepresents their identity in order to gain access to a variety of entitlements under their assumed name.

Although identity fraud is more likely to give rise to criminal liability, this is not always a straightforward matter as, contrary to popular perception, there is no general offence of fraud that could be deployed to convict those who misuse the identity of others. Instead, a whole range of criminal offences involve some level of fraudulent or deceptive conduct: Dodd (2000) notes that there are at least 150 common law or statutory offences that involve fraud, dishonesty or deception. These tend to relate to fraud or deception as to a particular fact or activity rather than criminalising generally fraudulent behaviour. For example, an individual will attract liability under section 36 of the Criminal Justice Act 1925 for making a statement they know to be untrue, i.e. that they are the person entitled to be associated with a particular set of identity information, in order to obtain a passport. In 2001, it was determined that 0.18 per cent of passport applications (approximately 11,700) were fraudulent while the Passport Agency detected 214 applications for passports made in the name of a deceased person (Hansard, 16 January 2006, col. 1115W). Despite this, there were only 16 prosecutions in 2001 under section 36 of the Criminal Justice Act 1925 thus illustrating that the difficulties lie not just in classifying and detecting criminal conduct involving identity but also in identifying and apprehending the 'invisible' person responsible.

Overall, the answer to the question 'is identity theft or identity fraud a criminal offence?' is 'it depends'. It is not an offence per se to impersonate another person or to misrepresent your own identity but it becomes an offence in certain circumstances. The majority of identity fraud will incur criminal liability simply because it is largely carried out in order to achieve an unlawful purpose. This may be using another's credit card to purchase goods or services, using another's identity to gain employment or obtain state benefit, or purporting to be another person and obtaining credit or incurring debt in their name.

The unifying feature of all these incidences of identity fraud is the misuse of another's identity in order to access something to which the impostor in their own right has no entitlement. However, because the law focuses on the entitlement rather than the fraudulent behaviour, irrespective of its aim, there is a diffusion of liability across a whole raft of different offences that gives an impression of fragmentation and, consequently, inadequate protection against identity fraud. The reality is that the real challenge for the authorities in dealing with identity fraud arises not from the diverse offences for which liability can be imposed but in identifying and locating the person responsible. This is a significant problem in the physical environment despite the fact that a person can be identified by means such as photographs, fingerprints or DNA, but these problems are magnified exponentially when the fraudulent use of identity transfers into the virtual arena (see Smith, this volume; Aas, this volume).

Legal identity and the Internet

This chapter has outlined the nature of legal identity and its vulnerability to hijacking by others that results from the historically tenuous link between an individual and the information that comprises their legal identity. Until the recent problematisation of identity, mere possession of identity information or documentation would suffice to authenticate the legal identity of the possessor despite the absence of any evidence that there was a genuine relationship between the individual and the identity they purported to be entitled to use. In short, identity theft and identity fraud were beneficial and straightforward, thus the proliferation of the misuse of identity is hardly surprising. However, increased awareness of identity theft and identity fraud has led to the exercise of a greater level of vigilance concerning personal information among the public. Simple measures such as shredding documents and increased wariness in the disclosure of personal information place at least some impediment in the way of those who would misuse this information. Moreover, organisations and service providers are conscious of the need to be more cautious in investigating the authenticity of purported identity. This has created an ethos of prudence as society becomes ever more aware of the need to protect the integrity of identity by controlling personal information. Furthermore, advances in technology have led to the evolution of increasingly sophisticated systems of authentication that facilitate the detection of fraudulent behaviour and enable information to be disseminated almost instantaneously. Unfortunately, this increased ability to detect identity theft in the physical world largely corresponded with the advent of a virtual world in which identity is inherently more amorphous:

> The Internet has become a significant social laboratory for experimenting with the constructions and reconstructions of self that characterise postmodern life. In its virtual reality, we self-fashion and self-create. (Turkle, 2004: 180; cf. Jewkes, 2003)

The Internet offers unique transformative possibilities as the persona that is presented in the virtual world is detached from the constraints that render identity relatively static in the real world. For example, an individual is not restricted to a persona that is in accord with their own gender, ethnicity or age thus the potential for experimentation is unparalleled. Moreover, it is acceptable in the online environment to shield one's real identity and to deploy any number of aliases; just as consistency of identity is expected in the real world, opacity of identity is the norm in the virtual world. The increased fluidity of identity in the virtual world accentuates the schism that already exists between legal identity and the person to whom it relates and opens up a range of fraudulent possibilities. The link between an individual and their legal identity is further fractured by the nature of online interaction which is characterised by an absence of the sensory cues that habitually enable individuals in the real world to authenticate identity; the visual appearance of a person or the sound of their voice, for example, are absent. This problem is exacerbated by the ability to create an association between the amorphous identity and the individual to whom it purports to relate; an individual may use photographs or avatars to create a deliberately misleading impression as to aspects of their identity. In the absence of face-to-face interaction, subtle visual cues assume a greater importance hence contribute significantly to the potential for shielding, modifying or otherwise misrepresenting identity (cf. DiMarco, 2003).

The contribution of the Internet to the misuse of identity

It is clear that the link between legal identity and the individual to whom it relates is even more fragile in the online environment than it is in the physical realm and this renders the Internet replete with criminogenic potential. For the fraudster, there is little to prevent them from presenting whatever persona they choose and, from the perspective of the person with whom they interact, there is little to be done to either prove or disprove the authenticity of the purported identity. Moreover, the default position taken by many Internet users, in the absence of the traditional tools used to authenticate, is one of trust until suspicion seems warranted:

> It is much more difficult to verify identity or sincerity online and, paradoxically, many users appear to be more trusting of those met online than those they encounter in person. (Rowland, 1998: unpaginated)

This ethos of trust and the illusion of 'knowing' another created by the false intimacy of virtual communications provide fertile territory for the fraudster. Not only does the default position of trust render potential victims vulnerable to deception, their unwary acceptance of others at 'face value' (despite the absence of a face) leads to a lack of caution in sharing personal information that facilitates access to their legal identity, making it vulnerable to misuse by the fraudster.

This unguarded attitude can facilitate both identity theft and identity fraud (see Brenner, this volume). It was noted earlier in this chapter that identity theft occurs in the physical environment as it involves an individual wholly discarding their true identity and assuming the identity of another. That is not to say that the Internet makes no contribution to identity theft; in many cases, it provides the impostor with the means to identify a potential victim and gather much of the information necessary to assume their identity. Prior to the arrival of the Internet, the acquisition of the personal information that comprises the legal identity of another was a painstaking process often taking weeks or months that involved visiting the various repositories of information, conducting time-consuming manual searches and obtaining the supporting documentation. This information is now only a few keystrokes away, thus accelerating the process of assembling a new legal identity. The Internet affords those seeking to abandon their true identity a means of identifying a range of potential new identities and of obtaining genuine identity documents; for example, birth certificates can be ordered online and applications for other documentation can be made 'at arm's length' via the Internet, thus distancing the impostor, literally and figuratively, from their actions. It is also possible for fraudsters to use the Internet to corroborate their false persona; for example, Alan McIlwraith's putative military background was chronicled on the online encyclopaedia Wikipedia where he was described as 'a hero that the UK and NATO can look to in times of trouble', thus seeming to substantiate his claims to be a highly decorated military officer rather than an employee of a call centre (*Times*, 12 April 2006). Other examples include the purchase of websites and related email addresses to seemingly authenticate a fictitious employment history as well as the use of websites offering for sale fake identity documents.

Of course, the ability to conduct research into potential victims is not only of value in relation to identity theft; the access to personal information provided by the Internet also renders it invaluable in terms of identity fraud. Impostors are able to sift through the mass of official sources of identity information available online in conjunction with the personal information that individuals post about themselves on personal websites, message boards, blogs or sites such as Friends Reunited. This enables the fraudster to identify a suitable victim and to acquire sufficient information to assume their identity. The depth of research that is needed is contingent upon the nature of the fraud that the impostor wishes to perpetrate. For example, an individual intent on committing financial fraud is likely to target someone who has the appearance of having a solid credit rating, such as a well-paid job and their own home, whereas the organisers of a marriage service for those seeking British citizenship are likely to approach those who appear in need of money so might focus on message boards devoted to debt. The Internet provides the means to conduct a focused search for a potential victim and to ascertain within a limited timeframe whether there is sufficient information available online to enable the impostor to assume their identity.

In addition to facilitating easy access to information that is already 'out there', the Internet provides the means to solicit identity information. For example, fraudsters may set up a trading website offering popular products at low prices in order to attract a high volume of visitors, some of whom will be seduced by the apparent bargain into entering their credit card details in order to make a 'purchase'. Not only do the non-existent goods never appear, the victim has provided their card details to the fraudster who can make further transactions or, even worse, use that information to obtain additional credit facilities in the victim's name. A similar technique operates through online auction websites such as eBay, which have been subject to numerous frauds (Yar, 2005: 81–4), where the victim purchases an item and is convinced by the seller to send a cheque or arrange a bank transfer by way of payment. The seller may even send the goods purchased to avoid alerting the purchaser's suspicions as the transaction was merely instrumental in attaining the primary purpose of acquiring bank account details. Once in possession of these details, the fraudster can use the Internet to obtain further identity information about the seller which can be used in combination with the bank details to make fraudulent credit card or loan applications.

The potential of the Internet for harvesting information to facilitate financial fraud is unsurpassed. It has become the method of choice for so-called information brokers to obtain information about individuals which they package up for sale to 'interested parties', i.e. fraudsters, in the knowledge that the gathering and passing-on of readily available information is not unlawful (provided they close their minds to its use at its destination). Information brokers use a range of methods to accumulate their information including facilities such as searchable databases based on the electoral register. Extensive use is also made of the unguarded informality of chat rooms where potential victims are identified and induced, through cleverly planned yet seemingly innocuous communications, into disclosing information that enables the impostor to assume their identity. This means of harvesting identity information is heavily reliant on the shielding of true identity provided by the Internet as the impostor assumes whatever identity characteristics are necessary to deceive the potential victim. Just as middle-aged paedophiles present themselves as children in order to groom their victims, fraudsters using Internet chat rooms adopt an appropriate persona that enables them to engage with their chosen victim. For example, some fraudsters target 'dating' chat rooms in the belief that users are more forthcoming with their personal information. They adopt an 'eligible and personable' identity using a gender-neutral username and then tailoring their identity characteristics (male/female, age, profession, location and even sexuality) to suit their chosen target. This technique is often used by fraudsters to elicit information that is then supplemented by searches of official sources. While chat room users are generally forthcoming with personal information, certain areas are regarded as off-limits; there is little prospect that someone will reveal their address in an open forum, for example. However, locating an individual's address is unproblematic once the fraudster has their name and general location and these details are readily revealed online. Recognising the value of chat rooms as a source of identity information, much of which would not be available other than directly from the individual, fraudsters have developed subtle ways of eliciting information without attracting suspicion and will devote time and effort to building up long-term online relationships both to gather information and to establish credibility in a particular Internet forum.

Fraudsters may modify their own identity with relative ease in order to elicit identity information online but the key value of the Internet in connection with identity theft and identity fraud is the way in which it shields the true identity of the fraudster from those with whom they interact online. In the physical environment, the link between legal identity and the person to whom it relates is stronger as characteristics such as gender, ethnicity and age impose limitations on the range of others whose identity can be assumed but these constraints are not applicable in online transactions. This enables a fraudster to impersonate anyone online provided they are possessed of the necessary identity information.

The ease of impersonating others or shielding one's true identity online is thus of central significance to the misuse of identity in the virtual environment. The appearance of anonymity it provides generates a sense of safety from the consequences of one's actions that prompts individuals to behave in the virtual world in ways that they would view as unthinkable in reality (DiMarco, 2003). Turkle's (2004) exploration of the way in which individuals immerse themselves in their online environment, suspending disbelief in its lack of actuality, provides insight into the way in which the Internet can lead to a bifurcation of the real and the simulated world. In other words, individuals may feel that the consequences of their online actions cannot follow them once they leave the virtual world; this aura of unreality associated with online conduct has been termed the 'disinhibition effect' (Suler, 2004) and it could go some way to explaining why individuals who would not contemplate engaging in criminal behaviour in the real world do so using the Internet:

> For the most part, people [online] only know what you tell them about yourself ... you can keep your identity hidden ... That anonymity works wonders for the disinhibition effect. When people have the opportunity to separate their actions from their real world and identity ... they feel less vulnerable about opening up. Whatever they say or do can't be directly linked to the rest of their lives. They don't have to own their behaviour by acknowledging it within the context of who they 'really' are. (Suler, 2004)

Therefore, just as the Internet offers positive possibilities for users to develop new facets of their personality, it also confers the opportunity to develop negative, i.e. criminal, characteristics without the feeling of insecurity or vulnerability that would be attached to analogous behaviour in real life. Moreover, the fragmenting of the self into the real and the virtual encourages disassociation from the negative feelings that accompany engaging in reprehensible behaviour as the physical manifestation of the individual distances them from the actions of their online counterpart: 'those behaviours aren't me at all' (Suler, 2004). For example, one first-time fraudster who used credit cards 'borrowed' from a family friend to make online purchases sought to dissociate himself from his actions by turning his computer off in a manner comparable with ending participation in an online game, while another viewed the income generated from his crude eBay fraud as so tinged with unreality and so unconnected to his 'real' self that he was surprised to be held accountable (*Independent*, 12 October 2004).

Conclusion

Although legal identity has always been vulnerable to appropriation by impostors, opportunities for identity theft and identity fraud in the real world have become increasingly limited as a result of advances in technology that serve to strengthen the link between a collection of information and the individual to whom they relate. Moreover, growing awareness of the threat of identity misuse has led to increased vigilance over identity information while the proliferation of authentication systems has made the impersonation of another in the real world a perilous enterprise. However, the virtual environment created by the Internet weakens the adherence of legal identity to its rightful owner and confers on the fraudster a far wider range of potential victims; in the fragmented spatiality of the Internet, anyone can impersonate anyone else. Moreover, conventions of Internet use normalise the shielding of identity thus the absence of an ability to authenticate identity does not attract the same suspicion as it does in the real world and there appears to be an ethos of trust and of face-value acceptance that is advantageous to the fraudster (see Brenner, this volume). It is little wonder that criminal behaviour flourishes in this environment; not only does it convey a sense of anonymity that offers to protect the fraudster from detection, it also frees individuals to act in uncharacteristic ways that they would not contemplate in real life. The benefits of spatial and symbolic distance leading to disassociation have long been recognised. Dante consigned the inventor of the catapult to the inner circle of hell as he recognised that it would be easier for warriors to kill without having a visual link with their victim; similarly, the Internet conveys an aura of distance between action and consequence that allows the fraudster to disassociate themself from their online behaviour.

It seems that impostors have adapted their strategies to take advantage of the fraudulent possibilities presented by the Internet. Whether this is using the Internet to streamline the research process and pass off others' work as one's own, to elicit identity information, or to impersonate a victim online, fraudsters are making full and creative use of the criminogenic potential of the virtual environment. Although little can be done to restrict access to official databases of information to the law-abiding user, the fraudulent potential of the Internet could be reduced if ordinary users exercised greater caution with their personal information (see Brenner, this volume). Particularly vulnerable are users of chat rooms who seem not to question the authenticity or motives of fellow users. Information is the life-blood of identity theft and identity fraud and the Internet has become the dominant means by which this information circulates among members of society. As it is difficult, at the present time, to envisage the curtailment of this information flow by any official means, it is imperative that users exercise greater vigilance in their online dealings with others to protect their legal identity from abuse.

References

Burr, V. (2003) *Social Constructionism*. Hove: Routledge.

Clarke, R. (1994) 'Human identification in information systems: management challenges and public policy issues', *Information Technology and People*, 7: 173–96.

DiMarco, H. (2003) 'The electronic cloak: secret sexual deviance in cybersociety', in Y. Jewkes (ed.), *Dot.cons: Crime, Deviance and Identity on the Internet*. Cullompton: Willan.

Dodd, N. J. (2000) 'The psychology of fraud', in D. Canter and L. Allison (eds), *Profiling Property Crimes*. Dartmouth: Ashgate.

Finch, E. (2003) 'What a tangled web we weave: identity theft and the internet' in Y. Jewkes (ed.), *Dot.cons: Crime, Deviance and Identity on the Internet*. Cullompton: Willan.

Foucault, M. (1979) *Discipline and Punish: The Birth of the Prison*. New York: Vintage International.

Goffman, E. (1968) *Stigma: Notes on the Management of Spoiled Identity*. Harmondsworth: Penguin.

Jewkes, Y. (2003) *Dot.cons: Crime, Deviance and Identity on the Internet*. Cullompton: Willan.

Jones, G. and Levi, M. (2000) *The Value of Identity and the Need for Authentication*. DTI Office of Science and Technology Crime Foresight Panel Essay for 'Turning the Corner'.

Jung, C. (1988) *Two Essays on Analytical Psychology*. Princeton, NJ: Princeton University Press.

Locke, J. (1690) *Essays on Human Understanding*, Book II.

Marx, G. T. (2001) 'Identity and anonymity: some conceptual distinctions and issues for research', in J. Caplan and J. Torpey (eds), *Documentary Individual Identity*, Princeton, NJ: Princeton University Press.

Rowland, D. (1998) 'Cyberspace – a contemporary utopia' *Journal of Information Technology Law* 3 (online at: http://www.law.warwick.ac.uk/jilt/98-3/Rowland.html).

Semmens, N. (2005) 'When the world knows your name: identity theft and fraud in the UK', *Scottish Journal of Criminal Justice Studies*, 11: 80–91.

Steinhardt, B. (2004) 'Privacy and forensic DNA data banks', in D. Lazer (ed.), *DNA and the Criminal Justice System: The Technology of Justice*. Cambridge, MA: MIT Press.

Suler, J. (2004) 'The online disinhibition effect', *Cyber Psychology and Behaviour*, 7: 321–6.

Torpey, J. (2000) *The Invention of the Passport: Surveillance, Citizenship and the State*. Cambridge: Cambridge University Press.

Turkle, S. (2004) *The Second Self: Computers and the Human Spirit*. Cambridge, MA: MIT Press.

Williams, R. (2001) *Making Identity Matter: Identity, Society and Social Interaction*. Durham: Sociology Press.

Yar, M. (2005) *Cybercrime and Society*. London: Sage.

Chapter 4

Biometric solutions to identity-related cybercrime

Russell G. Smith

Introduction

In recent times, identity-related crime has received considerable public attention. In the news media, reports regularly appear of credit card numbers and other personal information being taken from databases and misused. In the United States in May 2005, for example, the processor of payment card data, CardSystems Solutions Inc., had its database breached and credit card account information including magnetic stripe data and cardholder names relating to over 40 million accounts were stolen (Krim and Barbaro, 2005). Between January and December 2005, Consumer Sentinel, the US complaints database developed and maintained by the Federal Trade Commission, received over 685,000 consumer fraud and identity theft complaints, 37 per cent of which concerned identity theft (see Finch, this volume). Consumers reported losses from fraud of more than US$680 million in 2005 (Federal Trade Commission, 2006). Cases involving identity-related cybercrime continue to come before the courts with most instances facilitated through the misuse of computer passwords.

One of the essential elements in the commission of most forms of cybercrime is the need to disguise one's identity in order not to be located by police once the crime has been committed. Developments in information and communications technologies (ICTs) have now made the task of hiding one's identity relatively easy. These technologies enable offenders to log onto computers using someone else's identity, or to conceal their activities through weaving or looping through various Internet Service Provider (ISP) locations. Perhaps the greatest area of risk lies in taking out an online service in the first instance, as few telecommunications carriers or ISPs carry out extensive enrolment identity checks on new customers. The use of scanners, editing software and laser printers all make the task of creating and manipulating documents used to establish identity, such as passports, birth certificates and drivers' licences, relatively simple.

Identity-related cybercrime takes place when an individual defeats the user authentication strategies of a networked system, whatever they may be, and successfully identifies himself or herself as someone else – whether in the guise of a real other person or under cover of a totally fabricated identity. Depending upon the nature of the transaction, circumventing an authentication system may allow an individual to obtain a benefit to which he or she is not entitled, or to avoid a detriment or responsibility which may arise as a result of being identified as oneself. Examples extend from obtaining benefits from the government dishonestly, through loan fraud, to avoidance of fines or tax liabilities. Even the security of frequent flyer and other loyalty schemes have been compromised electronically, while in Australia electronic highway toll collection schemes have been defrauded. It is the deliberate use of deception to obtain a benefit or avoid a detriment that makes the user's actions fraudulent.

The conventional means of countering such problems is to require individuals to identify themselves by producing or disclosing something that they *have* (such as a card or other token), something that they *know* (such as a password or PIN), something related to *who* they are (such as a fingerprint or other biometric), or something indicating *where* they are located (such as an address or phone number). Of course, there are other means of identification, such as the use of a person's name and a variety of behavioural and psychological characteristics. Depending upon the degree of certainty with which one needs to establish a person's identity, one or more of these various methods may be relied upon. Often only one method of information will be used, although so-called 'two-factor authentication' is now becoming the gold standard. Each, however, has its own vulnerabilities and risks, which are able to be exploited by those who want to act illegally.

The precise way in which identity-related cybercrime is perpetrated, and the ease with which it can be carried out, will depend on the type of authentication system that is in place. In particular, it will depend on the nature of the data which are associated with individuals, and how easy they are to obtain and/or to replicate. For example, to defeat knowledge-based systems it is necessary for an offender to ascertain and use the piece of information that the user knows, such as a password or PIN. This information may be learnt directly from users who may share their passwords with friends or co-workers. Alternatively, a user may be tricked into revealing information through 'social engineering' – that is, by persuading the user to reveal information in the belief that it is required for some legitimate purpose, such as a regular verification check by a bank, or by pretending to be a researcher who is conducting a survey. Information can also be guessed or 'cracked' through the use of computer technology, or may be obtained through practices such as 'shoulder-surfing' (where an individual watches a person entering their password or PIN into a machine) or 'dumpster-diving' (where an individual searches through a person's rubbish for relevant information).

Different challenges are faced by those who seek to defraud a token-based system. As such systems rely on the association of people with a physical object, circumventing them will generally require an individual to acquire the required token. This can be done either by stealing or purchasing a legitimately manufactured token, or forging a copy. The ease with which such objects can be counterfeited will depend on the nature of the object, and any document security features (such as holographic images) that have been incorporated. Although the use of such security features may make it more difficult to defraud token-based systems, with advances in computer technology it is usually possible for a determined identity thief to bypass even the most secure systems and counterfeit documents containing the appropriate security features (Smith, 1999). Even if documents cannot be successfully counterfeited, it may still be possible to buy or steal them.

This chapter examines the various considerations that need to be addressed in deciding whether to continue to use conventional systems of identification that rely on tokens, knowledge or location as evidence of identity, or whether to replace or supplement these approaches with biometric systems. The focus is on the risks of identity-related fraud that arise when people gain access to computer networks (so-called logical access) which lies at the heart of most types of cybercrime.

Biometric identification and authentication

Due to the vulnerabilities of knowledge-based and token-based systems, a number of organisations and government agencies are moving to 'biometrics'. The United Kingdom Biometrics Working Group (2002: 4) defines biometrics as 'the automated means of recognising a living person through the measurement of distinguishing physiological or behavioural traits'. In other words, biometric systems are based on who a person is, rather than what a person has or what he or she knows. Whether by fingerprint, voiceprint, iris pattern or a number of other characteristics, it is possible to measure an individual's personal attributes to help identify them.

Currently, fingerprint recognition comprises the largest share of the marketplace, followed by hand geometry, iris recognition and facial recognition. This makeup of the biometric market is likely to change as the more recently developed technologies, such as facial recognition and iris recognition, become more accurate and less expensive. The range of biometric technologies currently available are summarised in Table 4.1.

In recent years, biometrics have been used for a range of logical access control applications. These include: electronic voting in Mexico, Uganda and Yemen (employing facial recognition), and in Brazil, Costa Rica, Dominican Republic, Honduras, Italy, Jamaica, Nigeria, Panama and Peru (employing fingerprint recognition); personal computer logon applications (employing fingerprint recognition); network access control at banks and hospitals in the United States, and at schools in Sweden (employing fingerprint recognition); at the Federal Aviation Authority and the Office of Legislative Counsel of the House of Representatives, and at hospitals in the United States (employing iris recognition); at a publishing company in the United Kingdom, and an insurance company in the United States (employing voice recognition); cellular telephone security (employing fingerprint and voice recognition); ATM and EFTPOS access in Germany, the United Kingdom and the United States (employing iris recognition); and e-commerce customer authentication at banks in Belgium, Brazil, Ireland, Israel and the United States, as well as at retail outlets such as the Irish Farmer's Association in Ireland and the Home Shopping Network in the United States (employing voice recognition).

In recent times with ever-present concerns over terrorism, a number of countries have decided to issue compulsory identity cards, some of which include a biometric identifier. In Australia, on 24 October 2005, a biometrically enabled passport was first made available in which the personal information currently recorded on a passport is now kept on a computer chip embedded in the centre pages of the passport. Already some 2,500 e-passports have been issued in Australia, and trials are being conducted involving airline staff and some others which enable them to use facial recognition technology in conjunction with the e-passport to proceed through customs controls at airports (Nash, 2005). The Special Administrative Region of Hong Kong has developed multi-use ID 'smartcards' which contain basic biometric information such as thumbprints and a photograph, and are capable of multiple functions including use as drivers' licences and as library cards (Benitez, 2002; *South China Morning Post*, 2002). A pilot programme for a biometric ID card was also implemented in Britain in relation to asylum seekers some time ago (McAuliffe, 2002), although proposals to introduce a national biometric identity card failed in early 2006 (see BBC News, 2006; LSE Department of Information Systems, 2005).

Biometric systems entail two processes: enrolment and matching. In the enrolment phase, an individual's biometric characteristic (such as a fingerprint) is acquired for the first time. The image acquired will usually be converted into a 'template', against which subsequent comparisons are made. In the matching phase, an individual's biometric characteristic is captured again. This 'live template' is compared against previously

Table 4.1 Biometric technologies

Major technologies	Minor technologies	Emerging technologies
Facial recognition – uses still, video or web cameras to identify individuals by using characteristics of the face, such as the distance between the eyes, the width of the nose, the depth of the eye sockets and the size and shape of the chin.	*DNA matching* – compares DNA samples in their entirety. Is used in a forensic capacity, but cannot yet be used as a real-time biometric identifier.	*Blood pulse measurement* – uses a small infrared sensor placed on the tip of a finger to identify individuals by using their blood pulse signatures.
Fingerprint recognition – uses optical, capacitive or ultrasound scanners to identify individuals by using the patterns of ridges and valleys found on the surface of the fingertip.	*Facial thermography* – uses infrared cameras to identify individuals by using heat patterns emitted from the face due to the branching of blood vessels.	*Ear shape recognition* – uses cameras to identify individuals using the shape of the projecting portion of the outer ear. Faces many obstacles for personal identification purposes, such as interference caused by hair or headwear.
Hand geometry – uses hand scanners to identify individuals by measuring the three dimensional shape of the hand, including the width, height and length of the fingers, as well as the distance between joints, and the shape of the knuckles.	*Keystroke pattern recognition* – uses software to identify individuals by analysing the way in which they type, examining factors such as the latencies between successive keystrokes, keystroke durations, finger placement and pressure applied to the keys.	*Gait recognition* – uses cameras or radars to identify individuals by the way they walk. Has many problems to overcome, such as gait being obscured by clothing, and problems with the angle of acquisition. Gait may also not be unique to each individual.
Iris recognition – uses high-quality cameras capable of infrared imaging to identify individuals by using the characteristics of the coloured rings around the pupil of their eyes.	*Retina recognition* – uses retina scanners to identify individuals based on the blood vessel pattern on the back of the eye.	*Nailbed identification* – uses light and an interferometer to identify individuals by using the vertical ridges beneath fingernails.

Table 4.1 *Continued*

Signature recognition – uses special pens and 'pads' to identify individuals based on either the appearance of their signature ('static signature recognition') or the series of movements involved in the signing process ('dynamic signature recognition').	*Vein recognition* – uses scanners which emit near-infrared light to identify individuals using the pattern of blood vessels in the back of the hand.	*Odour recognition* – uses an odour-sensing instrument ('electronic nose') to identify individuals based on their smell. Has many problems to overcome, such as the use of perfumes and deodorants, and changes in odour due to diet or medical conditions.
Voice recognition – uses audio capturing devices, such as telephones or microphones, to identify individuals by using the characteristics of their voice.		*Skin pattern recognition* – uses near-infrared light and a spectroscope to identify individuals by measuring the optical pattern which is reflected from the skin.

enrolled data, seeking a match. The key question for biometric systems operating in verification mode is 'are you who you claim to be?' Other issues arise in the contexts of using biometrics for identification and 'watch list' checking, such as for border control and immigration purposes (Aas, 2006).

Evaluating biometric systems

The ways in which biometric systems can be evaluated differ depending on the particular type of biometric technology to be tested, as well as the purpose for which it is being used – whether for identification or surveillance. No single test has been developed which can accurately measure all issues across different biometric devices in a uniform way. Because of this multiplicity of ways in which biometric systems can be evaluated, it is not readily possible to determine which is the 'best' biometric, because some systems will perform well on one measure but will be outperformed on others. The choice of which biometric system to deploy, if any, will depend on the particular needs and priorities of the organisation, including the location and purpose of the system and the number and nature of the people who will be using it.

Policy-makers are faced with a wide range of considerations when deciding whether or not to implement biometric solutions to identity-related cybercrime. On the one hand, they must evaluate a considerable and ever-increasing body of technical evidence relating to the performance of biometric technologies, while on the other hand a range of social, legal and practical considerations need to be addressed including privacy, data security, user acceptance and cost. Compelling evidence of performance should not, however, overwhelm these non-technological considerations. There are ten key issues to consider which will be discussed in the remainder of this chapter (see also Smith 2006).

Enrolment

At the outset, it is important to bear in mind that the traditional ways in which identity is established will still be required during the enrolment phase of a biometric system. A person's biometric does not, by itself, provide evidence of identity: 'Biometric systems can only confirm or determine a claimed identity – one established upon a system at enrolment – as opposed to revealing a "true" identity' (International Biometric Group, 2003: 17). To this end, it is important to ensure that appropriate identification documents are still provided and background checks made prior to enrolment as the integrity of a biometric system is only as good as the quality of the enrolment data (Dunstone, 2003). If care is not taken in the enrolment phase, it will continue to be possible for a person to defraud the system, defeating the purpose for which biometrics are used.

Moreover, a real danger arises if a person can successfully bind their biometric data to a stolen identity, because this will allow them to continue using the stolen or fabricated identity for a variety of fraudulent purposes, with little risk of detection. It will generally be accepted that because a person can provide a biometric that matches the assumed identity, they must be that person. This may have a significant detrimental effect on the person whose identity has been stolen and can take a long period of time to correct.

Some of the most difficult issues relate to the creation of databases of personal information, and the enrolment of individuals within them. The techniques of deception often reach back to the very creation of the records entailed in a system of identification. If a false identity can acquire the trappings of legitimacy from the very start, it makes a much more effective tool for the identity fraudster, being practically impossible to detect.

With established databases, for example those held by large government agencies such as registries of births, deaths and marriages or revenue departments, there is an ongoing need to cleanse the data to ensure that the information recorded about individuals is correct. Some changes that occur may be legitimate, such as changes of name on marriage or through formal change of name procedures. Others, however, are dishonest. In Australia, the Report of the House of Representatives Standing Committee on Economics, Finance and Public Administration (2000), *Numbers on the Run*, reported the finding of the Australian National Audit Office that there were 3.2 million more Tax File Numbers than people in Australia and 185,000 potential duplicate tax records for individuals. The ATO currently believes that there are over 25,000 duplicate tax file numbers which form part of 6.5 million inactive tax file number records (Australian Taxation Office, 2004: 6).

Performance

There are a number of ways in which the performance of biometric systems can be measured. These include collecting and analysing the following measures:

- *Failure to enrol rate (FTER)* – this measures the proportion of users who, for some reason, cannot enrol in a particular biometric system.

- *Failure to acquire rate (FTAR)* – this measures the proportion of cases where a user seeks to provide a biometric to match against their previously enrolled template but the system cannot acquire an image of sufficient quality.

- *False match rate (FMR)* – this measures the probability that a sample will be falsely declared to match the template of another person.

- *False non-match rate (FNMR)* – this measures the probability that a sample will be falsely declared not to match the template of the user who provided the sample.

- *False accept rate (FAR)* – this measures the proportion of cases in which an impostor is falsely accepted by a biometric system.

- *False reject rate (FRR)* – this measures the proportion of cases in which a genuine user is falsely rejected by a biometric system.

- *Equal error rate (EER)* – this is usually the point at which the false reject and false accept rates are equivalent. In some cases, it can also refer to the point at which the false match and false non-match rates are equivalent.

It should be noted that while these measures are widely used, their use is not always consistent. Evaluations are also often carried out within the industry promoting the technology in question, casting doubts on the objectivity of some reports. This makes it vital for policy-makers to inspect any biometric evaluation report closely before accepting its results. In addition, while each of the above-mentioned measures can be used to evaluate biometric technologies, they are not the only possible ways of evaluating biometric systems.

Efficiency

An important consideration for all identification systems is their ability to deal with extremely large numbers of individuals quickly. It is possible to assess speed in a number of ways. These include looking at the time taken to enrol a person, to acquire their characteristics, to verify information provided or to conduct the matching process. Biometric systems vary considerably in relation to their processing speeds, although they are invariably quicker than manual processing of individuals using token-based or knowledge-based systems or when using plastic cards. Where, however, systems fail for some reason, considerable time may be taken to rectify the problem. The problem of data overload also needs to be considered prior to implementing an electronic system on an international scale.

Data security

The implementation of biometrics in any case is not a simple matter, and the two models of storage of biometric information each offer their own challenges and risks. On the one hand, biometrics applications for verification may compare the individual's body – whether it be a fingerprint, face, hand or iris – directly to the template recorded on a card or other *portable medium*. If this is the case then defeat of that medium's security features may allow replacement or alteration of the template, unbeknown to the system administrators. For facial recognition, depending on the model used, this might be as straightforward as photo substitution or as complex as cracking strongly encrypted data.

If, on the other hand, the comparison is to a template held on a *central database*, that database would represent a high-profile target for hackers, organised criminals and other parties. Securing that information, for example using public key encryption, and ensuring inside parties are not able to access and alter information inappropriately represents a major challenge. In recent times, various large-scale information databases, including client details held by major credit card companies and respected commercial providers, have been defeated or compromised by outsiders and insiders alike. To anticipate the points of susceptibility to interference is the essential challenge of implementing biometric applications on a wide scale.

Spoofing

Spoofing refers to techniques developed or adapted to challenge the biometric in question. There are three main ways in which a system can be attacked (Thalheim et al., 2002). The first involves the creation of an artificial biometric. This involves putting artificially created data into the regular sensor technology of the system. For example, a fake finger could be used to deceive a fingerprint scanner, or a photograph used to deceive a facial recognition system. For this approach to work, it is necessary for the impostor to obtain a copy of the biometric that they wish to use. This could be done, for example, by taking a photograph of the person to be imitated.

The second, known as relay attacks, involves the use of artificially created data. However, instead of obtaining the relevant data by copying the biometric to be used, this method involves capturing the relevant data as they are input into the sensor through use of a device such as a sniffer program. This is a device which can be attached to the back of a computer (for example, in the USB port), which can obtain information as it is input into the computer. The data captured can then be replayed in order to deceive the system. A researcher at the Australian National University in 2002, for example, demonstrated how fingerprint verifiers could be circumvented by presenting a template resembling that electronically stored in the device (Baker, 2002).

Finally, there are database attacks which seek to compromise the databases in which the data are stored. This will usually need to be done by someone who has administrator rights over the database, although it could be done through an external attack on the database (hacking). One way such an attack could take place is where an individual who works on the development of the system forges user data that are reactivated at a later date to their advantage. For example, a person could match his or her own fingerprint to a false identity, which could then be used for fraudulent purposes.

The first of these methods is the main focus of literature in this area, as it is the most likely avenue for spoofing. People are more likely to attempt to spoof a fingerprint recognition system by using a rubber finger, or a voice recognition system by using an audio recording, than they are to hack into the database itself. Many technology developers have attempted to create countermeasures to prevent such attacks. The most common of these countermeasures is what is known as 'liveness' testing. Many systems have some form of technology capable of checking that the biometric characteristic being measured belongs to a live person. For example, fingerprint scanners may test the temperature of the finger, while iris scanners may search for a pulse or rapid eye movements. Such systems have a dual advantage: they can help to prevent spoofing, as well as potentially preventing some forms of crime displacement (see below). Unfortunately, there is little research on the steps that have been taken to prevent the less common forms of attack. There are also few evaluations that measure the ability of systems to repel concerted attacks. One of the few studies in this area was conducted by three German researchers who attempted to spoof a number of different devices (Thalheim et al., 2002). While some of the devices caused them slight difficulties, with a little persistence they managed to compromise each device investigated.

Facial recognition systems, for example, have yet to be tested against people seriously motivated to evade detection through prosthetic and cosmetic adjustments to their facial shape and size. Indeed, there have been reports that transplant surgery and immune system drugs may very soon enable faces to be transplanted. This might not currently be considered a realistic threat, and in any case is unlikely to occur on a sufficiently wide scale to affect most systems. Yet, in view of the global awareness of how far terrorists may go in furtherance of their aims, such concerns need to be taken into consideration.

Privacy

While some have claimed that biometrics can be a privacy-enhancing technology (Biometrics Institute, 2002), there is a general perception that the use of such technologies is likely to invade privacy. Some of the main privacy fears include concerns that biometric information will be gathered without permission or knowledge or without explicitly defining the purpose for which it is required, and that information may be used for a variety of purposes other than those for which it was originally acquired ('function creep'), shared without explicit permission or used to track people across multiple databases to amalgamate information for the purpose of surveillance or social control (General Accounting Office, United States, 2002).

The decision to issue compulsory biometrically enabled identity cards in some countries has led to vocal opposition from advocates of privacy who raise the grave consequences of essential information being misused such as occurred during the Nazi regime in the Second World War. One writer refers to 'the singular ease with which population registration systems have been mobilised for genocidal purposes' (Seltzer, 1998: 544). Any use of biometric systems thus needs to comply with privacy principles and privacy legislation (Crompton, 2002). In Ontario, for example, policies were developed to govern the use of biometric systems designed to prevent welfare fraud. The following privacy protective provisions were included in the Canadian Social Assistance Reform Act (Cavoukian, 1999: 5): any biometric information collected under the Act must be encrypted; the encrypted biometric cannot be used as a unique identifier, capable of facilitating linkages to other biometric information or other databases; the original biometric must be destroyed after the encryption process; the encrypted biometric information only can be stored or transmitted in encrypted form, then destroyed in a prescribed manner; and no program information is to be retained with the encrypted biometric information. The Act also required that systems should be unable to be implemented that could reconstruct or retain the original biometric sample from encrypted biometric information, or that could compare it to a copy or reproduction of biometric information not obtained directly from the individual.

User acceptance

Past experience has shown that the efficiency and accuracy of biometric systems can be reduced if those required to use the system are not willing to accept the technology: 'user attitude can make or break the implementation of a biometric system' (United Kingdom Biometrics Working Group, 2002: 7). Some people may find the process of providing personal information in public distasteful. This was one reason given for the reluctance of retailers to make use of a cheque fraud prevention initiative which required customers to leave their fingerprint on cheques before they would be accepted by retailers (see Pidco, 1996). Similarly, users may associate fingerprints with policing and criminality and feel reluctant to use fingerprinting systems. Still others may believe that systems which scan irises or retinas may harm their eyes (despite clear evidence to the contrary). Both end users and administrators of systems may be reluctant to make use of them. Accordingly, the need arises to educate users about the reasons why the system has been introduced and how it might benefit them. User concerns relating to privacy and security of data storage, as well as the safety of using some devices, especially eye-based biometrics, would also need to be addressed.

Rectification

Another problem associated with biometrics arises from the fact that once a system has been compromised, it may be difficult to rectify the problem. While a new PIN can always be issued, new fingerprints cannot. Any error, corruption or systematic failure of the biometric identifier will be as permanent and irrevocable as the 'correct' identification is supposed to be. Even if the enrolment process remains error-free, a biometric is effectively a 'PIN you can never change' – and compromised once is compromised for all time (Biometrics Institute, 2002). Meanwhile, the ostensibly greater security afforded by the use of the biometric may lead to overconfidence in its accuracy, which could make any cases of successful identity fraud that much more damaging.

Cost

There is a wide range of costs involved in the implementation and use of biometric systems. It is especially important to consider recurrent costs, which can often outweigh the costs of infrastructure and initial implementation. Often however, these differing cost considerations are grouped together and presented in simplistic charts, such as that contained in a report from the International Biometric Group (2003) which seeks to compare a range of considerations relating to different biometrics in one chart. Although simple to read, it could be grossly misleading.

Cost considerations associated with the implementation of a biometric identity card in the United Kingdom recently led to proposed legislation being defeated in the House of Lords. The Home Office had estimated that the scheme would cost approximately £584 million to run each year, with each combined biometric passport and identity card costing £93 (BBC News, 2006). However, a report by the Department of Information Systems at the LSE argued that the government had not given full cost estimates for establishing the scheme and that its overall costs would depend on how government departments chose to use the card scheme. The LSE report estimated that the scheme would actually cost between £10.6 billion and £19.2 billion over ten years, excluding public or private sector integration costs and potential cost overruns, if the government followed its original plans (LSE Department of Information Systems, 2005).

Displacement

Finally, the use of biometrics as a crime reduction strategy, like many other crime reduction techniques, carries with it the risk that displacement may occur. Displacement has been defined as: 'a change in offender behaviour, along illegitimate means, which is designed to circumvent either a specific preventive measure or more general conditions unfavourable to the offender's usual mode of operating' (Gabor, 1990: 66). One academic described the problem of displacement of crime as follows:

> Fear of displacement is often based on the assumption that offenders are like predatory animals – they will do what ever it takes to commit crimes – just as a rat will do whatever it takes to steal food from the cupboard. (Eck, 1998)

If it is assumed that potential offenders act on the basis of some rational calculation in which they balance up the likely risks and benefits to be derived from a potential course of conduct, then as some types of crime are seen to become too difficult to commit, other easier targets may be considered.

The use of biometrics for logical access control could result in offenders obtaining access to computers through bribery or coercion of IT personnel or other gatekeepers within organisations, or forcing users under threat of violence to permit the offender to have access by presenting their biometric under duress. We have already seen the occurrence of this with duress being used by offenders against users at ATMs to compel them to withdraw cash. Failure to comply has even resulted in users being killed in some countries.

Conclusions

This chapter has identified some of the considerations that need to be taken into account when deciding whether or not to implement biometric systems in order to minimise risks of identity-related cybercrime. The concern is that the introduction of a new technology may make matters worse – either with respect to the specific crime problem sought to be addressed or by creating new risks through the infringement of privacy or displacement to other forms of more serious crime.

Careful thought also needs to be given to what biometric technologies cannot do. Of greatest importance is the fact that they cannot validate identity upon initial enrolment. If checks are not in place to validate the evidence of identity produced upon enrolment, then the subsequent use of a biometric authentication system may make identity-related crime easier to perpetrate and more difficult to detect. Offenders may simply put their energies into creating a false identity and using that when enrolling in a biometric system.

The decision about which biometric technology, if any, to implement is not a simple one. There is a wide range of factors which need to be considered, including the performance of the system, its ability to be compromised, the ease of using such systems and user concerns about issues such as privacy and security. In addition, the cost-effectiveness of rolling out a biometric system must be determined, with consideration given to both implementation and recurrent costs. These should be carefully weighed against the cost of using other viable alternative methods of identification, such as knowledge or token-based systems, in light of the particular security needs of the organisation.

Of great importance from the point of view of policy-makers, however, is the need to balance the evidence that exists in support of, and against, any given system in relation to each of the various considerations outlined above. Policy-makers should avoid the temptation solely to focus on the seemingly convincing evidence of technical performance provided by the industry concerned. Technical performance is only one criterion, and even this can be measured in a wide range of ways. Instead, evidence needs to be sought out and scrutinised concerning the range of other legal, social and ethical considerations governing the use of any given system. Unfortunately, it is these aspects which have yet to be fully researched.

Note

The views expressed in this chapter are those of the author alone and do not represent the policies of the Australian government. Assistance in conducting research for this chapter was provided by Jamie Walvisch, Dr Yuka Sakurai and Stuart Candy.

References

Aas, K. F. (2006) ' "The body does not lie": identity, risk and trust in technoculture', *Crime, Media, Culture: An International Journal* 2 (2): 143–58.

Australia, House of Representatives Standing Committee on Economics, Finance and Public Administration (2000) *Numbers on the Run: Review of the Australian National Audit Office Audit Report No 37, 1998–99 on the Management of Tax File Numbers*. Canberra: Parliament of the Commonwealth of Australia.

Australian Taxation Office (2004) *Compliance Program 2004–05*. Canberra: Australian Taxation Office.

Baker, L. (2002) 'Rule of thumb: don't rely on new security systems', *ANU Reporter*, 33: 9 (online at: http://www.anu.edu.au/pad/reporter/volume/33/09/acrobat.pdf).

BBC News (2006) 'Lords defeat for ID cards scheme', *BBC News Online*, 17 January (online at: http://news.bbc.co.uk/go/pr/fr/-/1/hi/uk_politics/4616356.stm).

Benitez, M. A. (2002) 'ID card contract awarded', *South China Morning Post* (Hong Kong), 27 February, p. 2.

Biometrics Institute (2002) 'The impact of biometrics on privacy', an interview with Dr Roger Clarke (online at: http://www.biometricsinstitute.org/bi/interviews.htm).

Cavoukian, A. (1999) 'Privacy and biometrics' (online at: http://www.ipc.on.ca/docs/pri-biom.pdf).

Crompton, M. (2002) *Biometrics and Privacy: The End of the World as We Know It or the White Knight of Privacy?* Presented at Biometrics-Security and Authentication Conference, 20 March. Sydney: Biometrics Institute Conference.

Dunstone, T. (2003) 'The use of biometric technology in airports' (online at: http://www.biometricsinstitute.org/bi/Articles/0303_AirportReview1.pdf).

Eck, J. (1998) 'Preventing crime at places', in L. W. Sherman, D. Gottfredson, D. Mackenzie, J. Eck, P. Reuter and S. Bushway, *What Works, What Doesn't, What's Promising*. Washington, DC: National Institute of Justice.

Federal Trade Commission (2006) *Consumer Fraud and Identity Theft Complaint Data, January–December 2005*. Washington, DC: Federal Trade Commission.

Gabor, T. (1990) 'Crime displacement and situational prevention: toward the development of some principles', *Canadian Journal of Criminology*, 32: 41–73.

General Accounting Office, United States (2002) *Technology Assessment: Using Biometrics for Border Security*, GAO-03-174, November. Washington, DC: General Accounting Office (online at: http://www.gao.gov/new.items/d03174.pdf).

International Biometric Group (2003) *Biometric Market Report 2003–2007*. New York: IBG.

Krim, J. and Barbaro, M. (2005) '40 million credit card numbers hacked', *Washington Post*, 18 June, A01 (online at: http://www.washingtonpost.com/wp-dyn/content/article/2005/06/17/AR2005061701031_2.html).

LSE Department of Information Systems (2005) *The Identity Project: An Assessment of the UK Identity Cards Bill and its Implications*. London: London School of Economics and Political Science.

McAuliffe, W. (2002) 'Asylum seekers get first UK biometric ID cards', *ZDNet Australia*, 5 February (online at: http://www.zdnet.com.au/newstech/security/story/0,2000024985,20263301,00.htm).

Nash, B. (2005) *Utilising the Latest in Biometrics Technology to Enhance Your Forensic Capability*. Paper presented at the IIR Conference 'Combating Identity Fraud', 1 November, Sydney.

Pidco, G. W. (1996) 'Check print: a discussion of a crime prevention initiative that failed', *Security Journal*, 7: 37–40.

Seltzer, W. (1998) 'Population statistics, the Holocaust, and the Nuremberg trials', *Population and Development Review*, 24 (3): 511–52.

Smith, R. G. (1999) 'Identity-related economic crime: risks and countermeasures', *Trends and Issues in Crime and Criminal Justice*, No. 129. Canberra: Australian Institute of Criminology.

Smith, R. G. (2006) 'Identification systems: a risk assessment framework', *Trends and Issues in Crime and Criminal Justice*, No. 324. Canberra: Australian Institute of Criminology.

South China Morning Post (Hong Kong) (2002) 'ID card plans raise issue of carrier privacy', 17 January, p. 11.

Thalheim, L., Krissler, J. and Ziegler, P.-M. (2002) 'Body check: biometric access protection devices and their programs put to the test', *c't Magazine* (Germany), no. 11, May (online at: http://www.heise.de/ct/english/02/11/114/).

United Kingdom Biometrics Working Group (2002) 'Use of biometrics for identification: advice on product selection' (online at: http://www.cesg.gov.uk/site/ast/biometrics/media/Biometrics%20Advice.pdf).

Chapter 5

Internet child pornography: international responses

Yvonne Jewkes and Carol Andrews

Introduction

This chapter will draw primarily on research from the UK and New Zealand, with additional data from the USA, Canada and Australia, to discuss Internet child pornography, the offenders who use it and the responses of, and difficulties faced by, the police in investigating and prosecuting those responsible. While Internet-related forms of child sexual abuse can take many forms, we are primarily concerned with the downloading of abusive images for personal gratification, the trading of child pornography and the concomitant use of the Internet (e.g. via newsgroups and bulletin board systems) by individuals to communicate with like-minded others. The chapter is thus chiefly interested in the Internet circulation of sexualised images of children, including those involving explicit, aggressive and abusive acts as opposed to seemingly 'innocent', non-sexualised pictures that are used by adults for sexual gratification. In other words, and to employ the terms used by investigators when categorising evidential material, it is 'indecent' and 'obscene', as opposed to 'indicative' material that we are primarily concerned with. Although our focus is on individuals who consume (rather than produce) abusive images of children, like much of the other literature in this field, we do not propose to make a distinction between those who download child pornography and paedophiles. In countries that have initiated sex offender registers (including all the countries mentioned above), offenders found guilty of possessing child pornography are required to register as sex offenders even if they are not 'contact offenders'. Furthermore, recent research suggests that exposure to child pornography is a factor in the development of sexual offending against children, with 40 per cent of arrested consumers of child pornography found to have also sexually victimised children, according to a recent American study (Wolak et al., 2005; see also Araji, 2000; Taylor and Quayle, 2003; DIA, 2004). We would further argue that it seems a spurious distinction to make given that the trade in sexualised images of children could not exist without a constant supply of new images. As the Director of the new Child Exploitation and Online Protection (CEOP) Centre has noted, 'anyone who puts these pictures of children online not only offends against that child today but every time these images are viewed' (Jim Gamble, quoted in the *Guardian*, 19 April 2006).

The chapter is divided into five parts: first, we briefly discuss the paradox of societies that fetishise youth and sexuality at the same time as condemning paedophiles as the bogeymen of our age; second, we examine the nature and content of offensive material; third, we discuss the demographics and behaviours of offenders; fourth, we explore the role of the police; and fifth, we outline some of the particular difficulties facing police in the successful investigation and prosecution of individuals who download sexually abusive images of children.

Cultural hypocrisy?

The question of what constitutes child pornography might, at first, appear relatively straightforward (and will be explained with reference to Taylor et al.'s (2001) typology of child pornography below) but it is worth saying something first about the nature of abusive images of children within a wider context. The popular media constructs the behaviour of adults who are sexually attracted to children and adolescents in unambiguously negative terms: they are 'perverts', 'monsters' or 'evil sex pests' (Greer, 2003). On occasions, such salacious reporting has led to incidents of community 'direct action' and vigilantism against people suspected (sometimes wrongly) of paedophile activities, assaults which are then in turn reported in a continuous loop of punitive and vindictive media discourse. Yet the reality of adult–child relations is almost certainly more complex and more uncomfortable than such black-and-white representations suggest, given that the sexualisation of children and the blurring of boundaries between expressions of childhood and adult sexuality has reached unprecedented levels (Greer and Jewkes, 2005). The construction of the paedophile as society's number one folk devil sits uncomfortably within a culture which, in other arenas (such as fashion, beauty and art), fetishises youthful bodies. As Silverman and Wilson (2002) point out, the vogue for small girls to dress as adult women and adult women to dress as small girls suggests that children carry a broad appeal to many adults who are not paedophiles, and would frankly be offended by the suggestion. By way of example, some of the Spring/Summer 2004 collections created by the fashion houses of Paris and Milan were themed around Nabokov's novel *Lolita*, the story of a middle-aged man's quest to seduce a twelve-year-old girl. Containing fantasy sequences and sexualised imagery of the pre-pubescent heroine, the book caused outrage at the time of its publication in 1955 and remains controversial today. Commenting on the designs of John Galliano, one newspaper summed up the 'look' under the headline 'Lolita knocks our socks off again': 'This designer's models came down the catwalk in quite the most fluffy baby-doll dresses the world has ever seen. These were paired with bright white bobby socks . . . and matching silk Mary-Jane shoes' (*Independent*, Review Section, 22 April 2004, p. 14, cited in Greer and Jewkes, 2005). Silverman and Wilson pose two rhetorical questions that hint at the underlying discomfort provoked by such cultural statements: why is it that our society 'discovered' the paedophile at exactly the same time as this process of sexualising our children seemed to gain pace (2002: 182)? And why does our society collectively collude with the idea of 'stranger danger', when we are all too aware that most children will be abused by someone they know?

The suggestion that sexual attraction to children may not be the preserve of a few grubby, inadequate loners but is actually a widespread social phenomenon was graphically illustrated by 'Operation Ore' launched in May 2002. In brief, a Texas-based subscription website called Landslide was operating as a portal to pornography sites containing abusive images of children and babies. The seizure of Landslide's database by police and the US Postal Inspection Service yielded the names and credit card details of some 390,000 subscribers in 60 countries, including around 35,000 subscribers in the United States, over 2,300 in Canada and over 7,200 in the United Kingdom. Investigations are ongoing in Australia, where 206 suspects have been identified, and in New Zealand 103 individuals have been convicted. Throughout the police investigation of the British subscribers to Landslide, the archetype of the grubby, socially inadequate, middle-aged man has been notable by its absence. Instead, those investigated have included high-profile celebrities, teachers, MPs, a prison governor, teenagers and women. The British subscribers represent a small fraction of the 390,000 individuals in 60 countries who subscribed to this one portal, but it has been suggested that as many as 250,000 Britons continue to use child pornography sites (Cullen, 2003; Jewkes, 2003a). So what *is* child pornography and who commits offences involving abusive images of children?

What is Internet child pornography?

Drawing on both legal and psychological data, Taylor et al. (2001) have constructed a model for understanding the nature of Internet child pornography and its escalating levels of severity. Although most of us would agree on a basic definition of child pornography as images depicting children and young people in a sexualised way, Taylor et al. point out that what is meant by 'sexualised' can vary depending on whether or not a purely legal position is adopted. For these researchers, legal definitions are limited because legislature differs from country to country and cannot take account of varying cultural, moral or political meanings attached to the word 'pornography'. In addition, legal definitions tend to emphasise obscene or sexual content as an essential quality of the images, thus overlooking the fact that any image can be sexualised or fantasised over: what makes the image important to the offender is the psychological role it plays in arousal and masturbation. Add to this the wide variation in tactics employed to select and 'groom' victims, and in avoiding detection, and all that can be said with any certainty is that, while legal definitions give us a starting point in helping to understand what child pornography is, they tend to 'necessarily reduce what might be a complex definitional issue to something simple and identifiable and create what are inevitably rather blunt instruments in application' (Taylor and Quayle, 2003: 30; cf. Taylor et al., 2001: 95; Smallbone and Wortley, 2001).

The work of the COPINE project (Combating Paedophile Information Networks in Europe) and its principal researchers, Max Taylor and Ethel Quayle, based within the Department of Applied Psychology at University College Cork, has generated a vast database of over 80,000 still images that are publicly available on the Internet, as well as more than 400 video sequences. From this database and the research team's work reviewing and categorising material, Taylor et al. (2001) have produced a typology or taxonomy of material available on the Internet based on ten levels of severity (see Table 5.1).

Taylor and Quayle's analysis of these images – which combine archive material that is more than 15 years old, images that are between ten and 15 years old, as well as more recent and new pictures – illustrate five discernible trends. First, the age of victims is reducing (which Taylor et al. suggest is because younger children are less able or likely to disclose the abuse than would older children). Second, there is an increase in 'domestic' production (where the settings are family rooms) although it is not clear whether this indicates a changing trend from the abuse of victims unrelated to the offender to victimisation by a family member, or whether it is simply a consequence of more sophisticated technology which has increased the production of images in the safety and comfort of the home (DIA, 2004). Third, more than half the victims are girls, although in the 'new' pictures, boys are increasingly prevalent (26 per cent of boy photographs in the level 7 and above categories are new, compared with 7 per cent of girl photographs). Fourth, there are ethnic and racial dimensions to victimisation. At level 7 and above, children of both sexes

Table 5.1 Taxonomy of different kinds of child pornography

Level	Name	Description of picture qualities
1	**Indicative**	Non-erotic and non-sexualised pictures showing children in their underwear, swimming costumes, etc. from either commercial sources or family albums; pictures of children playing in normal settings, in which the context or organisation of pictures by the collector indicates inappropriateness.
2	**Nudist**	Pictures of naked or semi-naked children in appropriate nudist settings and from legitimate sources.
3	**Erotica**	Surreptitiously taken photographs of children in play areas or other safe environments showing either underwear or varying degrees of nakedness.
4	**Posing**	Deliberately posed pictures of children fully, partially clothed or naked (where the amount, context and organisation suggests sexual interest).
5	**Erotic posing**	Deliberately posed pictures of fully, partially clothed or naked children in sexualised or provocative poses.
6	**Explicit erotic posing**	Emphasising genital areas where the child is either naked, partially or fully clothed.
7	**Explicit sexual activity**	Involves touching, mutual and self-masturbation, oral sex and intercourse by child, not involving an adult.
8	**Assault**	Pictures of children being subject to a sexual assault, involving digital touching, involving an adult.
9	**Gross assault**	Grossly obscene pictures of sexual assault, involving penetrative sex, masturbation or oral sex involving an adult.
10	**Sadistic/ bestiality**	(a) Pictures showing a child being tied, bound, beaten, whipped or otherwise subject to something that implies pain. (b) Pictures where an animal is involved in some form of sexual behaviour with a child.

Reproduced from Taylor and Quayle (2003); original source Taylor et al. (2001).

are most likely to be white Caucasian, with Asiatic children more likely to appear in posed images (levels 5 and 6). Additionally, there is a 'marked absence' of black children across the age groups and severity levels, although Taylor et al. do not have evidence or surmise why this might be the case. Finally, in recent years there has been an increase in the number of photographs of East European children. This last trend appears to be linked to the growing global trade in these images. Whereas the 'market' for abusive images of children has historically been a matter of private circulation among individuals who are known to each other and who form 'clubs' with like-minded associates, the Internet has facilitated the relatively anonymous buying and selling of child pornography like any other commodity. This commercial exploitation of children has been aided by the fact that many countries in Eastern Europe have no specific laws governing the production or circulation of such material. For example, Russia has become a major source of child pornography despite not actually being a major source of the material. Quite simply, despite estimates that less than one per cent of offensive content is actually produced in Russia, numerous criminal groups from other countries use Russian Internet sites to broadcast child pornography around the world (Jewkes, 2005).

While applying slightly different criteria, an American study of child pornography found in the possession of offenders who had been arrested between July 2000 and June 2001 shows a similar pattern of consumption. Fifty-eight per cent of images depicted very young children (younger than five years old); more girls than boys were pictured; 92 per cent of offenders possessed images that, according to Taylor et al.'s criteria would be graded at level 6 or above while 71 per cent had pictures that would rank as level 8, 80 per cent had pictures that would rank as level 9 and 21 per cent had images that would rate as level 10 (Wolak et al., 2005).

The database of video clips held by COPINE demonstrates a similar pattern of victimisation and abuse to the still images. Writing in 2001, Taylor et al. note that, while the Internet is playing an increasingly important role in the distribution of offensive material, it is video technology that remains the principal primary production medium for child pornography. Of course, the technologies are compatible and, as Taylor et al. imply, advances in technology simply allow better quality images to be downloaded on the Net. Furthermore, they note that the Internet is facilitating the emergence of new ways of abusing children. With reference to the Orchid Club, a group of paedophiles arrested in the United States in 1996 (although containing members from the US, Europe and Australia), they describe how, using a digital camera, one of the group members transmitted real-time images of a child being sexually assaulted and responded to requests from the club's members in directing the abuse, a modus operandi that has become more common in the intervening decade thanks to peer-to-peer (P2P) technology (Taylor et al., 2001: 97). While membership of these kinds of 'clubs' usually requires a relatively high degree of dedication and commitment (for example, the infamous Wonderland club is said to have required thousands of new images as a prerequisite for joining) the 'casual' user of abusive images of children can find them more freely available on newsgroups, bulletin board systems (BBS), Internet relay chat (IRC) forums, web pages and web browsers, and email files distributed through list servers (listservs) (for explanations of these terms see Jewkes, 2003a).

Who are the offenders?

The offence of downloading pornographic pictures of children from the Internet brings to the fore a range of issues that make it unusual, if not unique. It is a sexual crime in which the offender may have no contact with the victim. Insufficient research currently exists on the relationship between 'lookers' and 'doers' (that is, those who behave as voyeurs and those who actually sexually abuse children), but it may be that the Internet facilitates some kind of justification or neutralisation in the minds of many offenders who might not otherwise have sought sexual gratification from exploitative images of children (variously explained as 'I only looked to see what all the fuss is about/because I had a latent memory of being sexually abused as a child/because I was doing research', etc.) or that the Internet has simply made more accessible an activity that previously entailed a high degree of personal risk or expense (King, 1999). The Net also provides a 'meeting place' where some offenders justify their behaviour with reference to the fact that 'they're not the only ones doing it' or 'it's just fantasy . . . I'm not doing anything else' (Quayle and Taylor, 2003).

Although research is expanding in this area, offences involving abusive images of children on the Internet are very difficult to study because of the anonymity provided by the technology and the fact that it is a global phenomenon in which producers and consumers can be on different sides of the world. The majority of research data on child sexual offending derives from clinical studies of convicted offenders undergoing treatment. This in itself raises problems, as Smallbone and Wortley note:

> Although such studies have produced a large and rich empirical literature, it is unclear the extent to which these findings can be generalised, even to the larger population of convicted offenders. The reliability and validity of these data are typically compromised by the absence of confidentiality, since such offenders would normally be aware that information provided by them may affect decisions concerning their progress in treatment and their release from prison. (Smallbone and Wortley, 2001: 1–2)

In addition, the dominance of clinical understandings of offender behaviour in this area suggests a model of Internet use as an illness or pathology and relegates it to an extreme end of a continuum of behaviour (Quayle and Taylor, 2003), a representation contradicted by the arrests made during police operations such as Ore. A survey of arrests for Internet-related sex crimes by law enforcement agencies in the US provides useful data about the demographics of offenders but is clearly limited by its exclusive focus on offenders who have been arrested (Wolak et al., 2005). Further limitations of existing research are that they tend to use small samples, and they rarely compare findings from different samples and across different jurisdictions (Smallbone and Wortley, 2001). There is also significant discrepancy and diversity between studies in terms of the characteristics isolated (for example, not all studies note offenders' marital status or sexual orientation). As a result, little is known about the demographics of offenders, and whether people who download child pornography share the same characteristics and behaviours as contact offenders. Furthermore, psychological profiling reveals that those who use the Internet to obtain indecent images of children may have extremely varied levels of emotional loneliness, self-esteem, congruence with children and so forth (Middleton et al., 2005). Having said that, and not withstanding their weaknesses, a number of interesting findings emerge from these studies and, when studied together, some comparative issues can be noted.

Perhaps the most obvious characteristic of those who download Internet child pornography is that they are usually Caucasian males. Research does indicate that a small but significant number of offenders are women, adolescents and children (including children who have themselves been abused), but it is currently impossible to estimate with any accuracy the numbers involved, due partly to the probable under-reporting of female-perpetrated and child-on-child offences (Taylor and Quayle, 2003). Not surprisingly, then, the other overriding characteristic is that most offenders are over the age of 25 years (Wolak et al., 2005). For example, a study of 62 cases in New South Wales, Australia, reveals that nearly 80 per cent of offenders were over the age of 30, and nearly half were over 40 years (Krone, 2005). In New Zealand, however, the age profile of offenders is somewhat younger than that of any other country in which research has been undertaken. The most recent research compiled by the Censorship Compliance Unit using data involving 202 cases found that offenders between 15 and 19 years of age accounted for approximately one quarter of all offenders (24.3 per cent) and made up the largest single age grouping. Over half of all offenders were under the age of 30 at the time of investigation. On the face of it, there is no clearly discernible reason why New Zealand should have a younger demographic profile of offenders who download abusive images of children than other countries, although National Censorship Compliance Manager, Steve O'Brien, suggests that the reason is that the CCU are proactive in targeting offenders using Internet relay chat or peer-to-peer networks which tend to attract younger offenders with a high level of computer skills who are more aware of virus protection and firewalls (personal email correspondence). Websites, by contrast, tend to be favoured by older offenders because they are more straightforward to access and, in O'Brien's words, 'promise so much' (ibid.). In the New Zealand study, the relatively low age of typical offenders was supported by findings about occupation. Students made up the largest occupational group identified, with the second most commonly identified profession being those involved in the field of information technology (16.7 per cent). Although the majority of offenders (74.5 per cent) had no previous criminal history the number of offenders who had committed sexual offences (8.82 per cent) was of particular concern (Sullivan, 2005). While it was not possible to draw any causal link between viewing child pornography and offending against children, an association between the two offences was suggested by the findings. Offenders were found to favour three distinct types of objectionable material: violent images of all manner of subjects; degrading and dehumanising images of all manner of subjects; or solely paedophilic images. The number of images held by offenders varies considerably, but in one case in New Zealand a man had three networked computers searching the Internet for child pornography, which he then copied onto compact disks. He had amassed tens of thousands of images (Wilson, 2003).

The New Zealand Censorship Compliance Unit also measures the degree to which the offenders had access to children through occupation or lifestyle. In common with other studies, a significant number of offenders (81 individuals or 40 per cent of the sample) were identified as having some form of regular contact with children or young people. Examples of abusers identified included a soccer coach, the headmaster of a local primary school, a babysitter, a caregiver, a teacher's aide and one offender who lived across the road from a private girls' school and whose wife worked in a childcare centre (Sullivan, 2005; Andrews and Wilson, 2004). This finding, together with evidence from other studies of 'sex tourism' (i.e. frequent trips to third-world or former Eastern Bloc countries; Lanning, 1987), would appear to further problematise the finding that the majority of users have not committed contact offences.

In Switzerland a smaller study was conducted by psychologists in Lucerne (Frei et al., 2005) who analysed 33 cases of 38 individuals identified as having used Landslide to download illegal images of children. In this study, the mean age of offenders was 39.8 years, but in all other respects the findings mirror those of the CCU in New Zealand. In addition, the Lucerne study found that a high proportion of offenders (33 per cent) were unmarried without ever having had an intimate partner, 27 per cent were married and 24 per cent lived with a partner. Sixty per cent had no children and more than two-thirds had no prior conviction. Fifty-one per cent cited 'curiosity' as their motive with the second most common reason for the offence being 'research' (15 per cent) which, studies suggest, is a typical excuse for the consumption of child pornography (Lanning, 1987; Frei et al., 2005). In terms of behaviours, there is some evidence that the Internet has obsessive qualities, and that offenders frequently engage in excessive, compulsive online activity. One of the attractions cited is a feeling of power, control or mastery that comes from downloading and distributing offensive material (Young, 1998), while another is 'collector syndrome'. For example, Quayle and Taylor's (2001) interviews with offenders demonstrate that many individuals who amass large numbers of sexualised images of children are driven by a desire to 'complete' their collections, and describe their trading as being like a collector of baseball cards, stamps or fine art.

The only conclusion about Internet child pornography offenders that can be drawn from international research, then, is that, while almost exclusively male and usually reported to be white professionals, in all other ways offenders are a diverse and heterogeneous group, a point underlined by Wolak et al. in their report on one of the largest research studies of Internet-related child pornography cases (concerning 1,713 arrests across the United States):

> While the great majority were men older than 25 ... there was considerable variety among arrested CP possessors. Many were older than 40, but some were juveniles. Their incomes ranged from poverty to wealth and their levels of education ran the gamut. Many had fewer than 100 graphic images, but some had more than 1,000. More than one-quarter maintained organised child-pornography collections, but most did not. One-third were known child-pornography distributors, but investigators noted that distribution was often hard to prove. Some committed other sex crimes against minors besides CP possession. A few were diagnosed as being mentally ill or had diagnosed sexual disorders, some had identified drinking or drug problems, and there was evidence that some were involved in other kinds of deviant sexual activities not involving children like bestiality and sadism. But many were not in these categories. (Wolak et al., 2005)

How is it policed?

Much policing of cyberspace is not concerned with 'the police' at all, but rather non-police regulatory bodies (Internet service providers, global interest groups and hotline providers, private security firms set up specifically to protect business interests and so on). Even the police themselves are becoming part of a more diverse assortment of bodies with policing functions, and the array of activities we term 'policing' is becoming increasingly diffuse within and between nation-states (Jewkes, 2003b). For example, the most recent initiative in the UK is the establishment of the Child Exploitation and Online Protection (CEOP) Centre which has brought together specialists from the NSPCC, Microsoft, AOL and Internet charities, as well as the police. Supported by another new policing body, the Serious Organised Crime Agency (SOCA), CEOP is also linked to counterparts in Australia, Canada and the US, as well as Interpol, via an organisation called the Virtual Global Taskforce (http:// www.virtualglobaltaskforce.com). Just as the policing of terrestrial space has demanded a 'joined up approach' between individual citizens, private sector agencies and the police, so too has the policing of cyberspace become a pluralistic endeavour, encompassing a wide range of different bodies whose primary aim may be to protect Internet users or to enforce the law. The international police coordination body, Interpol, and its European equivalent, Europol, also support cross-border investigation and act as conduits for the pooling of intelligence and expert knowledge, although with debatable levels of success (Jewkes and Andrews, 2005). In the US, a similar multi-agency approach to law enforcement exists. While most cases involving possession of child pornography begin at state or local level, these agencies frequently look to federal agencies and ICAC (Internet Crimes Against Children) Task Forces for assistance and support. The majority of cases involve more than one law-enforcement agency, with around half of all cases involving assistance from federal agencies (Wolak et al., 2005). As in the UK, the need for cooperation across multiple agencies and jurisdictions at local, state and federal levels heightens the need for staff to be specially trained on an ongoing basis (ibid.).

So, while a review of the literature on policing Internet-related child sexual abuse reveals that much of it is not concerned with 'the police' at all, but is about non-police regulatory bodies, a great deal of discussion that *is* explicitly concerned with the police service's role in combating this – and indeed cybercrime more generally – is scathing about their commitment to the task (Goodman, 1997; Hyde, 1999). Yet, great strides have been made in recent years and it is certainly not the case that all police officers are Luddites seeking to thwart progress within the force. Since the first UK police operation targeting paedophiles using the Internet for networking purposes code named Starburst was conducted by Greater Manchester Police in 1998, there have been a number of successful investigations including, to name but a few: Cathedral (an international operation which exposed the notorious 'Wonderland Club' in 2001); Artus (in which an international paedophile network known as the 'Round Table' was uncovered in March 2002); Magenta (in which 27 people were arrested in the UK in April 2002); Amethyst (a nationwide swoop by Ireland's Sexual Assault and Domestic Violence Unit in May 2002); and Twins, an operation involving police from seven countries working in partnership across multi-geographical jurisdictions, to identify and prosecute offenders engaged in serious sexual abuse of children.

The launch of CEOP in April 2006 will further endorse the police's commitment to combating the Internet trade in child pornography. Under the directorship of Jim Gamble, previously Deputy Director General of the

National Crime Squad, the Centre aims to take a tough line on paedophiles who use the Internet to facilitate abuse. Their remit is broad: specialists within the Centre will set up fake paedophile websites and use undercover police officers to pose as children on Internet chatrooms; powerful new face recognition software will be used to match images and trace abusers and locations; the Centre will have a permanent presence in countries with identified problems such as sex tourism (initially Cambodia) and will work with local police to identify offenders; a 24-hour online facility will enable anyone to report potential paedophilic activity at the click of a mouse; the Centre will provide education in Internet safety for parents and children; officers will go into schools; and they will work with the computer industry to develop new products and services that prevent children from being exposed to abuse (*Guardian* 19 April 2006; http://www.ceop.gov.uk). The online reporting facility was instrumental in securing CEOP's first successful arrest and prosecution, when a woman in Nottinghamshire, UK, reported via the http://www.virtualglobaltask force.com site that her 14-year-old daughter had been sexually abused after being groomed on the Net. In June 2006, the judge in the trial of 21-year-old Lee Costi endorsed the tough message of the CEOP Director by sentencing Costi to nine years in prison on three counts of sex with children, three counts of Internet child grooming, five of making indecent images of children and one of possessing over 40 indecent images.

While the police have a mandate to investigate Internet-related child sexual abuse in most countries, the situation is rather different in New Zealand where 'policing' Internet child pornography is the responsibility of the Censorship Compliance Unit (CCU), part of the government Department of Internal Affairs (DIA). The CCU carries out proactive Internet investigations in newsgroups, chat rooms and peer-to-peer applications to detect New Zealanders who are involved in the distribution of objectionable material on the Internet (Sullivan, 2005; Andrews and Wilson, 2004). It also conducts profiling research based on questionnaire data completed by the CCU inspectors and based on their observations of, and interviews with, offenders. They claim that this results in higher success rates: unlike the police in other countries who may give these offences low priority in relation to 'real-world' crimes, the CCU is responsible for investigating a relatively narrow range of offences and is therefore better placed than many law enforcement agencies elsewhere to develop specialist intelligence and technical expertise (DIA, 2004). In February 2005 the New Zealand Parliament amended the censorship laws, setting much higher penalties for cases involving objectionable material. Penalties for possession of objectionable material have increased to a jail term of up to five years or a fine of up to $50,000. Penalties for distributing objectionable material have increased from a jail term of up to one year to a jail term of up to ten years. In 2005 the CCU were averaging more than two convictions a month (http://www.dia.censorship.govt.nz).

What are the problems of policing and conviction?

Elsewhere we have outlined in detail the problems that hamper the police in England and Wales, based on a review of the literature and interviews with nine key police personnel, eight of whom worked on Operation Ore (Jewkes and Andrews, 2005) and, in this concluding section, we present a condensed version of our findings. While our focus was primarily England and Wales, many of the problems we highlighted are common to law enforcers around the world. To summarise, then, we identified ten obstacles that present serious challenges to the investigation and prosecution of Internet child pornography. First is the problem of *jurisdiction* already mentioned. Much paedophilic Internet content comes from sites hosted in other countries, making it virtually impossible for a police force in one country to investigate or bring a successful prosecution against individuals in another (cf. Jewkes, 2003b, for a fuller account of the problems of jurisdiction).

Second, law enforcers may be hampered by the inadequacy of *legislation* in their own jurisdiction. For example, the UK police are authorised only to search for, and seize, tangible evidence. This requirement, as laid down in the Computer Misuse Act 1990, can be counterproductive to the investigation and prosecution of cybercrimes where evidence may be regarded as intangible (Goodman and Brenner, 2002). Furthermore, and again as previously noted, the notions of 'obscenity' and pornography' are socially, culturally and historically constituted, and legal definitions are frequently imprecise enough to impede the proper application of due process. A further aspect of UK legislation that causes difficulties for the police in that country is the fact that they are not legally entitled to 'entrap' a suspect. New legislation has created a charge of 'grooming' (that is, the seduction of children over the Internet with intent to obtain underage sex). This legislation enables the police to carry out 'sting' operations by posing as children in Internet chat rooms and then arranging to meet the unsuspecting groomers at a 'real' location. In other jurisdictions, 'stings' have proved successful; for example, in Perth, Australia, 48 per cent of adult suspects targeted were arrested while meeting their victim (http://news.ninemsn.com.au). For many commentators such operations are little more than honeypots and blur the distinction between lawful and unlawful police procedure. Consequently, in the UK, a number of legal defence teams have constructed cases around the certainty that the police acted in a manner that actually caused the defendant to commit the crime charged.

A third obstacle to the successful policing of Internet child pornography is the *composition* of many police forces who have to operate across national boundaries as well as global jurisdictions. For example, each of the 43 police forces in England and Wales has its own organisational structure and, although regional collaboration exists between forces, policing in England and Wales has retained a strongly decentralised, local character that largely emanates from each force's historical evolution and geographical location (Mawby and Wright, 2003). One consequence of the local nature of policing is that, although there is a degree of structural correspondence between forces, there is little standardisation in the names, roles, remits and locations of units and departments. Of course, the difficulties faced by police officers working within geographical boundaries in the 'real' world are infinitely magnified in the borderless world of cyberspace and the differing sizes and structures of national police forces only inflates the complexity of the task. To take the example of another country, Canada's investigation into their own Landslide subscribers, Operation Snowball, resulted in the arrest of less than 5 per cent of suspects in its first two years, leading one investigator, Detective Sergeant Paul Gillespie, to underline the problems inherent in investigations that rely on collaboration between federal, provincial and municipal forces: 'International co-operation is a dream – national co-operation is a nightmare' (cited in Akdeniz, 2003: 3).

A fourth difficulty facing the police concerns *competence*. While CEOP employs only those with the highest level of technical expertise, the police in general are renowned for their resistance to change and progress. Although a few forces now have specialist units concentrating expertise in computer-related crime, for example Hi-Tech Crime Units or Computer Crime Units, the vast majority of police forces in England and Wales do not have their own distinct and easily identifiable 'cybercrime unit' dedicated to investigating only computer-mediated crimes. Some forces employ one or two specialist personnel with 'high-tech' expertise within the much broader context of, for example, a Serious Crime Unit, Scientific Support Unit or Forensic Investigation Unit. Other forces have departments which gather intelligence on major crimes, usually in support of a force CID or Fraud Squad. However, even within units that amass expertise within the broad field of cybercrime, the officers working within them may not have the specialist skills and training required when dealing with the production, distribution and consumption of abusive images of children. Only three forces – West Midlands, Greater Manchester and London's Metropolitan force – have dedicated paedophile units which not only conduct proactive and reactive operations against those who manufacture and distribute paedophile material via the Internet, but also carry out operations against high-risk predatory paedophiles operating within the 'real' (as opposed to virtual) community.

A fifth problem facing the police in their battle to combat child pornography on the Net is that of *resources*. In 2001 the National Hi-Tech Crime Unit (NHTCU) was established to work in cooperation with local police forces across the UK as part of a wider £25 million strategy funded by the British government. However, several commentators have criticised the government for throwing a relatively large amount of money at the NHTCU and local forces during the start-up phase, and subsequently being less than forthcoming when the scale of the problem became apparent. When Operation Ore elicited the names of 7,272 offenders the police requested extra resources to enable them to carry out preliminary routine work (estimated at £2 million). However, the Home Office turned them down, saying that it was a matter for the police to manage within existing budgets. As a result of the inexorable pressures on police resources, thousands of paedophiles have been let off with a caution because police cannot cope with the huge volume of cases (Bright, 2003). Meanwhile, specialist units such as the Met's have been forced to concentrate on what have been termed the 'low-hanging fruit' which need fewer resources and may require less complicated investigations in order to yield results (Goodman, 1997), in this case individuals who download and pass on abusive images of children or who use Internet chat rooms to prey on young victims. Meanwhile, the more difficult task of policing the producers and distributors of child pornography is largely ignored (Jenkins, 2001). It is perhaps with some justification, then, that the Censorship Compliance Unit in the New Zealand government's Department of Internal Affairs can claim they are more successful in locating offenders than their policing counterparts in other countries. Like the police in the UK and elsewhere, the New Zealand CCU pick up many offenders either via international web sting operations or because the individual concerned has taken their computer to be fixed by a local repair technician who has then discovered objectionable material on it. However, the CCU do not rely on such fortuitous circumstances and claim that their more proactive procedures yield results beyond the initial investigations:

> In Britain they catch the dedicated physical offender (who normally is an older offender) and then subsequently look at what's on his computer. We had an excellent catch at the beginning of the year, where we caught a guy in Gisborne, we seized everything including a couple of video cameras. He fully admitted possessing 'child sexual abuse images' but it was not until we examined the cameras that we found that he was indecently assaulting two local children. The children were interviewed but denied the offending had occurred (which is often the case). The offender has been remanded in custody awaiting sentence where he is likely to get 5 years on our charges and say 7 on the Police charges. Point being that his physical offending may never have come to light if we had not picked him up in a web sting. (O'Brien, personal email correspondence)

A sixth challenge facing the police, which is subtly but inextricably linked to funding, is that the whole subject of cybercrime tends to be met with *public apathy*. It is frequently public opinion which drives government priorities in the form of performance indicators and targets and, like the more general category of white-collar crime, cybercrime seems remote and intangible, especially when compared to offences such as interpersonal violence, street crime or sexual assault in the 'real world'. It might justifiably be argued that abusive images of children on the Internet are an exception to this rule of general apathy and that, while cybercrime has, on the whole, failed to cause public consternation, the figure of the paedophile preying on victims in chat rooms and on dedicated porn sites *does* haunt the public imagination. Indeed, it is frequently asserted that paedophilia is the moral panic of our age. Yet however strongly the public feel about child sex abuse and about paedophiles preying on children in chat rooms, the existence of unquantifiable numbers of sites trading in abusive images of children, the origins of which are either unknown or in countries that seem geographically and culturally distant from our own, does not elicit the level of vehement reaction as does, say, the release into the community of a convicted paedophile. Responses to computer-mediated images of children in pornographic poses or being sexually violated by adults reflect the universal public denial of child abuse that takes place within families (two scenarios which are far from mutually exclusive). Unless it is 'our' children who are at risk from strangers outside the home, we are, for the most part, simply not interested (Jewkes, 2004). Consequently, in these times of fiscal constraints and appeals for more community policing programmes to tackle the mundane offences that elicit most fear, police chiefs are unlikely to direct precious resources into a type of crime that is costly, difficult to investigate, intangible to many and thus low down on most people's priorities for their police service.

Public indifference to such crime is mirrored in the attitude of many senior police personnel who simply do not view cybercrime (even when it involves the sexual exploitation of children) as 'real' police work. The seventh obstacle to policing child pornography on the Internet identified by Jewkes and Andrews (2005) is thus *police culture*. Many police, practitioners and other professionals who work with sex offenders feel ill-equipped to ask questions about their downloading activities because of their own unfamiliarity with the technology involved and their ignorance of the motivations of paedophiles who use the Internet (Quayle and Taylor, 2002). But more fundamentally, the 'fuzziness' surrounding the concept of cybercrimes such as Internet pornography is exacerbated by the fact that many of today's police managers have risen up through the ranks of a force they first joined in a pre-computer age and continue to think they can 'get by' without having to devote additional resources to cybercrime because that is what has been done in the past (Goodman, 1997). While technophobia may be no more prevalent within the police than it is in the public at large (itself a point of debate for many commentators; see Jewkes, 2003b) a lack of computer savvy *is* a serious problem for the police, and is compounded by insufficient training on either computer usage or computer crime (Goodman, 1997; Hyde, 1999; Woods, 2002). Jewkes and Andrews (2005) note that poor (or non-existent) training programmes in information technologies for police officers may emanate from the occupational culture of the police as well as from fiscal constraints. The point is illustrated by a Senior Investigating Officer who comments: 'We don't need to know the intricacies. We just need to know enough to conduct a proper interview' (Jewkes and Andrews, 2005: 54) Even those officers assigned to Operation Ore received little formal training that equipped them for their new role. In many cases they were selected because they had a reasonable working knowledge of computers gained from personal interest and usage but, having been assigned to Ore, many received no further instruction and were left to their own devices. As one detective constable put it: 'It is only my own interests which have allowed me to understand what computers are all about as I have taught myself' (telephone interview, 1 July 2003).

The weak commitment to training is exacerbated by the speed with which computer technologies move forward. The eighth challenge to the police is thus *technological advancement*. Peer-to-peer file-sharing technology is a particular concern for investigators as it facilitates real-time images of abuse, creates immediate new images and makes investigation and prosecution fraught with difficulty. File-sharing is also, for the most part, free, easy to use and readily accessible, making it attractive to individuals who wish to swap images without the risks involved in a traditional organised paedophile network where a third party is involved, passwords are necessary, decryption skills may be required and a very large collection of 'new' images may be a condition of membership (Gillan, 2003). Moreover, abusers are increasingly growing wise to the work of forensic analysts and, while some successes have been made by investigators pinpointing clues (such as telephone directories) in the background of images, much abuse now takes place in completely empty rooms and locations devoid of artefacts that could give the police useful leads (ibid.). Of course, any residual technophobia within the police may gradually dissipate as more computer literate individuals, who have grown up in a world in which computer technologies are integral and taken for granted, join the police. The police may currently feel most comfortable following a paper trail, but as they increasingly come to appreciate the benefits offered to them by computer technologies (for example, through the effective implementation of an e-policing strategy) they may become more open-minded about the possibilities of the Internet. However, the extent to which the police are falling behind in the cat and mouse game they are being forced to play is illustrated by the fact that Scotland Yard officers 'stumbled across by accident' the sharing of files showing real-time child sexual abuse during another type of inquiry (ibid.).

The ninth problem for the police in this area concerns the policy of *rotating key personnel* (in the UK tenure has recently been reduced from eight to three years), a strategy designed to circulate ideas, prevent corruption and protect investigating officers from trauma. In practice, rotation of personnel can result in a need to constantly train new staff while removing experienced individuals who have a strong residual knowledge and proven expertise. When appropriate levels of understanding and skill are already sparse, it seems to make little sense to move experts on to other units and replace them with officers who must be trained up from scratch. The rationale behind rotation is itself questionable. After one day on a specialist unit, an investigating officer may have been exposed to hundreds of images of child abuse. Be it one day or many years, the officer is unlikely to forget those images. But by retaining the eight-year term, fewer individual officers would be exposed to the material and, overall, trauma would be kept to a minimum number of officers.

Finally, a tenth obstacle to the successful policing of Internet-related child sexual abuse concerns the *under-reporting* of such crimes. As alluded to elsewhere in this chapter, reasons for the under-reporting of abuse include the inherently unequal power relations that exist between adult offender and child victim, the evidence suggesting that victims are getting younger, the social stigma attached to being a juvenile victim of sex offences, the privatised nature of offending and the anonymity afforded by the Internet.

Concluding thoughts

The subject of abusive images of children on the Internet throws up a number of paradoxes and contradictions. Sexualised images of children have circulated in society for many years and were relatively common among collectors in the Victorian era when there was less public censure regarding the sexualisation of children (Pearsall, 1993). Famous children's writers of the time J. M. Barrie (creator of *Peter Pan*) and Lewis Carroll (author of *Alice In Wonderland*) have been subjected to revisionist scrutiny questioning the morality they displayed both in their depictions of children in art and in their relationships with children in life. In contemporary society, opprobrium is most vehemently articulated via the pages of the popular press at celebrities such as Gary Glitter (convicted for child abuse offences in Vietnam in March 2006) who work in creative industries which commodify youth for the consumption and gratification of all of us, while simultaneously being directed at judges for passing 'lenient' sentences on paedophiles and being 'out of touch' with public sentiment. Yet despite the hysterical tone adopted by a media that are happy to peddle overtly sexualised images of young people in other contexts, the issue of Internet-related sexual exploitation of children remains a somewhat hazy and intangible concept in the collective public conscience. Because of the highly disturbing nature and socially taboo status (to most people, at least) of child–adult sex, media audiences are not confronted with the kinds of images that might force them to acknowledge these crimes, apply pressure on police and regulatory bodies and press for intervention programmes to treat offenders. As such, even the levels of fear and anxiety that might be expected to accompany reports of child sexual abuse are not as apparent as those elicited by, for example, terrorists and suicide bombers, whose actions (and their aftermaths) are graphically depicted in news reports. In addition, the obstacles facing the police, and the challenges in securing convictions across geographical territories, cultural boundaries and legal jurisdictions, make the problem of child pornography a worrying yet somewhat tenuous concern. What is beyond doubt is that the cases which come to the attention of the police, regulatory authorities, clinicians and academic researchers are likely to represent a very small tip of a very large iceberg.

References

Akdeniz (2003) Akdeniz, Y. (2003) 'Regulation of child pornography on the Internet', www.cyber-rights.org/reports/child.htm.

Andrews, C. and Wilson, D. (2004) *Internet Traders of Child Pornography and Other Censorship Offenders in New Zealand: Updated Statistics*, November, Department of Internal Affairs.

Araji, S. K. (2000) 'Child sexual abusers: a review and update' in L.B. Schesinger (ed.) *Serial Offenders: Current Thought, Recent Findings*, Boca Raton: CRC Press.

Bright, M. (2003) 'Sex offenders let off the hook', *Observer* 28 September, www.guardian.co.uk.

Cullen, D. (2003) 'Child porn list leaked to Sunday Times' (online at: http://www.theregister.co.uk).

DIA (2004) 'Internet traders of child pornography and other censorship offenders in New Zealand: updated statistics (November)' www.dia.govt.nz.

Frei, A., Erenay, N., Dittmann, V. and Graf, M. (2005) 'Paedophilia on the Internet: a study of 33 convicted offenders in the Canton of Lucerne', *Swiss Medical Weekly* 135: 488–494 .

Gillan, A. (2003) 'Race to save new victims of child porn', *Guardian*, 4 November (online at: http://www.guardian.co.uk).

Goodman, M. (1997) 'Why the police don't care about cybercrime', *Harvard Journal of Law and Technology*, 10, Summer: 465–94

Goodman, M. and Brenner, S. (2002) 'The emerging consensus on criminal conduct in cyberspace', *International Journal of Law & Information Technology*, 10 (2).

Greer, C. (2003) *Sex Crime and the Media: Sex Offending and the Press in a Divided Society*. Cullompton: Willan.

Greer, C. and Jewkes, Y. (2005) 'Images and processes of social exclusion', *Social Justice*, special edition, 32 (1): 20–31.

Hyde, S. (1999) 'A few coppers change', *Journal of Information, Law and Technology* (JILT) (online at: http://elj.warwick.ac.uk/jilt/99-2/hyde.html).

Jenkins, P. (2001) *Beyond Tolerance: Child Pornography on the Internet*, New York: New York University Press.

Jewkes, Y. (ed.) (2003a) *Dot.cons: Crime, Deviance and Identity on the Internet.* Cullompton: Willan.

Jewkes, Y. (2003b) 'Policing cybercrime', in T. Newburn (ed.), *Handbook of Policing*, Cullompton: Willan.

Jewkes, Y. (2004) *Media and Crime: A Critical Introduction.* London: Sage.

Jewkes, Y. (2005) 'Cybercrime', in E. McLaughlin and J. Muncie (eds), *The Sage Dictionary of Criminology*, 2nd edn. London: Sage.

Jewkes, Y. and Andrews, C. (2005) 'Policing the filth: the problems of investigating online child pornography in England and Wales', *Policing & Society*, 15 (1): 42–62.

King, S. (1999) 'Internet gambling and pornography: illustrative examples of the psychological consequences of communication anarchy' *CyberPsychology & Behavior* 2(3): 175–193.

Krone, T. (2005) 'Child pornography sentencing in NSW' *High-Tech Crime Brief no. 8*, Australian Institute of Criminology, www.aic.gov.au/publications.

Lanning, K. V. (1987) *Child Molesters: A Behavioural Analysis*, 2nd edn. Washington, DC: Center for Missing and Exploited Children.

Mawby, R.C. and Wright, A. (2003) 'The police organisation', in T. Newburn (ed.) *Handbook of Policing*, Cullompton: Willan.

Middleton, D., Beech, A. and Mandeville-Norden, R. (2005) 'What sort of person could do that? Psychological profiles of Internet pornography users', in E. Quayle and M. Taylor (eds), *Viewing Child Pornography on the Internet.* Lyme Regis: Russell House.

Pearsall, R. (1993) *The Worm in the Bud: the World of Victorian Sexuality.* London: Pimlico.

Quayle, E. and Taylor, M. (2001) 'Child seduction and self-representation on the Internet', *CyberPsychology and Behavior* 4: 597–608.

Quayle, E. and Taylor, M. (2002) 'Child pornography and the Internet: perpetuating a cycle of abuse', *Deviant Behaviour* 23: 331–362.

Silverman, J. and Wilson, D. (2002) *Innocence Betrayed: Paedophilia, the Media and Society.* Cambridge: Polity Press.

Smallbone, S.W. and Wortley, R.K. (2001) 'Child sexual abuse: offender characteristics and modus operandi', *Trends and Issues in Crime and Criminal Justice no. 193*, Australian Institute of Criminology, www.aic.gov.au/publications.

Sullivan, C. (2005) *Internet Traders of Child Pornography: Profiling Research*, October, New Zealand, Department of Internal Affairs.

Taylor, M. and Quayle, E. (2003) *Child Pornography: An Internet Crime.* Hove: Brunner-Routledge.

Taylor, M., Holland, G. and Quayle, E. (2001) 'Typology of paedophile picture collections', *Police Journal*, 74 (2): 97–107.

Wilson, D. (2003) *Censorship in New Zealand: The Policy Challenges of New Technology*, New Zealand, Department of Internal Affairs (online at: http://www.dia.govt.nz).

Wolak, J., Finkelhor, D. and Mitchell, K. J. (2005) *Child Pornography Possessors Arrested in Internet-Related Crimes: Findings from the National Juvenile Online*

Victimization Study. Washington, DC: Center for Missing and Exploited Children.

Woods, P. (2002) *E-policing*, www.e-policingreport.com.

Young, K.S. (1998) 'Internet addiction: the emergence of a new clinical disorder', *CyberPsychology & Behavior* 1(3): 237–244.

Chapter 6

The role of computer forensics in criminal investigations

Robert Moore

Introduction

Computer forensics is a relatively new term to those outside the field of computer science. The term refers to the use of computer science techniques to recover evidence from computerised devices and then to present that evidence in criminal trials. With more criminal activities containing some element of computer-related assistance, understanding of computer forensics and data recovery are becoming increasingly important. The role of computer forensics, however, extends beyond the realm of criminal investigations. Corporate companies are also finding uses for the technology to maximise worker productivity and minimise illegal activities by employees. This chapter will examine the basics of computer forensics, including: what is meant by the term 'computer forensics'; how computers store data; how computer forensics programs operate; how the computer forensics process itself works; and finally the admissibility of computer forensics-related evidence. The chapter will also briefly address some of the problems associated with integrating computer forensics programs into law enforcement agencies.

What *is* computer forensics?

Crime changes with society. Nowhere is this more prevalent than in the area of computer-related crime. As society has become more dependent on computer technology, so too have the criminal elements of society. As discussed throughout this volume, there are increasing reports of computer-assisted identity theft, hacking and distribution of child pornography. Unlike traditional crimes, cybercrimes often fail to provide physical evidence but instead, may leave evidence that is digital in nature. Eoghan Casey (2000) has termed this collection of digital evidence the 'cybertrail'.

Additionally, there are an increasing number of traditional crimes that involve computers and digital evidence. Take for example the recent case of the American serial killer known as the BTK Killer (because of his desire to bind, torture and kill his victims) who was captured as the result of a computer disk. Following his crimes, the killer would send letters to newspapers and television stations. His last letter was sent to a news station on a 3.5-inch floppy disk. The contents of the letter revealed very little about the killer, but important evidence was recovered from the disk which, under forensic analysis revealed remnants of documents that had been deleted. One of these documents was a church newsletter and after locating the church, investigators were able to determine that the individual who designed the newsletter was Dennis Rader. Used in conjunction with additional evidence uncovered during the investigation, investigators were able to determine that Dennis Rader was indeed the BTK killer (Heying, 2005).

This case demonstrates the use and benefits of computer forensics in criminal investigations. Computer forensics thus refers to the combination of computer science and legal principles to recover digital information from computers that can be used as evidence in criminal and civil proceedings. It should be noted, however, that computer forensics is not just used in criminal scenarios such as the BTK case. Many large corporations have found uses for computer forensic services (Nelson et al., 2006), including determining if their employees are utilising company computers for illegal or personal activities. At least one computer forensics company has developed a program that allows network administrators to monitor and recover deleted files without having to physically access the employee's computer. All data recovery and analysis takes place over the company's network.

In order to better appreciate the importance of computer forensics, it is necessary to understand more about what computer forensics actually is and is not. As previously stated, the term computer forensics refers to the combination of computer science and legal principles. Computer forensics programs are designed to recover deleted files, hidden files, website activity and a variety of other forms of digital evidence stored on computers. There are a variety of software programs available today to allow computer forensics analyses. In the beginning the majority of these software programs were DOS-based programs (Nelson et al., 2006). This meant that in order for a user to conduct a forensic analysis they had to be familiar with DOS-based commands and DOS-based computer environments. While this was not really a problem in the area of computer science, it did present problems for the field of law enforcement. The use of computer forensics in criminal investigations was more limited because of the intricate and technologically sophisticated nature of computer programs. Quite simply, many law enforcement agencies did not employ officers who were familiar enough with computers to engage in complicated analyses (see Jewkes and Andrews, this volume).

Large law enforcement agencies, or those agencies that could afford to pay better salaries, *did* maintain officers who were familiar with computer-related technologies. Unfortunately, however, the majority of law enforcement agencies did not succeed in retaining these individuals for financial reasons. In the early days of computer forensics, computers and the Internet were not as well used by the general public. As a result, individuals who had education and training in these areas were more likely to take higher paying salaries in the computer industry. Therefore, while criminals were becoming more familiar with the capabilities of computers and the Internet, law enforcement personnel were not (Jewkes and Andrews, 2005).

Recognising this as a problem, and building on the fact that, in most homes, computers have Microsoft Windows operating systems, more computer forensics companies have abandoned DOS-based software programs. The new forensic packages are Windows based and contain a GUI (Graphical User Interface), which is a 'techy' way of saying that the software features are activated by pointing the cursor and using a mouse to select options. Instead of typing in a complex series of commands to access a suspect disk, users can click on an icon within the software program and the commands are executed by the program. With these newer, more user-friendly software programs available, more law enforcement agencies are recruiting officers with a sufficient understanding and training in the area of computer forensics analysis.

Several companies, such as AccessData (makers of the Forensic Tool Kit) and Guidance Software (makers of the EnCase forensics package), have even focused their tools on law enforcement users. As a result of this targeting, these two companies are considered the more popular choices for law enforcement purposes in the United States. The training provided by them focuses on not just the technical aspects of computer forensics, but also the investigative and legal aspects of a computer forensics investigation (Guidance Software, 2006; AccessData, 2006).

Basics of file storage

Computers store data on circular disks known as platters. Some disks, such as hard disks stored inside of central processing units, are made up of multiple platters. When data is saved to the hard disk, the data is actually inscribed onto one of the platters through the use of a read/write head. These platters are divided into sectors and clusters. Sectors are made up of a small amount of data, normally 512 bytes. These bytes represent characters of a data file; normally one byte represents one character. A cluster is a collection of bytes and the smallest form of data storage. When data is saved to a disk the data is saved in clusters. This means that if a cluster is 2 KB in size, then it is made up of 4 sectors – 512 bytes $\times 4 = 2048$ KB (Casey, 2000).

If a file is 8 KB in size, and the hard disk uses 2 KB sized clusters, then the file would require four clusters. This method of saving files requires that an entire cluster be utilised when a file is saved. Therefore, if a file is 9 KB in size then five clusters are required for the file to be saved to the disk. This is true even though 1 KB of the last cluster is not being used. The extra space between where the file ends and the cluster ends is referred to as *slack space*, and is a very important concept in the arena of computer forensics (Vacca, 2002). Clusters are organised by the computer operating system's file operating system. Because of the physical layout of a disk, an entire file's contents may not necessarily be saved on the same platter. As a result, the operating system must know where all of a file's components are located so that when the file is opened it can be reassembled from the disk. This file operating system is referred to as the *file allocation table*, commonly denoted as FAT.

The file allocation table not only maintains a record of where on the platters a file is stored, but also which files are currently in use and which files have been deleted. Because file data is actually written onto the surface of the disk, deleting a file from use does not allow for the file to be actually erased. Instead, when a file is deleted by the operating system's user the file allocation table will note that the file is no longer being used and that the space on the disk can be used for the saving of new files. When a new file is saved and the space is needed for the new file, the read/write head will inscribe the data over the old data. The disk operating system then only reads the most recently stored data when a file is opened.

This method of storing data is why users who have accidentally deleted important files can sometimes recover their files by restoring them from the deleted folder. In Microsoft Windows this deleted folder is referred to as the recycle bin. When a Windows-based computer has a file deleted, the file's space is not immediately set aside for reuse. Instead, the file allocation table makes a note that the file has been deleted but that the file's space is not ready for reuse. If the recycle bin on the computer is emptied, then the operating system will make a note that the file's space is now available for use by another file. The file allocation table accomplishes this through the hexadecimal naming of files. Files that are deleted and no longer being used are designated by the 'E5' hexadecimal value (Casey, 2000). For example the file taxes.doc, when deleted, might appear to the operating system as E5axes.doc.

Frequently, once a file has been deleted, the space occupied by the file will be used to save a smaller file. When this occurs remnants of the original file may be stored in the slack space. Consider the following example. An original file is saved to a disk that is 32 KB in size. If the operating system utilises 2 KB clusters, then 16 clusters would be needed to save the original file. After the 32 KB file is deleted, a 31KB file is then saved in the space originally used for the 32 KB file. As a result, there is 1 KB of the original file stored in the area of the disk not utilised by the new file. This data stored in slack space can often contain valuable evidence. However, one problem with this concept is that newer operating systems are utilising smaller and smaller clusters, meaning that fewer amounts of data are stored in this slack space.

How computer forensics programs operate

Computer forensics programs work by examining the file allocation table used by a computer disk and looking for files and remnants of files on the disk. In the same manner that the file allocation table looks for files designated with the 'E5' hexadecimal value, these forensics programs look for the same value and then report these files as deleted files that can sometimes be recovered by users of the forensics program. Further, these forensics programs allow users to examine every bit of space on a disk. This means that not only deleted files are recoverable, but remnants of files stored in the slack space are also recoverable.

Many of the computer forensics programs currently on the market allow users to identify deleted files and file remnants by displaying these characters in a different colour of text, such as blue or red. Users of the forensics program are then able to determine whether a file was still stored on the disk at the time of its collection, or whether a file was deleted in an attempt to remove or hide evidence. Further, evidence that was thought to be deleted may be stored in the slack space and recovered by investigators.

Because these computer forensics programs allow for recovery of all data stored on a disk, there are other forms of evidence recoverable from a suspect's disk. The first to be discussed is evidence of electronic communications. Emails that are saved to a computer are treated as any other file and assigned space on a disk. It should be noted, however, that many email programs do not require downloading to a disk. These email services, referred to as webmail programs, allow users to store their emails on servers provided by the email company. Examples of these email programs are Hotmail, Yahoo mail, AOL mail and Google's new webmail. There are some new programs that are seeing increased use, especially among universities and business professionals, that allow users to download their emails from a server, yet still gain access to emails as if they were web-based. However, these programs are primarily powered through Microsoft's Outlook Express.

While downloaded emails are stored on a disk in the same manner as other files, there are some differences depending on the email program used to download the file. Some email programs encrypt messages, requiring that the user of the computer forensics program know where to look for remnants of email files and how to remount these files in a manner that allows for them to be read. Recent versions of computer forensics programs such as Forensic Tool Kit and EnCase have made this process easier, but recovering email messages – and the attachments that often accompany emails – can still be time consuming.

Another area of evidence that is recoverable is that of web activity. Any time a user visits a website, data is transferred to the computer. This data is stored in several different places, one of which is the cache folder. In the early days of the Internet, cache folders were very important because Internet connections were much slower than they are today, and as a result cache folders allowed for faster web surfing. The folders worked as follows. When a user directed their web browser to a particular website, data from the website was stored in the cache folder. If the user should return to the same website then the operating system would note that the site had already been visited and would access some of the data from the cache folder instead of the website. This sped up the user's access to the web page.

This cache folder can be used by computer forensics investigators to reassemble the websites that a user has visited. In some cases the data stored within the cache folder can allow an investigator to reassemble a page in such detail that he or she can view the webpage exactly as the original user viewed the page. Further, to assist with this process, a list of websites visited by a user can sometimes be retrieved from the disk.

A final area of evidence worth discussing is evidence related to files that have been printed from a suspect's computer. When a user selects the print option, the operating system will copy the file's contents into a temporary memory. The file contents are then transferred to the printer and printed. Computer forensic investigators can sometimes recover copies of the images printed by reassembling the image sent to the printer. In much the same manner as slack space, some parts of the data may have already been written over, while other parts can allow investigators to view the printed image just as the original user viewed the image.

The computer forensics process

The forensic investigation process begins with the imaging of a suspect disk. An image is nothing more than a forensic copy of the suspect disk. A copy is utilised during investigations because data can easily be modified or deleted. By examining a copy of the suspect disk, there are no changes to the disk's data. Further, the original disk can be safely stored in a law enforcement agency's evidence vault, while allowing the imaged copy to be examined in the lab (Kruse and Heiser, 2002).

There are several different methods of making a forensic image of a disk. First, there is the copy feature built into the Linux operating system. Linux, an open-source alternative to Microsoft Windows, is preferred by some computer forensics professionals because of the many built in features and the ability to modify the program as needed. A second method of creating an image involves the use of a commercial imaging device. These devices allow investigators to connect the suspect drive and a blank disk, transferring the data between the two disks at incredible speeds. A third method of imaging a disk is through the use of a software imaging program. Many computer forensics programs now include the option of imaging a suspect drive. These images work by compressing the data stored on the suspect disk and then converting the data into an evidence file that can then be uploaded into the computer forensics program.

An important concept in the computer forensics process is that of the *bit copy image*. The term bit copy image refers to a copy of a suspect disk that contains every bit of data stored on the original disk (Nelson et al., 2006). Traditional copy features built into operating systems only allow for active files to be copied. For example, returning to the concept of slack space discussed earlier, if the copy feature of Microsoft Windows is used, then the copy of the file will only include the new data and not the remnants stored in slack space. A bit copy feature will copy not only the active file but every bit, sector and cluster exactly as it is on the original suspect disk. This is of utmost importance because a variety of evidence can be stored within the slack space.

Verifying files and imaged data

Once an imaged copy of a suspect disk is made, the next step in the forensics process is to verify the imaged files. This is necessary because more and more users are attempting to masquerade file names and file types. An example of this is when an individual will take a Microsoft document file that is normally labeled with the .doc file name extension, and change the file name extension to that of another format. One such format would be the .jpg file name extension, which is normally used to denote an image file. This modification of the file extension confuses the operating system. When the operating system is asked to list the file, it will display the file as if it is the file format indicated by the file extension. When a Microsoft Windows user clicks on the My Documents folder, document files are displayed as a document icon and image files are displayed as a picture icon. When a user changes a document file's extension to an image file extension, the Windows Operating System will display the document name with a picture icon. Unless a user clicks on the icon to activate the file's contents, the file will continue to appear as an image and not a document.

During the verification process, the computer forensics program will examine each file stored on a disk in order to verify that the file in question is not being masqueraded as another file type. This is possible because of information stored in a file's header data. Every file contains unseen data that indicates the type of data stored within the file. This header information is larger in some file formats, thus explaining why a document file in Microsoft Word is often larger than a document file stored in Corel WordPerfect. As the forensics program examines each file's header, the program compares the information found in the header file with the file extension. If there are any discrepancies, the program will flag that file for review by the investigator. The investigator can then conduct an examination to determine exactly what type of file is stored on the computer. This process has been especially useful in locating image files that have been renamed as other file formats such as documents or spreadsheets.

The verification process also involves verification that no data has been modified from the original disk. This is crucial when later attempting to have the evidence introduced during a trial. If the evidence cannot be shown to be the same as that taken from the suspect then the evidence will not likely be admissible at trial. One of the more commonly accepted methods of verifying the integrity of data involves the use of the MD5 algorithm, a mathematical depiction of a disk's contents. Once an MD5 value has been generated for a disk, any changes to the disk's data contents will result in a drastic change in the MD5 value for that disk.

Consider the following example. A forensic investigator images a suspect's hard disk and then generates a hash value for the file test.com. The test.com file contains the following sentence – this is a test. The MD5 value for this file would appear similar to the following: 12eokja4kazkjdjoekale1lkjlp30azm. By changing the sentence, even slightly, the MD5 value will change dramatically. So, if the test.com file is changed to contain the following sentence – htis is a test – the MD5 value could appear as follows: 1ajck3zcoeiajahtaweazcm1k08as91x. Notice that the two values are not even close in similarity, despite the fact that only two characters have been modified.

There has been some discussion in recent years concerning the possibility of duplicating an MD5 hash value (Deering, 2006). While it is theoretically possible, most computer scientists seem to agree that such duplication would require a very large number of computers operating at full power for an undetermined amount of time. So, while duplication is possible it is still very unlikely. With this in mind, MD5 still remains the predominant choice for data and file verification. Many of the more popular computer forensics programs continue to use the algorithm. This verification process can either involve an entire disk or can be conducted on a file-by-file basis.

The forensic investigation

Once a disk image has been created and the data's integrity has been verified, the next step is the actual forensic investigation. It is during this stage that the imaged disk is examined bit by bit for evidence. Newer forensics programs have sped up this process, but fully examining a 100 gigabyte (or larger) hard disk still requires a significant amount of time. One method of speeding up the search involves the use of keyword search utilities. These programs work by searching all areas of an imaged disk, including the allocated and unallocated spaces of the disk. The slack space is also searched during this process. Keyword searches are extremely useful when looking for information related to offences such as narcotics trafficking, identity theft or hacking-related crimes.

For crimes such as downloading abusive images of children, there are other search utilities, such as the image search feature. This feature creates an index of all images stored on an imaged disk. The forensic investigator can then search through the gallery of images by viewing thumbnails. These images can be saved to the forensic report or opened with the use of another image viewer. Opening an image with an outside software program can be beneficial if the investigator believes that an illegal image (e.g. pornography) is placed under a legal image. When the image is opened by a traditional image viewer program, only the legal image is displayed. If a user knows that there is another, hidden image beneath, they can reveal it using the right software program. One of the most common programs used by downloaders of child pornography to hide illegal material seems to be Adobe Photoshop, presumably because of its ease of use.

Some forensic programs have even attempted to make the examination process easier by adding in script programs that perform some of the more complicated functions. EnCase, by Guidance Software, has script programs that allow investigators to search a disk for evidence of credit card numbers, phone numbers, specific email addresses, etc. Likewise, there are script programs for small image files, large image files and even video files. Other forensic programs, such as Forensic Tool Kit, have an option that allows investigators to view email by merely selecting the email tab.

The forensics report

The final stage of the forensics process is the compilation of the report. This is where the results of the entire process are compiled into an easy-to-read format. Sections of data from the imaged disk can normally be saved to the report, allowing readers to gain an understanding of not only how many keywords are present on the disk but also the context in which the keywords are being used. Images analysed during an investigation can also be included in these reports. By combining sections of text and images, along with any other evidence uncovered during an investigation, an investigator can present a defendant with a stack of documents detailing exactly how strong the case is against the accused. If the investigator has found a sufficient amount of evidence the report may be used to prevent the defendant from continuing with his opposition to the charges. Criminal prosecutors love well organised reports, so many of the newer forensics programs now include report features with a variety of cosmetic options allowing images, documents, web page information and other evidence to be saved as it is viewed by the investigator. At the conclusion of the investigation the report can then be edited by another word processing program to make the document appear more professional and organised.

Legal issues associated with computer forensics

Despite the obvious benefit of computer forensics services, there are still some who question whether such techniques are sufficient to meet the legal standard necessary for the admission of evidence. In the United States this issue has been addressed in a couple of different areas of criminal law and procedure. First, there has been the issue of whether computer-generated evidence obtained by a computer forensics investigator should be admissible because of the fact that such evidence can be so easily modified or deleted. A second argument is related to whether law enforcement officers who are not computer scientists should be allowed to conduct such examinations without more training and education in the areas of computer science.

Some of the issues related to admitting digital evidence have been addressed by the criminal courts. The general consensus is that while digital evidence is susceptible to manipulation, there are methods of ensuring that the evidence is untainted. One way of ensuring that the evidence has not been tampered with involves the use of hash values. If an investigator generates a hash value for a file or disk, a subsequent file hash should be the same if there have been no changes to the file. According to Kruse and Heiser (2002) the MD5 algorithm is as accurate, if not more accurate, than DNA testing. As such, courts that have accepted the admission of DNA evidence could allow the admission of digital evidence. The use of an image to conduct forensic examinations is also helpful in countering claims of evidence tampering. Should the issue of authenticity be raised during a trial, then the original evidence could be brought in and compared to the imaged copy of the evidence. Generally, however, the use of a hash value will preclude the need to bring in the original evidence.

The issue of training is an area that is still being debated. Certainly computer forensic investigators need training in the area of criminal investigations involving computers and the Internet (Jewkes and Andrews, 2005 and this volume). However, many of the debates appear to revolve around the extent of training necessary for computer forensic investigators. Do computer forensic investigators need to have a degree in computer science or advanced training in the field? Of course, the more training received, the better examination an investigator can conduct. However, software utilities such as the scripts built in to new forensic packages conduct many of the advanced examinations themselves, allowing lesser skilled individuals to conduct more thorough investigations.

This issue was addressed in the US court decision of *United States* v. *Scott-Emuakpor* (2000). In this case the court was asked to determine whether evidence admitted by two Secret Service agents, and recovered from a suspect's computer, was admissible because the agents admitted at trial that their knowledge of computer systems was limited to their training in forensic recovery. The court ruled that the agents' testimony, and the subsequent introduction of evidence recovered from computers, was admissible because the agents had received training in the area of computer forensics and data recovery. In the United States this decision has resulted in more and more computer forensics vendors offering training courses to law enforcement personnel, as well as to other purchasers of their products.

With this training, law enforcement personnel asked to testify at trial are capable of getting on the stand and indicating that they have received training in the recovery of digital evidence. Further, some companies and organisations have developed certified forensic examiner programs that allow users to complete a rigorous course of study and then receive certification as an expert in data recovery. Individual software companies often tailor these certification programs to include expert designations in the use of the company's particular software program.

Another procedure that can assist investigators in getting digital evidence admitted in criminal trials is the development and upkeep of an evidence transaction log (Kruse and Heiser, 2002). This log provides information such as the following:

- where the digital evidence was recovered from and which investigator was responsible for the forensic examination;

- the date and time digital evidence was removed – this information relates to exactly when the digital evidence was removed from the evidence vault and when the evidence was returned to the vault;

- the reason the digital evidence was removed – here the investigator removing the evidence will detail exactly why the evidence was removed from the vault;

- where the digital evidence is being taken to – the investigator will use this section of the transaction log to detail where the digital evidence will be taken during the analysis;

- exactly who removed the digital evidence – this section is where the investigator will sign his or her name, as well as the name of any third party persons who will take part in the analysis of the digital evidence.

The creation of this transaction log is useful when defending against claims of evidence tampering. By logging everyone who has come into contact with the digital evidence from the time of its collection until the actual trial, an investigator can argue against claims that someone not involved in the case has manipulated the evidence. If such a claim is made, then the investigator merely has to bring out the evidence transaction log and call in each person who has touched the evidence. Each person then testifies as to the role they played in the investigation. However, it is recommended that, wherever possible, the number of individuals involved in the analysis – and therefore called to testify in court – should be minimised and, where possible that only one investigator should take part in a forensic examination.

The future of computer forensics investigations

Unfortunately, the number of computer-assisted crimes continues to rise and, as the number of incidents increases, so too does the need for a greater and more sophisticated level of investigation. With this increased requirement for skilled investigations comes a greater need for the number of individuals trained to conduct forensic investigations of computers and networks. More companies are manufacturing computer forensics software, but there are still problems associated with getting these software programs into the hands of criminal investigators.

One problem is related to the number of law enforcement officers interested in conducting computer forensic-related investigations. While the software companies have continued to make forensic packages that are easier to use, there is still a great deal of tediousness involved in examining a computerised device for digital evidence. Some agencies may have a hard time convincing an officer(s) that computer forensic investigations are necessary, let alone exciting. Additionally, there is the fact that dedicating oneself to investigating computer-related crime means that an investigator will have to continually study computers, networks, the Internet and criminal activities. It seems that as fast as law enforcement determines how best to handle a particular computerised crime, the technology or the techniques used by criminals changes, causing law enforcement agencies to once again struggle to catch up. As has been noted in relation to the UK police, the problem is not restricted to the failure of law enforcement agencies to offer salaries to computer graduates that are commensurate with other sectors: it is relatively easy to take good officers and give them adequate training in computer technologies, but it is much more difficult to take computer 'whizzkids' and turn them into good investigators; it requires a 'different mindset that can be difficult to reach' (spokesperson for the UK National Hi-Tech Crime Unit, quoted in Jewkes and Andrews, 2005: 50). One solution used by larger law enforcement departments in the US is the use of reserve or auxiliary officers who are highly trained computer scientists. These officers are volunteers who wish to serve as agents of law enforcement (Harrison et al., 2004).

Once an agency has selected someone to investigate computer-related crime, the next issue remains the cost of computer forensic training and certifications. Many of the larger software companies offer certification courses and training in the use of their software. However, these companies do not offer these services for free. Agencies may be required to pay anything from US$500 to US$2,000 dollars for training and, in general, the classes are held out of town, so there are related transportation, lodging and payroll costs. Certification programs are similar in price, but do provide investigators the opportunity to testify in court that they have received extensive training in computer forensics, or at least the specific computer forensics program used by an agency.

Computer forensics is a relatively new weapon in the war on digital crime but with computers becoming more and more ingrained into the lives of individuals around the world, the need for forensics increases daily. However, there are several problems associated with the use of this technology, which this chapter has highlighted. They range from providing investigators with training and equipment, to finding personnel interested in investigating such criminal activities in the first place. Computer forensics requires a commitment to ongoing review and resourcing. As criminal activities continue to evolve, hopefully so too will computer forensics technologies and techniques.

References

AccessData (2006) AccessData training (retrieved on 1 March 2006 from: http://www.accessdata.com/training/).

Casey, E. (2000) *Digital Evidence and Computer Crime: Forensic Science, Computers and the Internet*. New York: Academic Press.

Deering, B. (2006) Data validation using the MD5 hash (retrieved on 17 February 2006 from: http://www.forensics-intl.com/art12.html).

Guidance Software (2006) Training and certification (retrieved on 1 March 2006 from: http://www.guidancesoftware.com/training/index.asp).

Harrison, W., Heuston, G., Mocas, S., Morrissey, M. and Richardson, J. (2004) 'High tech forensics', *Communications of the ACM*, 47 (7): 49–52.

Heying, T. (2005) 'Computer disk may have cracked BTK case', MSNBC (retrieved on 15 February 2006 from http://www.msnbc.msn.com/id/6988048/).

Jewkes, Y. and Andrews, C. (2005) 'Policing the filth: the problems of investigating online child pornography in England and Wales', *Policing & Society*, 15 (1): 42–62.

Kruse, W. and Heiser, J. (2002) *Computer Forensics: Incident Response Essentials*. New York: Addison-Wesley.

Nelson, B., Phillips, A., Enfinger, F. and Steuart, C. (2006) *Guide to Computer Forensics and Investigations*. Boston: Thompson.

United States v. *Scott-Emuakpor*, 2000 WL 288443 (WD Mich. 2000).

Vacca, J. (2002) *Computer Forensics: Computer Crime Scene Investigation*. Hingham, MA: Charles River Media.

Chapter 7

Teenage kicks or virtual villainy? Internet piracy, moral entrepreneurship, and the social construction of a crime problem

Majid Yar

Introduction

When it comes to Internet crime issues, it can fairly be suggested that the 'problem' of online piracy has been one of the two most hotly debated topics, seldom far from the public gaze over recent years (the other being child pornography – see Jewkes and Andrews, this volume). While the unauthorised sharing of copyrighted materials has a decades-long history, it was only in 1999 that widespread controversy ignited over this isssue, making the online file-sharing service Napster into something of a cause célèbre. Internet piracy (especially in relation to music) provides, I would suggest, an exemplar of how new crime problems are being socially constructed in the era of the Internet. Moreover, the phenomenon of music downloading, and the varied social responses to it, can be located at the intersection of a number of sociologically interesting issues, for example the commercialisation of the Internet, the role of capitalist interests in shaping crime problems and responses to them, the development of youth identities through consumption of popular culture, and the social dynamics of labelling and resistance. Of central importance here is the process of 'moral entrepreneurship' (Becker, 1963), a concerted enterprise on the part of empowered social actors to redefine the boundaries and limits of transgression; such entrepreneurship typically articulates and supports some sectional social, political, economic or cultural interest (Hall et al., 1978; Goode and Ben-Yehuda, 1994). In the case of music piracy, we see the ways in which organised economic interests (the recording industry and its allies) have attempted to create a new moral consensus about music downloading as a form of harmful criminal activity, and those (predominantly young) people who engage in it as 'parasites' and 'thieves'. However, as we shall see, such endeavours have not been straightforwardly successful in constructing piracy as a crime problem; rather, they have been met with strategies of resistance that refuse and contest this process of labelling, turning claims about theft and immorality back upon the entrepreneurs themselves.

Piracy: the history of a problem

As Atton (2004: 195–6) and Marshall (2004: 191) note, there is a long-standing tradition of illicit copying and sharing of popular music, a practice which took off in the 1970s with the widespread availability of home cassette recorders. Music fans would copy tapes for their friends, and the most ardent enthusiasts of particular artists would produce and trade 'bootleg' recordings of concert performances. In the past, such activities by fans were not consistently subject to rigorous control, with some artists tolerating or even encouraging bootleg recording, viewing it as a valuable means for cementing fans' loyalty to the artist and finding new audiences for their music. Moreover, as Marshall (2002: 9) notes, accepting such practices may also give performers an 'underground cachet', suggesting that they are artists first and foremost, and not unduly motivated by commercial considerations. However, recent years have seen attempts to institute much more strict limitation of informal and unauthorised recording (see, for example, IFPI, 2005), not least because recording companies have come to see the extensive profit potentials in commercial release of live recordings (be they in the form of records, tapes, CDs, videos or DVDs). Paralleling the prohibition of bootlegging, the music industry started to campaign in the 1980s against the phenomenon of home taping, wherein commercially released recordings would be copied onto cassette tape. Such taping was attributed with responsibility for a notable dip in record sales in the late 1970s, and inspired the (in)famous 'Home Taping is Killing Music' campaign by the British Phonographic Industry, the trade body representing the collective interests of UK recording companies (Woods, 2005: 8–9). This was the opening skirmish in what has developed into an ongoing ideological and rhetorical battle between recording companies and media corporations on the one side, and music fans on the other (the latter sometimes aided and abetted by the musicians themselves). For example, fans responded to the 'Home Taping is Killing Music' campaign by sporting T-shirts bearing slogans such as 'Home Taping is Killing the Music Industry: And It's Fun!' Meanwhile self-avowed socialist and popular musician Billy Bragg responded with the claim that '*Capitalism* is Killing Music'. The campaign ultimately failed to make any significant inroads among fans and consumers, gathering more mockery and indifference than sympathy among the public. However, the more recent revival of such efforts in the form of anti-piracy campaigns has been pursued with much greater determination and ruthlessness, combining relentless public relations work with concerted legal action. Attention has been focused especially upon the Internet, which is viewed as an unprecedented threat to the recording industry's control over popular music.

To understand why the Internet has come to be seen in such alarmist terms, we must note some of its distinctive features as both a technological medium and as a set of social relations. First, technologically speaking, the 'old' system of cassette recording was limited by issues of quality degradation. The reproduction of recordings using this analogue format resulted in inevitable losses of musical detail, such that the copy was always of a poorer acoustic quality than the original; the problem only worsened if one made a copy of a copy. However, the advent of digital recording meant that the data comprising the recording became infinitely and perfectly reproducible, such that the copy would be indistinguishable from the source material; it is 'as pure and pristine as the original' (MPAA, 2003). Second, the development of encoding tools and formats, such as MP3, has enabled digitally recorded music (for example on CD) to be easily transferred to computer, transmitted via the Internet in concentrated data files, and decoded for recording onto CD. Third, there has been a process of convergence between different digital media (Miller, 2004), e.g. the incorporation of the CD format within home computers, which makes the computerised transfer of music significantly easier, even for those with relatively limited technical know-how. Fourth, the rapid spread of home computing, and the ever-falling costs of powerful computer hardware, has brought many more consumers into play as potential copiers of music (Yar, 2005a). Fifth, the ability to store and play music without recourse to making permanent 'hard copies' (for example on computer hard drives and portable MP3 players) further reduces the costs associated with copying and subsequently enjoying the music. Finally, it is worth noting the ways in which the Internet facilitates social interactions, exchanges and communications between an extended array of actors. In the past, music fans would likely be restricted to copying those recordings that could be borrowed from an immediate circle comprising family, friends and acquaintances. However, the Internet has massively extended this sphere of potential sources of material, such that individuals can now download and copy music from potentially millions of others, especially through file-exchange systems such as Napster (which will be discussed below in more detail).

It is in light of the above developments that the recording industry has proclaimed that Internet-based music copying represents a serious threat to the viability of the music industry. It is claimed that 81.5 million people (4.98 per cent of the world's Internet users) illegally downloaded music in the course of 2003. This piracy is deemed to have lead to an average *monthly* loss of $450 million to copyright holders throughout 2004 (DIG, 2004). Online file-sharing is held responsible for a 22 per cent drop in worldwide music sales between 1999 and 2004 (BPI, 2005: 4).

Napster and the rise of online 'piracy'

The controversy over online music copying took off in earnest in 1999, a few months after the launch of the Napster service. The brainchild of 19-year-old student Shawn Fanning, Napster was a simple yet powerful idea. The system worked thus. Users would register online and download the Napster software onto their PCs. This software would scan the users' hard drives for any digitised music (MP3) files and transmit a listing to the Napster central server. When users looking for a particular piece of music searched the Napster catalogue, it would inform them whether other members had a copy on their computers, and if they were currently online. If the answer to both queries was yes, then the searchers could send a request to the person in possession of the file to download a copy for themselves (Post, 2002: 107). Enthusiasm for the system grew rapidly, with some 70 million individuals using it to share music with others around the globe. However, by late 1999, US recording companies were locked in battle with Napster in the courts, claiming that the primary use of the system was to facilitate 'theft' of intellectual property in the form of unauthorised (and more importantly unremunerated) copying of music over which the companies held copyright ownership. The courts ultimately upheld the recording industry's complaint, and Napster agreed to pay the plaintiffs $26 million for past copyright violations, and a further $10 million in royalties for future sharing of copyrighted content (NPMA, 2001: 7). In order to pay such royalties Napster was transformed into a subscription-based service in which customers would pay to download tracks of their choice (a model for the more recent, and highly successful, iTunes service from Apple).

However, the Napster affair was far from the end of the battle against online music copying. Firstly, the popularity of Napster quickly spawned many similar file-sharing services, and recording industry bodies were kept busy pursuing them through the courts for alleged copyright violations. For example, the RIAA (Recording Industry Association of America) reached an out-of-court settlement for compensation with Audiogalaxy, a 'Napster-like clone', in 2002 (NMPA, 2002: 1). Moreover, the post-Napster development of file-sharing software posed even greater problems for regulating unauthorised copying. Napster and similar services were centralised in character in that they provided a single point of access through which users could find and copy music files. This meant that recording companies could easily identify a single organisation or entity against whom legal action could be taken; once that organisation desisted or was shut down, the file-sharing would stop. From 2000, new software such as Gnutella and Freenet became available, working on a decentralised network basis. In other words, file-sharing was undertaken by the network of interconnected users without a single central entity coordinating the traffic in files (May, 2002: 101–2). Consequently, recording companies were forced to pursue copyright violators on an individual basis, sending cease-and-desist orders and initiating lawsuits against individual music fans; for example, in January 2004 alone, the RIAA 'filed a new wave of copyright infringement lawsuits against 531 individual computer users' (RIAA, 2004). Moreover, as Marshall (2004: 109–10) notes, these systems were driven by a much more radical ideological perspective than Napster, having been specifically developed as part of an 'anti-property' ethos and adopted by a community of music enthusiasts explicitly attached to anti-corporate values when it came to the enjoyment of music and other cultural goods. Consequently, there has emerged a starker division and oppositional attitude when it comes to music file-sharing: the major music corporations (and some major recording artists) have effectively 'declared war' on those music fans they hold to be little more than criminals, while fans' attitudes have hardened in the face of this 'persecution', thereby turning copying into an act of resistance.

'Piracy' as ubiquitous cultural practice

Moving more firmly from the legal and technical to the social-cultural dimensions of the copying debate, one of the most notable features of Internet piracy is its apparent ubiquity. Far from being confined to a small class of 'professional criminals', piracy activity appears to be socially widespread and undertaken on a regular basis by individuals who would otherwise consider themselves 'law abiding citisens'. Participation in the illegal downloading of copyrighted materials appears to span persons from various social classes and walks of life. Some insight into the social distribution and engagement in Internet piracy is afforded by recent surveys and self-report studies; particularly noteworthy among such findings is the disproportionate involvement of young people in such offending (something that parallels the more general association of young people with computer crime – for discussion, see Yar, 2005b).

A recent US survey of professional workers reveals that only 26 per cent oppose software piracy 'in principle' (IPSOS, 2004). A UK-based poll in 2004, conducted on behalf of the Business Software Alliance, found that 44 per cent of 18–29 year olds owned pirated intellectual property; the figure for the 30–50 year age group was 28 per cent, and 17 per cent for the over 50s. The survey further found that 'there is little stigma to owning counterfeit goods' (Thomson, 2004). The findings of the UK government's 2003 Crime and Justice Survey reports that 9 per cent of people over 18 years old in the UK admit to committing technology offences such as 'illegally downloading software or music' (Budd et al., 2005: 25). Significant, then, is the apparent inverse relationship between age and propensity to commit copyright offences – the younger the age group, the more likely their involvement. Thus surveys of young people's attitudes toward computer-related activities such as downloading show high levels of participation and minimal reservation about doing so (Bowker, 1999: 40). A 2004 poll in the US found that 'more than half of all 8–18 year olds have downloaded music, a third have downloaded games and nearly a quarter have downloaded software illegally from the Internet' (Snyder, 2004: 1). A number of studies worldwide have found high levels of 'softlifting' (downloaded copyrighted software from the Internet) among college students and little weight attached to the 'legal and moral objections' (see discussion in Kini et al., 2003: 63–4). A 2004 survey of young people in Canada found that 47 per cent of 12–21 year olds intended to 'download music, video or software from the Internet over the next six months' (Jedwab, 2004: 1). It further found that 70 per cent of respondents 'deemed [it] acceptable to download music, video or software from the Internet' (ibid.). This relationship between youth and piracy has, as we shall see, shaped in significant ways the development of anti-piracy campaigns and initiatives.

Moral entrepreneurship and the construction of piracy

In order to fully grasp the dynamics through which piracy has been articulated as a crime problem, we need to reflect on the more general analyses about the social construction of deviance developed by criminologists. Starting with the work of Tannenbaum (1938), and later that of Kitsuse (1962) and Becker (1963), criminologists unpacked the ways in which socially and culturally generated labels served to create new categories of deviance and criminality, situating particular actors and their actions as dangerous, threatening and antithetical to social order and well-being. These accounts were based upon the insight (often overlooked in the everyday circulation of criminological and legal discourse) that 'crime' is more than a matter of legal, statutory prohibition (Lacey, 1995: 1; also Lacey, 2002). Rather, crime and criminality need to be understood as constructions that emerge from processes taking place beyond the sphere of legislation and judicial judgment. The identification of conduct as crime depends crucially upon a wider consensus that the behaviour in question constitutes a breach of acceptable social norms, that it partakes of some *moral* wrong-doing or injury that offends against a society and its members. This socio-moral underpinning of crime was well known to thinkers such as Durkheim, who noted that crime 'consists of an act that offends certain very strong collective sentiments' (Durkheim, 2003: 66), and that the effectiveness of legal prohibition is sustained by this feeling of offence. Thus laws which lose their grounding in social sentiments are liable to atrophy, languishing on the statute books and unenforced in practice; conversely, the mobilisation of censorious feeling against some category of behaviour may well be enough to institute a process of criminalisation, marking its transition from 'mere' social disapproval to formal prohibition, with all the force of the state's crime control apparatus arrayed against it.

Building on the work of labelling theorists, a fully worked account of criminalisation as a socio-cultural process was offered by Cohen (1972) in his influential study *Folk Devils and Moral Panics*. Cohen analysed 'moral panics' as excessive and unwarranted social and political responses to what come to be seen as major crime problems. Crucially, such perceptions do not follow from the objectively harmful character of acts, but through a process of meaning construction that is driven by what Cohen calls 'moral entrepreneurs'. Such individuals and/or groups typically have a stake in furthering the wider social perception that a new and dangerous crime problem is in the ascendancy, and that urgent action is required if it is to be tackled. Entrepreneurship, if successful, can generate considerable pressure upon the state and its agencies of social control, and lead to 'innovations' such as the formulation of new criminal laws and policing strategies. In what follows, I examine the construction of piracy as a crime problem as one such instance of moral entrepreneurship, a process in which interested parties attempt to redefine the boundaries of criminal, dangerous and deviant behaviour in an effort to shape public and political responses to cultural copying.

At the first level, we can note the ways in which practices of unauthorised copying have been linguistically recoded so as to furnish them with stronger criminal overtones. The use of the term 'piracy' to describe such activities is far from normatively neutral. Rather, as Drahos and Braithwaite (2002: 24–5) astutely observe, the term ought to be viewed not simply as a piece of legal terminology, but also as a rhetorical device which, by evoking associations with bloodthirsty seafaring brigands, is used to moralise copyright infringement as a 'serious crime'. This recasting of copying attempts to create a normative consensus that it offends against the agreed standards of decent and acceptable behaviour. This has been necessary precisely because copyright violations have been rendered socially acceptable by their ubiquity and the widespread perception that they are not genuinely 'harmful' in the manner of 'real crimes' (such as theft of personal property, homicide, rape, assault and so on).

In addition, it has now become commonplace to find in the discourse of copyright industries, trade bodies, governments and criminal justice agencies the claim that media piracy is linked with organised crime and terrorism (TraCCC, 2001; AACP, 2002). As a number of criminologists have noted, the term 'organised crime' is ill defined, but carries ready associations in the public mind with violent and ruthless criminal groups such as the Mafia (Levi, 1998; Woodiwiss, 2000). Hence, forging an association between piracy and organised crime helps to create a moral and emotive case against the former by drawing upon commonplace perceptions of the latter. This strategy is clearly attested in a recent report by the AACP, which begins by noting that:

> ... there continues to be reluctance among police, customs and trading standards services ... to regard intellectual property fraud as a priority, often being unaware of its association with organised crime ... (2002: 2)

'Raising awareness' thus becomes integral to the copyright industry's attempts to secure support for its agenda. Similar links have been asserted more recently between counterfeiting, piracy and terrorist groups. The FBI have explored claims that the 1993 bombing of the World Trade Center in New York was financed by sales of counterfeit goods (Paradise, 1999: 22); UK authorities have claimed that the IRA has financed its paramilitary activities through film piracy (ibid.; AACP, 2002: 14); drawing upon the post-9/11 momentum in the 'war on terror', the Anti-Counterfeiting Group has pushed claims that Al Qaeda has been financing itself through engaging in commercial counterfeiting (ACG, 2002: 2). Such claims have also become commonplace in the trailers that now routinely preface the cinematic exhibition of films and home DVDs. Whatever the truth of such claims, they must be seen as powerful rhetorical tools that are availed in order to create a public (and political) perception that there is a serious and dangerous criminal threat posed by piracy, which both justifies a prioritisation of intellectual property theft by criminal justice agencies and legitimates calls for further strengthening legal protections and criminal sanctions.

I have already noted that Internet copying has been particularly identified with young people. Consequently, it comes as no surprise that great efforts have been directed toward 'educating' adolescents and their parents about the 'immorality' of media copying and the potential criminal sanctions facing those apprehended for such activities. In recent years a number of bodies (representing the commercial interests of copyright industries) have produced anti-piracy campaigns aimed at 'educating' children aged between eight and 13 years. These include: the FA©E (Friends of Active Copyright Education) initiative of the Copyright Society of America, called 'Copyright Kids'; the SIAA's (Software & Information Industry Association) 'Cybersmart! School Program'; the BSA's (Business Software Alliance) 'Play It Cybersafe' program featuring the cartoon character 'The Copyright Crusader'; and the MPAA's 'Starving Artist' schools' road show. Such campaigns have been integrated into school curricula in the United States and elsewhere, thereby taking the struggle to define the moral meanings of piracy into the formal apparatus of the public education system.

The aforementioned campaigns can be seen to adopt a range of rhetorical strategies to challenge young people's indifference to Internet copying. Firstly, they regularly assert that immaterial cultural goods are essentially the same as tangible material goods; consequently, downloading and copying are said to be tantamount to stealing (Play It Cybersafe, 2005a). By suggesting a moral equivalence between the two activities, the campaigns seek to ride upon normative prohibitions about theft ('you wouldn't steal a CD ...') to dissuade potential copiers. Secondly, commonly held conceptions of harm are mobilised to evoke guilt amongst the audience. These campaigns make great play of the ways in which copying impacts negatively upon society. This is clearly exemplified in The Play It Cybersafe campaign, which has produced a comic strip featuring a mascot, Garret the Ferret, otherwise known as the Copyright Crusader. The comic tells the story of Shawn, an American fourth grader (eight years old) who is at his computer and about to make a copy of some software lent to him by his friend Erika. Garret suddenly materialises through his computer screen, and proceeds to tell Shawn that 'Companies lose billions of dollars every year. It also means people can lose their jobs.' Shawn (in a volte face akin to St Paul's on the road to Damascus) exclaims 'My friend's dad lost his job at a software company last year. I never thought about the bad things that can happen when I copy software' (Play It Cybersafe, 2005a: 3). The supposed social harms of copying are accompanied by claims about the harm done to the individual well-being of musicians and other artists. This argumentative strategy reaches its apotheosis in the 'Starving Artist' role-playing game designed for school children, and taken 'on tour' in 2003 in 36,000 classrooms across the US. The game invites students 'to come up with an idea for a record album, cover art, and lyrics' (Menta, 2003). Having completed the exercise, the students are told that their album is already available for download from the Internet, and are asked 'how they felt when they realised that their work was stolen and that they would not get anything for their efforts' (ibid.).

A final dimension of these campaigns is deserving of attention, namely the ways in which they attempt to recruit parents into the process of deviance construction and criminalisation by making them responsible for their children's behaviour. This strategy can be viewed as part of a more general trend in the reconfiguration of social control, what has been dubbed the 'responsibilisation' of citizens in relation to issues of law and order (Burchell, 1996; Garland, 2001: 124–7). In this situation, the burden of crime control is shifted away from the neo-liberal state and toward individuals (Muncie, 2005: 37, 39). This process has been particularly marked in relation to the responsibilisation of parents in an attempt to curtail youth offending (Kelly, 2001). Many of the programs examined here include 'guidance notes' for parents and guardians that displace responsibility for controlling children's piracy from formal agencies to the parents themselves:

> Explain copyright laws and talk to your child about why it is illegal [. . .] Help your child notice the copyright symbol [. . .] Encourage your child to make the right decisions when using protected works [. . .] Use positive reinforcement . . . (Play It Cybersafe, 2005b: 1)

Particularly noteworthy is the emphasis placed upon parental supervision:

> Stay close. An involved parent is the best teacher. (BSA, 2005)

> Supervise your child's time on the Internet. (Play It Cybersafe, 2005b: 1)

The suggestion that parents have a moral obligation to 'supervise' their children's activities in relation to copyrighted materials effectively institutes a regime of disciplinary surveillance within the home (Foucault, 1991); parents become the copyright industries' agents, recruited for the purposes of a moral pedagogy that promulgates and legitimates the industries' favoured understanding of property rights, and incrementally criminalises children's cultural and leisure activities:

> . . . there are very real consequences of violating copyright laws, including potential legal action against pirates . . . By educating [. . .] your children, you can protect your own family from these consequences . . . (Snyder, 2004: 4)

Moments of resistance

As Becker (1963) notes, it is by no means given that those targeted with stigmatising labels of criminality and deviance will automatically accept such labels. Rather, they may resist such efforts, seeking to deflect the label by defending their activities against those who seek to position them as 'outsiders'. Such reactions may be considered as instances of what Sykes and Matza (1957) call 'techniques of neutralisation'. These techniques serve as vocabularies of justification by which the potential 'deviants' deflect negative labels, turning accusations of moral delinquency back upon their accusers. Prime among these techniques are those of the 'denial of harm' (the assertion that no real social damage is caused by the behaviour in question) and 'denial of the deniers' (the assertion that those who mount accusations are themselves corrupt, immoral or otherwise hypocritical). Moments of reaction-resistance have clearly emerged in response to moral entrepreneurs' constructions of Internet copying as a form of criminality. Music fans, committed to the free circulation and appreciation of popular culture, have established websites where such rhetorical defences are mounted. For example, the activists of BOYCOTT-RIAA.com (2005) state that:

> Boycott-RIAA was founded because we love music. We cannot stand by silently while the recording industry continues its decades-long effort to lock up our culture and heritage by misrepresenting the facts to the public, to artists, the fans and to our government.

Through such responses, acts of copying and culture sharing are defended as principled stands against corporate interests who are charged with being the true 'villains' in the unfolding confrontation between producers and fans.

However, the lines of division within this battle to define criminality are further complicated by the indeterminate role played by recording artists themselves. On the one hand, artists have played a pivotal role in the entrepreneurship that has sought to define Internet copying as harmful and socially unacceptable. For example, the controversy over Napster's file-sharing service first hit the headlines as a result of legal action taken by the band Metallica (Marshall, 2002: 9). Other prominent anti-Napster performers included Madonna and Mick Jagger. In contrast, other artists have made common cause with file-sharers, choosing instead to direct their criticisms against the recording companies rather that the fans. In 2000, rock musician Courtney Love (singer with Hole and widow of rock icon Kurt Cobain) launched what has been dubbed the 'Love Manifesto', a critical reflection on intellectual property theft, artists and the recording industry. Love began her 'Manifesto' thus:

> Today I want to talk about piracy and music. What is piracy? Piracy is the act of stealing an artist's work without any intention of paying for it. I'm not talking about Napster-type software ... I'm talking about major label recording contracts. (Love, 2000)

She went on to claim that standard practice within the recording industry deprives musicians of copyrights, and the monies advanced to artists are largely recouped from them by the industry under 'expenses' for recording and promotion. As a consequence, the musicians see little return from their efforts and, she opined, 'the band may as well be working at a 7-Eleven' (ibid.). In fact, it has been argued that piracy is in the financial interests of most recording artists; most performers make their living from concert performance, and this is best supported and promoted by having their music circulated as widely as possible, including via copying. As musician Ignacio Escolar has put it: 'Like all musicians, I know that 100,000 pirate fans coming to my shows are more profitable than 10,000 original ones' (Escolar, 2003: 15).

Conclusion

This chapter has explored the controversy that has emerged around the online sharing of popular cultural goods, especially musical recordings. It is clear that the piracy issue is one of the most high-profile Internet crime issues of recent years. Yet I have also set out to show the complex dynamics through which piracy has come to be *socially constructed* as a supposedly serious crime problem. Far from being self-evidently criminal or deviant, the problematic nature of online copying has of necessity required an elaborate rhetorical construction by those moral entrepreneurs who stand to benefit from the enforcement of copyrights. Such efforts seldom pass uncontested, and the piracy controversy offers a fine example of how those groups and individuals targeted with deviant labels seek to challenge the definitions favoured by the powerful, and to defend their cultural practices as legitimate and socially valuable. While anti-piracy campaigns *have* yielded returns in the form of legal and crime control innovations, it is by no means certain that they will ultimately succeed in villainising cultural copying on the Internet.

References

AACP (Alliance Against Counterfeiting and Piracy) (2002) *Proving the Connection: Links Between Intellectual Property Theft and Organised Crime*. London: AACP.

ACG (Anti-Counterfeiting Group) (2002) 'ACG Christmas Warning', December (online at: http://www.a-cg.com).

Atton, C. (2004) *An Alternative Internet: Dissent, Transgression and Creativity in a Digital Age*. Edinburgh: Edinburgh University Press.

Becker, H. (1963) *Outsiders: Studies in the Sociology of Deviance*. New York: Free Press.

Bowker, A. (1999) 'Juveniles and computers: should we be concerned?', *Federal Probation: A Journal of Correctional Philosophy and Practice*, 63: 40–43.

BPI (British Phonographic Industry) (2005) *Online Music Piracy: The UK Record Industry's Response*. London: BPI.

BSA (2005b) 'Five tips for raising children to be respectful cyber citizens', URL (accessed March 2005: http://www.bsa.org/usa/press/newsreleases/Five-Tips-For-Raising-Children-To-Be-Respectful-Cyber-Citizens.cfm).

Budd, T., Sharp, C. and Mayhew, P. (2005) *Offending in England and Wales: First Results from the 2003 Crime and Justice Survey*, Home Office Research Study 275. London: Home Office.

Burchell, G. (1996) 'Liberal government and techniques of the self', in A. Barry, T. Osborne and N. Rose (eds), *Foucault and Political Reason: Liberalism, Neo-Liberalism and Rationalities of Government.* London: UCL Press.

Cohen, S. (1972) *Folk Devils and Moral Panics.* London: MacGibbon & Kee.

Digital Intelligence Centre (DIG) (2004) 'Digital Intelligence Centre: Archived News' (online at: http://www.itic.ca/DIC/News/archive.html#2004-06-09, accessed March 2005).

Drahos, P. with Braithwaite, J. (2002) *Information Feudalism: Who Owns the Knowledge Economy?* London: Earthscan.

Durkheim, E. (2003) 'The normal and the pathological', in E. McLaughlin, J. Muncie and G. Hughes (eds), *Criminological Perspectives: Essential Readings.* London: Sage.

Escolar, I. (2003) 'Please pirate my songs!', in WSIS, *World Information: Knowledge of Future Culture.* Vienna: Institut für Neue Kulturtechnologien.

Foucault, M. (1991) *Discipline and Punish.* Harmondsworth: Penguin.

Garland, D. (2001) *The Culture of Control: Crime and Social Order in Contemporary Society.* Oxford: Clarendon.

Goode, E. and Ben-Yehuda, N. (1994) *Moral Panics: The Social Construction of Deviance.* Oxford: Blackwell.

Hall, S., Critcher, C., Jefferson, T., Clarke, J. and Roberts, B. (1978) *Policing the Crisis: Mugging, the State and Law and Order.* London: Macmillan.

IFPI (International Federation of Phonographic Industries) (2005) 'International bootlegging ring smashed in Europe' (online at: http:/www.ifpi.org/site-content/press/20020620a.html).

IPSOS (2004) 'Online software piracy poll' (online at: http://www.ipsos-na.com/news/pressrelease.cfm?id = 2452).

Jedwab, J. (2004) 'The lowdown on music downloading in Canada: youth regard Internet downloading of music, video and software as acceptable: only threat of legal action is effective deterrent' (online at: http://www.acs-aec.ca/Polls/18-10-2004-1.pdf).

Kelly, P. (2001) 'Youth at risk: processes of individualisation and responsibilisation in the risk society', *Discourse,* 22 (1): 23–33.

Kini, R., Pamakrishna, H. and Vijayaraman, B. (2003) 'An exploratory study of moral intensity regarding software piracy of students in Thailand', *Behaviour & Information Technology,* 22 (1): 63–70.

Kitsuse, J. (1962) 'Societal reaction to deviant behaviour', *Social Problems,* 9: 247–56.

Lacey, N. (1995) 'Contingency and criminalisation', in I. Loveland (ed.), *Frontiers of Criminality.* London: Sweet & Maxwell.

Lacey, N. (2002) 'Legal constructions of crime', in M. Maguire, R. Morgan and R. Reiner (eds), *The Oxford Handbook of Criminology,* 3rd edn. Oxford: Oxford University Press, pp. 264–85.

Levi, M. (1998) 'Perspectives on "organised crime": an overview', *Howard Journal,* 37 (4): 335–45.

Love, C. (2000) 'Love Manifesto' (online at: http://www.reznor.com/commentary/loves_manifesto1.html).

Marshall, L. (2002) 'Metallica and morality: the rhetorical battleground of the Napster wars', *Entertainment Law,* 1 (1): 1–19.

Marshall, L. (2004) 'Infringers', in L. Marshall and S. Frith (eds) *Music and Copyright.* London: Routledge.

May, C. (2002) *The Information Society: A Sceptical View*. Cambridge: Polity.

Menta, R. (2003) 'Let's play starving artist' (online at: http://www.mp3newswire.net/stories/2003/starvingartist.html).

Miller, V. (2004) 'Stitching the Web into global capitalism: two stories', in D. Gauntlett and R. Horsley (eds), *Web.Studies*, 2nd edn. London: Edward Arnold.

MPAA (Motion Picture Association of America) (2003a) 'Anti-piracy' (online at: http://www.mpaa.org/anti-piracy/index.htm).

Muncie, J. (2005) 'The globalization of crime control: the case of youth and juvenile justice: neo-liberalism, policy governance and international conventions', *Theoretical Criminology*, 9 (1): 35–64.

NPMA (National Music Publishers' Association) (2001) *News and Views*, Winter, no. 6032.

NPMA (National Music Publishers' Association) (2002) 'Recording Industry Association of America, National Music Publishers' Association reach settlement with Audiogalaxy.com', (online at: http://www.nmpa.org/pr/NMPA-RIAA-Audiogalaxy2.pdf).

Paradise, P. R. (1999) *Trademark Counterfeiting, Product Piracy, and the Billion Dollar Threat to the U.S. Economy*. Westport, CT: Quantam Books.

Play It Cybersafe (2005a) 'Copyright Crusader to the rescue' (online at: http://www.playitcybersafe.com/pdfs/Curriculum_CC-2005.pdf).

Play It Cybersafe (2005b) 'Parents' and teacher's guide' (online at: http://www.playitcybersafe.com/pdfs/TG-copyrightCrusader-2005.pdf).

Post, D. (2002) 'His Napster's Voice', in A. Thierer and C. Crews (eds), *Copy Fights: The Future of Intellectual Property in the Information Age*. Washington, DC: Cato Institute.

RIAA (Recording Industry Association of America) (2004) '531 more file sharers targeted in latest RIAA legal efforts' (online at: http://www.riaa.com/news/newsletter/021704.asp).

Snyder, M. (2004) 'Pirates of the 21st century' (online at: http://www.cyberplayitsafe.com/resources/21st-Century-Pirates.PDF).

Sykes, G. and Matza, D. (1957) 'Techniques of neutralization: a theory of delinquency', *American Sociological Review*, 22: 664–70

Tannenbaum, F. (1938) *Crime and the Community*. New York: Columbia University Press.

Thomson, I. (2004) 'Britain becoming a nation of pirates' (online at: http://www.crn.vnunet.com/news/1157189).

TraCCC (Transnational Crime and Corruption Centre) (2001) *Transnational Crime, Corruption and Information Technology*. Washington, DC: TraCCC.

Woodiwiss, M. (2000) 'Organized crime – the dumbing of discourse', in G. Mair and R. Tarling (eds), *The British Criminology Conference: Selected Proceedings. Volume 3* (online at: http://www.britsoccrim.org/bccsp/vol03/woodiwiss.html).

Woods, C. (2005) 'The piracy genie is out', *WORLDfocus: Fighting IP Theft*, May: 7–10 (online at: http://www.kilpatrickstockton.com/publications/downloads/ThreatResponse.pdf).

Yar, M. (2005a) 'The global "epidemic" of movie "piracy": crime-wave or social construction?', *Media, Culture and Society*, 27 (5): 677–96.

Yar, M. (2005b) 'Computer hacking: just another case of juvenile delinquency?', *Howard Journal of Criminal Justice*, 44 (4): 387–99.

Chapter 8

In the back of the net: football hooliganism and the Internet

Stefan Fafinski

Introduction

> No matter what the police or government do, or what happens on the Internet, football violence can only exist if two people are within touching distance of each other and one of them feels the desire to lash out. (Brimson, 2000: 144)

There is an immediate and obvious difference between real violence and virtual violence. However, the distinction between the real and virtual worlds in relation to football-related violence is not as clear cut as it appears at first. Technology has been used as a means of both regulating and controlling behaviour as well as a means of circumventing that regulation and control. This chapter will examine the transformation and displacement of football violence by the Internet. It will briefly consider the moral panic of the 1970s which inextricably linked football to violence and public disorder, before turning to the emergence of the Internet as a potential new means of organising and otherwise facilitating football violence against the backdrop of an ever-increasing number of control mechanisms: often-controversial legislation, regulatory restrictions, modernisation of football stadia and policing approaches.

Violence, panic and legislation

Concerns about the Internet have given new impetus to mediated anxieties about the 'football hooligan', but football-related violence is by no means a recent phenomenon. Indeed, measures have been taken or sought since the fourteenth century to deal with the problem of disorder relating to football. A 1314 proclamation of Edward II declared:

> Forasmuch there is great noise in the city caused by hustling over large balls, from which many evils may arise, which God forbid, we command and forbid on behalf of the King, on pain of imprisonment, such game to be used in the city in future. (cited in House of Commons Library Research Paper, 2000)

Pitch invasions and 'violent disturbances' occurred in the late 1800s although much of this violence was spontaneous:

> Loughborough had much the best of matters and the Gainsborough goal survived several attacks in a remarkable manner, the end coming with the score: Loughborough, none Gainsborough, none. The referee's decisions had caused considerable dissatisfaction, especially that disallowing a goal to Loughborough in the first half, and at the close of the game he met with a very unfavourable reaction, a section of the crowd hustling him and it was stated that he was struck. (*Leicester Daily Mercury*, 3 April 1899, in Frosdick and Marsh, 2005: 114)

The end of the nineteenth century also saw the first appearance of the word 'hooligan' in daily newspaper court reports:

> It is no wonder ... that Hooligan gangs are bred in these vile, miasmatic byways. (*Daily News* 26 July 1898)

As might be expected as a reaction to the great conflicts, the period between the First and Second World Wars and the decade following the end of the Second World War were relatively peaceful. However, from the mid-1950s to the early 1970s more incidents of violence at football matches began to arise, with fighting breaking out between supporters of opposing teams or on trains carrying supporters to away fixtures. While much of this violence was still largely disorganised and sporadic, the late 1970s and 1980s saw the appearance of organised 'firms' or 'crews' and the spread of violence abroad. Elliott et al. describe this change:

> A new trend of disorder as stylised viciousness rather than emotional overreaction seemed to emerge. Fighting, throwing missiles and obscene and racist chanting became perceived as more commonplace. Drunken groups of rival supporters seemed to be forever running rampage through town centres and on public transport. (1999: 17)

It is clear, then, that football matches have attracted violent troublemakers ever since the birth of the professional game in the late nineteenth century. Moreover, the media have played an important role in the depiction and dissemination of football hooliganism to the general public. Media coverage of football-related violence is highly complex and, through mass communication, the media serve as primary definers of what constitutes 'hooliganism' (Poulton, 2001). As Melnick states:

> The mass media in general can take major credit for the public's view of the soccer hooligan as a cross between the Neanderthal Man and Conan the Barbarian. (Melnick, 1986 cited, in Carnibella et al., 1996: 89)

Increasing use of tabloid headlines throughout the 1970s such as 'SAVAGES! ANIMALS!' (*Daily Mirror*, 21 April 1975), 'RIOT! United's fans are animals' (*Sunday People*, 29 August 1975) and 'Scandal of soccer's savages – warming up for the new season' (*Daily Mirror*, 20 August 1973) led to the creation of the stereotypical football hooligan becoming a new 'folk devil' in society:

> The football hooligan begets the football hooliganism problem. The establishment of a new folk devil leads to the development of a moral panic . . . Future incidents then appear within the framework of this moral panic as evidence of a trend, which is increasingly newsworthy in its own right. (Whannel, cited in Poulton, 2001: 124)

Moreover, the press have played an influential role in policy-making often leading to short-sighted measures which have succeeded only in moving violence from the terraces and on to the streets outside the football grounds (Frosdick and March, 2005).

Therefore, the moral panic spawned largely in the 1970s inextricably linked football to violence and public disorder at the same time as English football hooligans began organising their activities. In parallel to this panic, a number of legislative controls were brought into force in an attempt to control, or at least contain, the perceived problem. As Frosdick and Marsh point out, although football supporters are subject to the same body of criminal law as other members of society, they are unusual in that there is a 'whole raft of criminal legislation which is solely football related' (2005: 169).

The first significant piece of legislation was the Sporting Events (Control of Alcohol) Act 1985 which restricted the possession and sale of alcohol at 'designated sporting events', criminalising drunkenness inside football grounds and the possession of alcohol in any part of the ground from which a glimpse of the pitch might be seen. The alcohol prohibition occurred despite the conclusions of the Department of the Environment

Working Group that restrictions would mean that the 'majority of football clubs ... would unnecessarily be penalised financially and the vast majority of non-violent spectators would suffer as a result' (1984: para. 5.34). The ban was a result of 'policy-making driven by populism and moral panic rather than the facts' (Frosdick and Marsh, 2005: 127), seemingly a common theme in much of the legislative control. It is no coincidence that the 1985 Act received Royal Assent only two months after the Bradford stadium fire in which 56 supporters died and the Heysel stadium disaster in Belgium which claimed a further 39 supporters. Lord Justice Popplewell's reports into the two tragedies (Home Office, 1985, 1986) made no recommendations that alcohol should be banned, although it did concede that 'even if [alcohol] does not give rise to violence, it gives rise to disorderly behaviour' (Home Office, 1986: para. 4.77).

The Hillsborough disaster in April 1989 in which 96 supporters were crushed against a perimeter fence and killed was the subject of further government reports by Lord Justice Taylor (Home Office, 1989, 1990). These 'set out in considerable detail a complex range and chain of causal factors leading up to the disaster'(Frosdick and Marsh, 2005: 23) and precipitated the Football Supporters Act 1989 seven months after the disaster. The new Act covered matters of admission of spectators at designated football matches, proposed a national membership scheme and introduced restriction orders aimed at preventing hooligans from travelling to matches abroad. Shortly thereafter the Football (Offences) Act 1991 created three football-specific offences of throwing 'anything' or going onto the pitch without lawful excuse or authority and 'chanting of an indecent or racialist nature'. The three offences were recommended by Lord Justice Taylor in his final report on the Hillsborough disaster (Home Office, 1990).

As the implementation of the Taylor Report recommendations took place, including the removal of perimeter fencing and the introduction of compulsory all-seater stadia in the top division, the following season was extremely quiet in terms of violent or tragic incident. As Brimson comments, this was:

> So much so that there were even suggestions that, finally, the problem had been solved altogether, an idea the game and the police were happy to encourage ... [But] if football genuinely thought that hooliganism was a thing of the past it was only deluding itself (2000: 131).

However, the Taylor Report controls shifted the locus of violence from the higher divisions where the Taylor controls were mandatory to the lower divisions where terracing was still in place and hooligans who had deserted or been banned from the big clubs after Hillsborough made their way down the divisions (Brimson, 2000). Consequently, violent incidents began to increase again throughout the 1990s, peaking in 1998. This year saw, among other things, attacks on officials, where a Sheffield United fan jumped onto the pitch at Fratton Park and knocked out a linesman, the death of a Fulham fan at Gillingham, and an incident in which 20 Birmingham fans sprayed Norwich fans with CS gas and then attacked them with bar stools in a Norfolk pub (Brimson, 2000); the latter incident providing further evidence of the displacement of violence away from the grounds themselves. Yet again, the official response was a government document which was announced in November 1998 and which outlined proposals for further legislation in a bid to control the problem.

It is clear from the discussion so far that the period from 1980 to 1999 was characterised by an increasing tendency to legislate in reaction to media panic and a series of disasters. In response to this, the football 'firms' sought alternative means of staying ahead of the game. The cyberthug was about to appear.

The emergence of the cyberthug

Brimson comments on the entry of the Internet in the arena of football disorder as follows:

> [The November 1998 government consultative document] laid out plans for all kinds of new legislation to counter the growing threat. It was almost certainly designed to influence the 2006 World Cup bid. For those involved in the hooligan scene, the document was merely another challenge to be overcome, though many expressed doubt (wrongly, as it turned out) that these laws would ever come onto the statute books. If the idea had been to send a warning to those intent on causing trouble, it fell sadly short. For in the quest to stay ahead in the contest with authority, the hooligans had discovered a new weapon: the Internet. (Brimson, 2000: 140)

The media's interest in the use of the Internet in connection with football violence began in earnest in August 1999. In a *Sunday Mirror* article entitled 'Hooligan.com – high-tech soccer thugs meet up on the Internet' (1 August 1999), Tim Luckett claimed that:

> Football hooligans are using the Internet to run riot at matches. They are also in contact via mobile phones and pagers to co-ordinate meetings and even update each other on police activity.

This seems largely to have been based on comments from Bryan Drew, spokesman for the National Criminal Intelligence Service (NCIS) (www.ncis.co.uk):

These people are not mindless hooligans – they are organised groups. They have their own intelligence structures and communicate in the same way as law enforcement. They use technology – including the Internet – both in Britain and internationally to contact each other.

Away from grounds – and with activities communicated through mobile phones, pagers and the Internet – the hooligans remain a menace.

Drew's comments also suggest that the NCIS was acknowledging the displacement effect of regulation and technology in the form of CCTV on the locus of football-related violence. The NCIS figures for the 1998–99 season indeed showed an increase in football-related offences for the first time in six years from 3,307 in 1997–98 to 3,341 in 1998–99, representing an arguably insignificant rise of just over one per cent: some 34 extra arrests in absolute terms. The *Sunday Mirror* article then concluded with 'the list of shame for hooligan arrests', a breakdown of arrests by club for 1998–99. The NCIS figures did not quantify the extent of the contribution of the Internet to the increase.

Cardiff City v Millwall (1999)

Within a week of the *Sunday Mirror*'s claim that 'hooligans are using the Internet to run riot at matches' Millwall visited Cardiff City, newly promoted to Division 2, on the opening day of the 1999–2000 season. A BBC News 'Special Report' (1999a) described how 'scores' of fans clashed, resulting in riot police with dogs and horses cordoning off the centre of Cardiff as chairs and bottles were used as missiles and local business-people locked themselves indoors for their own safety. The incident itself, leading to 14 injuries and six arrests, might not have been unforeseen. Cardiff and Millwall had both achieved notoriety for their association with football violence. Despite their *combined* total of arrests for the previous season being less than that of the seldom-vilified Everton, Arsenal or Manchester United, Cardiff and Millwall claim some 14 'firms' between them and had been thrown together via some trick of the Football League's fixtures computer on the first day of the season. When the Wales against England element was also added to the equation, it was hardly surprising that the day did not pass without *something* happening. Yet, in the midst of the fracas, an anonymous caller to BBC Wales said that Millwall fans had pre-arranged fights with Cardiff fans over the telephone and that the Internet had been used to help organise the violence (BBC, 1999b).

The particular website in question was that of Paul Dodd, co-author of *England's Number One: Great Adventures of a Serial Soccer Yob* (1998), whose publisher describes him as 'Britain's most notorious football thug'. On this site, Dodd, a Carlisle United supporter, talked of 'the "buzz" – the feeling of getting the fist, boot or pint glass into the anonymous face of a rival yob' and boasted of having being jailed over 17 times (http://www.pauldodd.com). In the week before the match, a number of postings referred to the violence which actually transpired:

> 11 o'clock Cardiff Central – where we go from there, its up to u

> Get ready Taffies, we're coming to wreck your country. We're flying the flag of St George.

> let's get this straight. Cardiff are as hard as nails, but your missing the point . . . Millwall are coming to town, boys!

On the day of the violence, the bulletin board on Dodd's site contained a topic entitled 'Cardiff Millwall Live Commentary' with an exchange of postings from the afternoon of the game:

> YEAH IT'S BEEN KICKING OFF RIGHT NOW AS I SPEAK HAS BEEN ALL MORNING, TIME NOW 1:45PM LOADZA OB AROUND

> BACK SOON FOR AN UPDATE. DON'T MISS THE TEAR UP OF THE YEAR :)

> nothing happen, too many old bill, millwall well up for it

> YEAH YOUR RIGHT, TOO MANY OLD BILL. BUT IT'S GOING OFF IN PLACES. JUST WAIT NOW FOR AFTER THE GAME. MY MATE ON THE MOBEY RECKONS IT'S GETTING PRETTY HOT IN THE GROUND TOO.

This seems to suggest, then, a well-drilled army of cyberthugs using every form of technology available to them to arrange meeting points, coordinate activities and avoid the attentions of the police. It certainly captured the attention of the media. However, police opinion was divided between those in the front line and the 'official' NCIS view. Chief Inspector Mick Long, who was in charge of policing at the match, said that the police had been aware of what might happen and had increased their presence in an attempt to minimise violent incident. It is certainly arguable that the police would have known of the potential for hooliganism irrespective of the presence of the Internet bulletin board messages, just from the popular reputation of the sides involved, although Long did make some reference to the bulletin board messages stating that:

> There were several messages . . . we looked at that information, were able to make an assessment and were able to apply the necessary resources to keep the disturbances to a minimum and deal with them effectively, which I'm quite happy we did. (BBC, 1999b)

However, he went on to comment:

> The concept of a running commentary being done over the Internet is, to me, totally ludicrous. I can hardly see a six-foot-four hooligan skinhead with a brick in one hand and a laptop computer in the other, it's just a completely ludicrous image. I do think it's a case of media sensationalism. (BBC, 1999b)

The views of the NCIS were quite different to those of Chief Inspector Long. The NCIS expressed serious concern about the problem, with its spokesperson Gail Kent reporting that law enforcement was engaged in a 'technology race' with the troublemakers:

> I think [that hooligans are] just happy to use whatever they can get their hands on which makes organisation easier and obviously the Internet and mobile phones mean that they can have instantaneous contact with each other . . . As these fans become more organised and they're using these tools, so the police become more advanced in what they're able to do. (BBC, 1999b)

The media storm that resulted in the aftermath of Cardiff took an interesting turn the following week. Seemingly encouraged by the *Daily Star*, Paul Dodd's website was taken down by 'white hat hackers' (Richardson, 1999), their front page headline reading 'WE GAG WEB HATE SOCCER THUGS'. One of the hackers was quoted, saying:

> Once we had infiltrated the Web site we scrambled it. There is no way anyone can post a message calling fans to do battle any more. It is a dead site.

Moreover, the *Star* reported that, secretly, the police had 'endorsed' the illegal actions of the hackers, despite their seeming contravention of section 3 of the Computer Misuse Act 1990 which criminalises unauthorised modification of computer material and section 1 of the same Act criminalising unauthorised access to computer systems. This demonstrates a tacit acceptance of the cybervandal being a socially acceptable counter to the cyberthug. It is socially abhorrent even to imagine the Internet being used to instigate and organise football violence, but quite acceptable to turn a blind eye to a breach of the criminal law associated with, if not directly sanctioned by, a national newspaper in order to rid cyberspace of the one particular bulletin board behind one particular episode of violence. In any case, Paul Dodd's website was back in operation within two days of the hack.

Libertarian groups were also swift to dismiss the cyber hooligan panic. *Libero!* is a (now defunct) libertarian football supporters' association linked with the free-speech group Internet Freedom and the LM (Living

Marxism) group. It was formed in 1996 as a response to two events which the founder, Carlton Brick, considered to be the final supplanting of the irreverent atmosphere of football by 'a Sunday School mentality'. The first of these was the censure of Aston Villa goalkeeper Mark Bosnich who gave a Nazi salute to a section of the Tottenham crowd (a club traditionally followed by the large Jewish population living around White Hart Lane) that had been haranguing him throughout a match. The second? The less widely reported ban on sticks of celery at Gillingham FC. Gillingham fans had begun to offer celery (with an accompanying vulgar song) to their goalkeeper 'Big Fat' Jim Stannard in seemingly innocent banter regarding his size. Their club, however, decided that celery could be used as an offensive weapon, and that discarded celery could result in health and safety issues inside the ground. As a result, fans were subjected to celery searches with the ultimate sanction for possession being a life ban.

Duleep Allirajah of *Libero!* (1999) claimed that:

Football hooligans are high on Britain's 'most hated' list, along with neo-nazis and paedophiles. As the Internet has already been blamed for allowing paedophiles and Nazis to organise, it was only a matter of time before it was implicated in football violence . . . The hooligan panics are quite simply modern fairy tales.

This view was echoed by Chris Ellison (a pen-name of Dr Chris Evans), founder of *Internet Freedom* who wrote:

It seems the Internet has become the focus of people's fears, leaving journalists to spin nothing but modern fairy tales about cyber hooligans and the Big Bad Web. (1999)

The 'modern fairy tales' continued as, three months later, England and Scotland prepared to meet in the qualifiers for the Euro 2000 championships.

England v Scotland – Euro 2000 qualifiers (1999)

In October 1999, the Scottish *Daily Record* reported under the headline 'Thugs make plans to riot' that football 'casuals from across Britain' had been leaving messages on Paul Dodd's message board in advance of the two Euro 2000 qualifiers between Scotland and England the following month:

You wait and see the squad that's waiting for this battle. Years we've waited for revenge and we're going to get it . . . the happy kilt-wearing turf-ripping days are over.

Let's do the Jocks.

The England/Scotland divide was exploited by the NCIS which classified Scotland as a foreign country for the purposes of section 15 of the Football Supporters Act 1989 (as substituted by section 1 of the Football (Offences and Disorder) Act 1999, in force from 27 September 1999) . This enabled international football banning orders to be imposed on 111 known hooligans: in the words of an NCIS spokesperson:

> It means they will have to attend at a police station in England with their passports at a set time, decided by the Home Office; probably kick-off. (Milne, 1999)

The police presence at both games was considerable. Around 250 British Transport Police from England travelling with supporters were sworn in under Scots law to extend their jurisdiction across the border. Strict segregation was also in operation along with CCTV surveillance and undercover police officers.

Despite these measures, the first leg, which England won 2–0 at Hampden, led to 230 arrests (BBC News, 1999c). England lost the second leg, at Wembley, 1–0. There were a further 39 arrests and 56 injuries (BBC News, 1999d). Whether the scale of the arrests was related to the Internet baiting is debatable. As with the game between Cardiff and Millwall, the England versus Scotland games had a high volatility quotient largely based on international rivalry; indeed the propensity for violence breaking out when England played Scotland was one of the contributory factors that led to the demise of the Home International Championship in 1984, a time at which the Internet was in its pre-infancy. Moreover, the extent of the arrests could be the result of a harder line in policing: a line taken since there was so much media and public attention devoted to the prospect of violence that the police had to be seen to be in control.

Media fascination with football violence continued. In November 1999 the BBC broadcasted a documentary, *MacIntyre Undercover* about the notorious Chelsea Headhunters football hooligans and the Reading Youth Firm. It showed secretly filmed football violence and the organising of fights (although this organisation was done via mobile phone rather than the Internet). In the same month, after a Manchester United fan was badly beaten by a gang of Arsenal hooligans, a British Transport Police spokesman said:

> The organisers of the violence are not usually the ones caught up in it. The ones on the mobile phones provide the information to others and then step back while the minnows get involved. (Ultra News, 1999)

Where, then, was the Internet?

Euro 2000

The English Football Association welcomed the 'success' of the policing for the home match with Scotland. In the light of its (ultimately unsuccessful) bid to host the 2006 World Cup, a campaign entitled 'Football Yes, Violence No' was run prior to Euro 2000. This was a jointly coordinated campaign with the old England Members Club (now englandfans) which aimed to promote the positive side of English football and its supporters both at home and abroad. Positive messaging was also backed up with the threat of international banning orders reinforced under the Football (Offences and Disorder) Act 1999.

However, the spectre of the Internet was raised yet again in an April 2000 investigative report by Jason Burke and Denis Campbell of the *Observer*. This report claimed that:

> Dutch police are so concerned by the ease with which thugs can swap information on the Internet that they have set up a special unit to monitor its increasing use by hooligans. 'If everything we read [on the Internet] is true, then for football it will be the end of the world', said Henk van Groenenveld, head of the Dutch national bureau for hooligan intelligence. (Burke and Campbell, 2000)

Citing the England match against Germany in Charleroi as the 'most likely flashpoint for violence this summer', the report then discussed more postings on the grandfather of all hooligan websites, that of Paul Dodd. However, no evidence of anything other than racist taunting appeared to be evident:

> Don't fuck with England or you will get hurt. We will do you like we did in the war. My grandad probably killed your grandad. (Yeti)

> We all know you are tossers who wont show against England's finest. (Three Lions)

Rioting before and after England's 1–0 victory led to 965 English arrests and 464 expulsions. It is perhaps interesting to note that 36 international banning orders under the Football (Offences and Disorder) Act 1999 were issued prior to the tournament by magistrates; by contrast the German authorities issued banning orders on around 3,000 known hooligans to prevent them from travelling: although a number of German fans were arrested in Charleroi, the vast majority of those arrested were English fans.

The Football (Disorder) Act 2000

Despite the seeming under-employment of international banning orders in the run up to Euro 2000, the government considered that the violence displayed by England fans throughout the tournament necessitated further, and swift, remedial legislative action, which came in the form of the Football (Disorder) Act 2000. England were eliminated from Euro 2000 on 20 June, three days after the Charleroi riots against Germany, following a controversial 3–2 defeat to a late penalty against Romania. This game saw around 3,000 police officers on duty to manage the crowd of 30,000 supporters. The match passed without any notable violent incident.

Two weeks later, on 4 July, the Home Secretary, Jack Straw, announced plans to legislate further while acknowledging that 'legislation is only part of the answer to the wider problem'. The Bill was introduced into the House of Commons on 12 July, receiving Royal Assent 16 days later and coming into force on 28 August. It is perhaps no coincidence that it came into force just five days before a high-risk match between France and England in Paris on 2 September 2000.

The new Act amended the Football Spectators Act 1989 to make provision for banning orders, replacing and merging international football banning orders and domestic football banning orders. At the time 105 international banning orders and 455 domestic banning orders were in force. The removal of the distinction prohibited banned individuals from entering any premises for the purpose of attending regulated football matches in England and Wales *and* required them to report to a police station as directed during the period in which international bans were in force. Moreover, the Act also had the effect of requiring virtually all people subject to such banning orders to surrender their passports to prevent them attending proscribed overseas matches. The requirement for the order's recipient to surrender their passport was previously at the court's discretion. However, the new Act rendered this requirement mandatory unless the court believed that there were exceptional circumstances.

Two further powers were introduced on a temporary basis. The first of these extended the magistrates' power to impose a football banning order such that a ban could not only be imposed as a result of a football-related criminal conviction, but also in response to a complaint by the police in accordance with a civil procedure. The police were permitted to introduce a wide range of evidence, including CCTV, video and other evidence gathered overseas, in order to satisfy the court on two counts: firstly that the individual had 'at any time caused or contributed to any violence or disorder in the United Kingdom or elsewhere' and, secondly, that 'there are reasonable grounds to believe that making a banning order would help to prevent violence or disorder at or in connection with any regulated football matches'. It is perhaps worth noting that 'violence' and 'disorder' are defined as not being 'limited to violence or disorder in connection with football'. In other words, an individual who had contributed to disorder in an entirely non-footballing context could still find themselves having to surrender their passport if the police were able to satisfy magistrates that they might be linked with forthcoming disorder at a football match. The legislative definition of 'disorder' includes 'displaying any writing or other thing which is threatening, abusive or insulting'. This could, of course, potentially encompass threatening, abusive or insulting postings on the Internet although there are no reported cases of Internet postings being used as evidence to support a football banning order.

The second temporary power allowed the police to detain without arrest individuals who have previously caused or contributed to *any* violence or disorder in the United Kingdom or elsewhere if they reasonably believe the individual may participate in football violence or disorder. Under these circumstances, the police may issue a notice both preventing the individual from travelling and also requiring them to attend a banning order hearing at a magistrates' court within 24 hours.

The vast and sudden extension in police powers was checked, albeit very slightly, by the statutory time-limitation which restricted the temporary powers to a twelve-month period unless extended by the Secretary of State by order. This duly happened: first, for a further 12 months via the Football (Disorder) (Duration of Powers) Order 2001 (2001 No. 2646) and second, for a further five years (to 21 August 2007) by the Football (Disorder) (Amendment) Act 2002. The Violent Crime Reduction Bill, introduced in June 2005, proposed the removal of the time restrictions entirely.

The effect of the legislation

Despite the introduction of the new legislation, the media rumble continued, although with increasingly less evidence of the cyberhooligan. NCIS figures, released in August 2001, a year after the Football (Disorder) Act 2000 came into force, showed an 8.1 per cent increase in arrests for 'football-related offences' in England and Wales, rising from 3,138 in 1999–2000 to 3,391 in 2000–01. This increase was swiftly seized upon by the *Guardian*, in an article entitled 'Hooligan disease that clings to football' within which the Internet was briefly mentioned:

> The nature of the football hooligan and the trouble they cause has also changed. With closed-circuit television cameras and police in most grounds, more organisation now goes into arranging confrontations between rival gangs – over the Internet or by mobile phone – and they usually meet well away from stadiums. Almost 85 per cent of all football-related violence took place away from grounds last season. (Chaudhary, 2001)

Duleep Allirajah was equally swift to respond. In *Spiked*, the next day, he commented that:

> The effect of recent football legislation has been to redefine hooliganism much more broadly. For example, an offence only used to be classed as 'football related' if it occurred immediately before or after a game – but the Football (Offences and Disorder) Act 1999 extended this period to 24 hours either side of a match, or even longer for overseas games. (Allirajah, 2001)

Moreover, the definition of 'football-related disorder' had been extended by the Football (Disorder) Act 2000 to encompass offences such as mere public drunkenness, a lesser offence than public drunken disorderly conduct, or ticket touting. Therefore, not only were new offences brought under the football umbrella, but the NCIS itself admitted that more violence was taking place away from stadia. It was questionable at this stage whether the link between 'football' and 'football violence' was beginning to weaken.

The government view

An insight into the government's perspective of the situation was given in response to a written question in the House of Commons (Hansard col. 917W, 25 February 2002). Here Gillian Merron asked a three-fold question: first, what action the Secretary of State for the Home Department had taken to investigate whether special websites are used by hooligans to orchestrate football violence; second, what discussions he had had with police and ISPs to ensure that football hooligan websites could not be set up; and third, what investigations had been made into the number of football websites with links to paramilitary groups.

The response, from John Denham, stated quite categorically that the NCIS had been monitoring websites associated with football hooliganism and sharing information with local police forces. They had found 'no evidence that the sites [were] used to orchestrate football disorder, or that individuals who set up or visit the sites [were] directly involved in the phenomenon'. Moreover there were 'no plans to discuss hooligan websites with Internet service providers' since the material posted appeared 'to reproduce information and opinions which, however unpalatable, [were] already published legally in the United Kingdom' (Hansard col. 917W, 25 February 2002). Similar materials hosted abroad fell outside national jurisdiction, although arrangements of 'mutual assistance' were being developed as a requirement of the G8 action plan on high-tech crime.

The marked contrast between the NCIS view of 1999 that 'they use technology – including the Internet – both in Britain and internationally to contact each other' and of 2002 that 'there is no evidence that [Internet sites were] used to orchestrate football disorder' was clear. Is the cyberhooligan merely a contemporary manifestation of the 1970s folk devil transformed by technology?

Keyboard warriors or cyber-orchestrators?

Stuart Hall (1978) identified an 'amplification spiral' (Wilkins, 1964) in relation to football hooliganism. In brief, this occurs when exaggerated media coverage of a problem results in it worsening, a phenomenon that has been apparent since the mid-1960s and the postwar resurgence of football-related violence. Supporting this viewpoint, Murphy et al. (1988) argue that media constructions of matchdays and football grounds as potential flashpoints for violence has stimulated and shaped the development of football hooliganism. Poulton (2001), in relation to England fans, talks of the popular image of supporters as being shaped by media representation which

> continually perpetuates the convenient, but simplistic, stereotype that it itself helped to construct. Hysterical headlines, emotive language, evocative imagery and graphic photographs all help to frame the football fan-cum-hooligan as a member of a homogeneous group of 'drunken, tattooed, crop-headed oafs'. (*Sunday Mirror*, 18 June 2000) (Poulton, 2001: 122)

The contribution of the broadsheets should not be overlooked either. In response to the Euro 2000 incidents, a *Guardian* editorial considered that it was 'a shame the Belgian riot police were not equipped with real bullets ... can nothing be done to stop these people reproducing, should their appearance not be a sufficiently effective contraceptive' (22 June 2000).

There is strong support for the viewpoint that the football hooligan problem is both constructed and perpetuated by its media representation. As Poulton concludes 'the continuing media construction and representation of "football hooliganism" is self-sustaining' (2005: 43). The involvement of the Internet as a facet of this problem appears to have been a media flashpoint, initially sparked by the reporting of the 1999 match between Cardiff City and Millwall and supported, at the time, by the NCIS and subsequent reports involving a very small number of Internet sites. By 2002, the NCIS considered that there was no evidence of Internet orchestration of football-related disorder. However, the Internet remains a conduit for communication between football supporters, as indeed it does for a multitude of other groups. There are many so-called 'hooligan' websites in existence. Giulianotti (2001) considers that these exist as much to establish a history and identity for firms and provide a social setting in which 'lads' can interact, a 'subcultural public sphere' which is simultaneously exclusive and global. The proliferation of the Internet has provided a means of contacting like-minded people and official club websites coexist along with unofficial sites and hooligan sites.

All these sites are free of spatial or temporal constraints. Lads can meet online, in 'a permanently accessible hooligan context, whereas in earlier times, due to other domestic and social commitments (notably work and family) physically meeting with other lads would not be viable' (Giulianotti, 2001: 152). Moreover, although contributors to such sites are wary of infiltration by the police or journalists, they offer the individual an opportunity, over time, to build the trust of a group of people who they have never met. Remotely negotiating acceptance within the group – or 'getting in the know' in this way can circumvent many of the issues of building trust in the physical world by exploiting the sense of false intimacy created in the online environment. The use of a screen name, or user ID, also provides a means of refuge. If one line of discussion proves unfruitful, or trust is broken, or an individual is discredited, then it is straightforward to re-establish a new online identity and try again. 'Trying on' identities in the world of the virtual hooligan offers ample scope for eventual acceptance within the online community (see Finch, this volume).

An online group of like-minded individuals is one thing: football violence is another. Many of the forums consist of taunting individuals or the teams they follow. This exemplifies both the regulatory displacement and technological transformation of behaviour. Swearing at grounds could fall within the bounds of the Football (Offences) Act 1991. However, fans are inventive. For instance, following police remonstrations regarding the chant 'He's here, he's there, he's every-fucking-where! Martin Hicks! Martin Hicks!' in honour of a hard-working central defender was simply changed by Reading fans to 'He's here, he's there, we're not allowed to swear! Martin Hicks! Martin Hicks!' The logical extension of this is that the increasing regulation of swearing and taunting within stadia has led to an easier outlet online with its shield of anonymity and the potential for a plethora of consecutive or concurrent identities. Similarly, the increased regulation of behaviour within stadia via legal and technological means such as CCTV, combined with the ability to locate rival groups of fans elsewhere via mobile phones or pre-arranged contact through the Internet, has displaced football-related violence, not deterred or eliminated it. This regulation has also given rise to a greater need for those involved in the violence to organise their activities than had previously been the case.

It could be considered that the antagonism between cyber groups might ultimately displace physical hooliganism. However, the proliferation of keyboard warriors might simply encourage violence, as ultimately the verbal virtual violence becomes unfulfilling. An analogy could be drawn with cybersex. Just as Internet taunting will usually fall outside the law, Internet infidelity is not a ground for divorce; however, when cybersex becomes real (in the sense of it being a financial transaction) it attracts the attention of the law, in the same way as physical violence is criminalised. Internet antagonism is a virtual substitute for real life emotional activity.

The media construction of the cyberhooligan has depicted the Internet as a source of social evil. Interestingly, however, the media have been quick to employ the same technology for equally condemnable activity. During Euro 2004, the Swiss referee, Urs Meier, disallowed a last-minute goal that would have sent England through to the semi-finals of the tournament. The *Sun* printed his website and email addresses and Meier received more than 16,000 emails, some of which contained death threats. He was subsequently placed under police protection. It was not just the media that exploited the technology. The airline Fly.be sent an email that was criticised by the Advertising Standards Authority as 'irresponsible and offensive':

> WE WAS ROBBED!! But you won't be with fly.be's post EURO blues sale! As a mark of respect to our lads, and some of the worst refereeing in years, we have suspended services to Switzerland, his home country ... In fact, if you visit flybe.com now, you can link through to Mr Meier's own personal website and leave your feedback on his performance.

The link between the Internet and public disorder extends beyond football. The riots on the streets of Paris in 2005 were incited, debated and tracked via the Internet. Blogs contained messages which both prompted further violence and vehemently denounced it:

> The hate will turn around. I am sick of these bearded fascists. (Raslebo)

> Be calm, if not all of this will come to nothing. (Anon.)

In an interesting final twist, Staffordshire police published 17 photographs of people they wanted to identify after violence at a game between Stoke City and Birmingham City in February 2006 on the 'Crimestoppers Most Wanted' website.

Conclusion

The role of the Internet in relation to football hooliganism is multi-faceted. While it does not seem that it is used – and despite media reporting to the contrary has *ever* been used – as the primary means of orchestrating football hooliganism, it unquestionably provides a community for those involved with disorder and those who wish to be associated with it. If any violence does occur as a result of Internet activity, it is most certainly not often, almost certainly not provable and will be at the hands of some very dedicated individuals. Technological advances have been used to transform enforcement and security and at the same time have been used to circumvent these new means of enforcement, leading to the displacement of football violence away from stadia and into the virtual realm.

References

Allirajah, D. (1999) 'The myth of the cyber hooligan' (online at: http://www.netfreedom.org/news.asp?item=81).

Allirajah, D. (2001) 'The hooliganism hype' (online at: http://www.spiked-online.com/Articles/00000002D08.htm).

BBC News (1999a) Special Report: Rival football fans in 'pre-arranged' fight (online at: http://www.news.bbc.co.uk/1/hi/uk/414368.stm).

BBC News (1999b) Soccer hooligans organise on the Net (online at: http://www.news.bbc.co.uk/1/hi/sci/tech/414948.stm).

BBC News (1999c) Court date for arrested fans (online at: http://www.news.bbc.co.uk/1/hi/Scotland/520745.stm).

BBC News (1999d) Police claim play-off success (online at: http://www.news.bbc.co.uk/1/hi/special_report/1999/11/99/battle_of_britain/526141.stm).

Brimson, D. (2000) Barmy Army: The Changing Face of Football Violence. London: Headline.

Burke, J. and Campbell, D. (2000) 'Hooligans link up on the Net to plot mayhem at Euro 2000', Observer, 2 April.

Carnibella, G., Fox, A., Fox, K., McCann, J., Marsh, J. and Marsh, P. (1996) 'Football Violence in Europe: A report to the Amsterdam Group' (online at: http://www.www.sirc.org/publik/football_violence.pdf).

Chaudhary, V. (2001) 'Hooligan disease that clings to football', Guardian, 16 August.

Department of the Environment (1984) Report of an Official Working Group on Football Spectator Violence. London: HMSO.

Dodd, P. and McNee, I. (1998) England's Number One: Great Adventures of a Serial Soccer Yob. London: PIG.

Elliott, D., Frosdick, S. and Smith, D. (1999) 'The failure of legislation by crisis', in S. Frosdick and L. Walley (eds), Sport and Safety Management. Oxford: Butterworth-Heinemann.

Ellison, C. (1999) 'How the Net became a football hooligan' (online at: http://www.netfreedom.org/news.asp?item=88).

Frosdick, S. and Marsh, P. (2005) Football Hooliganism. Cullompton: Willan Publishing.

Giulianotti, R. (2001) 'A different kind of carnival', in M. Perryman (ed.), Hooligan Wars: Causes and Effects of Football Violence. Edinburgh: Mainstream.

Hall, S. (1978) 'The treatment of "football hooligans" in the press', in R. Ingham et al., *Football Hooliganism: The Wider Context*. London: Inter-Action Inprint.

Home Office (1985) *Committee of Inquiry into Crowd Safety and Control at Sports Grounds – Chairman Mr Justice Popplewell – Interim Report*. London: HMSO.

Home Office (1986) *Committee of Inquiry into Crowd Safety and Control at Sports Grounds – Chairman Mr Justice Popplewell – Final Report*. London: HMSO.

Home Office (1989) *The Hillsborough Stadium Disaster 15 April 1989 – Inquiry by the Rt Hon Lord Justice Taylor – Interim Report*. London: HMSO.

Home Office (1990) *The Hillsborough Stadium Disaster 15 April 1989 – Inquiry by the Rt Hon Lord Justice Taylor – Final Report*. London: HMSO.

Home Office (2005) *Football (Disorder) Act 2000 – Report to Parliament*. London: TSO.

House of Commons Library Research Paper (2000) 00/70 *The draft Football (Disorder) Bill* (13 July).

House of Commons Library Research Paper (2001) 01/73 *The Football (Disorder) (Amendment) Bill* (11 October).

Melnick, M. (1986) 'The mythology of football hooliganism: a closer look at the British experience', *International Review for the Sociology of Sport*, 21: 1.

Milne, S. (1999) 'Thugs make plans to riot', *Scottish Daily Record*, 16 October.

Murphy, P., Dunning, E. and Williams, J. (1988) 'Soccer crowd disorder and the press: processes of amplification and de-amplification in historical perspective', *Theory, Culture and Society* 5: 645.

Poulton, E. (2001) 'Tears, tantrums and tattoos: framing the hooligan', in M. Perryman (ed.), *Hooligan Wars: Causes and Effects of Football Violence*. Edinburgh: Mainstream.

Poulton, E. (2005) 'English media representation of football-related disorder: "brutal, short-hand and simplifying"?' *Sport in Society* 8 (1): 27.

Richardson, T. (1999) 'Footy fight site hit by white hat hackers', *The Register*, 16 August.)

Ultra News (1999) 'View from the terrace' (online at: http://website.lineone.net/~view_from_the_terrace/latnew2.html.

Whannel, G. (1979) 'Football crowd behaviour and the press', *Media, Culture and Society*, 1 (2): 327.

Wilkins, L. (1964) *Social Deviance: Social Policy, Action and Research*. London: Tavistock.

Chapter 9

Constructing crime: stalking, celebrity, 'cyber' and media

Maggie Wykes

Introduction

New media have always attracted popular, policy and journalistic attention, usually linked to attributing the new form with a threatening potential, either in relation to morality or law and order. Film, television, video and computer games were each subject to similar anxiety when introduced, mostly related to a perceived increased potential to repro-duce, distribute and access so-called harmful material (Barker and Petley, 1997). Since the mid-1990s the Internet has increased every aspect of that potential infinitely and is unsurprisingly subject to similar panicky debates around effect, damage and control. Like other media, the Internet has not only been accused of reproducing 'undesirable' material possibly causal of crime but also of generating new forms of crime. 'Cyberstalking' is one example, while the terrestrial equivalent 'stalking' has also arguably been metamorphed from 'deviance' to 'crime' at least partly as a result of the traditional news media. This chapter focuses on the way in which the media are consistently attributed a causal role in the construction of crime. Stalking, and its netspace equivalent cyberstalking, are both activities on the edge of 'criminal', and in some jurisdictions are not criminalised at all. They are thus activities that are ripe for exploring how and why certain behaviours become criminalised.

Activities on the edge: harassment, celebrity and crime

Stalking is a real activity that hovers on the borders of deviance and criminality depending on the jurisdiction, culture and even the prevailing morality within which it occurs. Although the categorisation of stalking as a crime of harassment is relatively recent in the UK (1997) there is a significant history of occurrences recorded in other discourses, particularly psychology and feminism.

Within psychiatry stalking has a range of definitions. *Obsessional* stalking usually occurs when one party seeks retribution against another for a perceived wrong. *Erotomanic attention* is when the stalker is deluded that there is a romantic bond between themselves and the victim. *Love obsession* is often targeted at a celebrity or otherwise famous person (Zona et al., 1993). Other stalker profiles include the *incompetent* who may lack ability to form normal relationships and the *predator* who seeks to control their victims, and who may plan, or even execute, assaults (Mullen et al., 1999). Despite the often extreme nature of these behaviours the stalking phenomenon remained within the confines of mental health discourses prior to the 1990s.

Feminist intervention was largely due to the perception that stalking behaviour is deeply gendered, sexualised and oppressive, and therefore relevant to any critique of patriarchy. Sexual harassment 'locates woman in her body ... makes her simply body' (Smart, 1995: 223) just as rape does. So, harassment is seen within feminism as part of a systematic sexualised oppression of women. Kelly and Humphries (2000) place harassment firmly in the realm of actual harm by tracing the origins of much intimate violence against women to either beginning or ending in harassment, frequently from ex-partners (pp. 10–13). They also acknowledge that despite the 'ordinariness' of much stalking, the introduction in Britain of the 1997 Protection from Harassment Act (PFHA) was probably impelled by high-profile celebrity cases that drew heavy media coverage. It was that coverage which also saw the imported US term 'stalking' overtake 'harassment' in the UK news. American celebrity Madonna's victimisation both pre- and post-dates the UK legislation:

> An obsessed fan has been stalking Madonna prompting the star to beef up her security ... It is not the first time Madonna has been plagued by a stalker – in 1996 Robert Hoskins was jailed for 10 years after threatening the 45-year-old singer with violence. (http://uk. news.yahoo.com/040625/140/ewo5o.html13/04/2005)

In the UK, the pop band the Spice Girls and Princess Diana are among those who once suffered from the attention of obsessive fans. In Diana's case, obsessive paparazzi arguably became 'stalkers', as pointed out by her brother Earl Spencer[1] at her funeral. They even possibly contributed to the accident in which she died as they pursued her Mercedes through Paris in a frenzied search for illicit photographs of her to sell to a media hungry for celebrity images. After her death, film star Sylvester Stallone commented: 'The press, by and large, are fantastic. We're talking about a small renegade group. They're stalkers, legalized stalkers' (http://www.cnn.com/WORLD/9709/01/diana.paparazzi/index.html, 07/07/2006).

Although harassment from an intimidating friend or ex-partner is the most common typology for the offence it is these high-profile newsworthy celebrity 'stalks' by 'someone unknown to them' which are the focus of the news because celebrity itself is newsworthy and so, of course, is crime, particularly if it is potentially sexual and/or violent and perpetrated by a stranger (Wykes, 2001; Carter, 1998). Despite its prevalence in intimate relationships, the *Guardian* even went as far as to suggest the offence is more terrible in the case of the small minority of stalking attacks committed by a stranger. It claimed : 'Those who are in the public eye face perhaps the most extreme form of attack because they are usually among the 5 per cent of victims whose stalkers are strangers to them' (27 April 1999). In addition, according to Kelly and Humphries (2000), the gendered aspect of stalking is underplayed in media accounts, in that the media label stalkers 'dangerous strangers obsessed with celebrity'. This doubly distances the act from real gendered relations and offending by ex-boyfriends or husbands not strangers against ordinary women not stars.

Stalking, crime and cultures

Yet perhaps because of the attention to celebrity, in the UK 'real' stalking was effectively criminalised under the Prevention of Harassment Act 1997 which can be summarised as follows:

> A person must not pursue a course of conduct which he knows or ought to know amounts to harassment of the other or occurs in circumstances where it would appear to a reasonable person that it would amount to harassment of that person ... For the purposes of this section – 'conduct' includes speech; 'harassment' of a person includes causing the person alarm or distress; and a course of conduct must involve conduct on at least two occasions. (http://www.hmso.gov.uk/acts/acts1997/1997040.htm)

Key is the fact that the subject of the stalk must feel intimidated or distressed by the attention. The maximum sentence is six months in prison, unless the victim is put in fear of violence on at least two occasions in which case it can be five years. The British Home Office acknowledged the crime in the 1998 British Crime Survey and found that 'overall, 11.8 per cent of adults aged 16–59 could recall being subject to persistent and unwanted attention at some time in their lives ... (0.61 million women and 0.27 million men)' (Budd and Mattinson, 2000). Only 'one-third of victims (33 per cent) considered what had happened to be a crime' and a further 37 per cent considered it to be 'wrong but not a crime'. Despite the discontinuities in interpretation, publicity about celebrity victims together with feminist concerns about the lack of attention to women's place in crime (Brownmiller, 1975; Smart, 1976, 1989; Edwards, 1987; Gelsthorpe, 1988; Hanmer et al., 1989) propelled stalking from being seen as a sexist nuisance or nastiness into a serious crime affecting mainly women.

Arguably, harassment has thus become a crime in the UK largely driven by resort to law by celebrity victims and the newsworthiness of their 'stalk' experience. In turn, that publicity has highlighted and legitimated serious feminist work, eventually placing more everyday, victimising harassment on the criminal agenda in many western cultures. For example, in the US and Canada concerns began in the early 1990s, with research during the first half of the decade showing that '8.1 percent of surveyed women and 2.2 percent of surveyed men reported being stalked at some time in their life ... A woman is three times more likely to be stalked than raped' (Tjaden and Thoennes, 1998). Such studies led to a rapid criminalisation process; as of November 1999, all 50 US states' legislatures, the District of Columbia, and the federal government had enacted laws making stalking a crime (Miller and Nugent, 2002). Malsch (2000) identifies differing responses in Europe, including Norway's definition that 'conduct violating another person's right to be left in peace' should be punishable by law. In Australia, legislation was adapted or introduced across the territories during the mid-1990s; for example, the Northern Territory, Criminal Code Act 1997, section 189, defines stalking as a criminal offence. In other parts of the world there is sometimes a strong western influence, particularly in previous colonies. In Hong Kong, the Law Reform Commission released the Stalking Report on 30 October 2000 recommending: 'A person who pursues a course of conduct which amounts to harassment of another, and which he knows or ought to know amounts to harassment of the other, should be guilty of a criminal offence' (http://www.hkreform.gov.hk/reports/stalk-e.htm, 14/04/2005). So, in many western countries a 'crime' has been constructed from what had previously been a 'deviant' behaviour and the same crime is variously defined in different legislatures which bring differing punishments to bear.

Yet stalking in other countries is not only *not* a 'crime' but sometimes seems not to be recognised as a problem at all. A web search for 'stalking in China' produced twenty sites mainly relating to hunting animals or 'stalking' the cause of the Sars virus. Link 'stalking' to Saudi Arabia and you get al-Queda: 'What al-Queda want is to see the international community fight amongst themselves, as they move through the shadows *stalking* their next victims' (http://www.saudi-american-forum.org/ Newsletters/SAF_Item_Of_Interest_2003_07_15.pdf). Stalking has different connotations in a news article in the *Asia Times* online: 'The "vice" police are notorious for stalking the streets searching for any form of "un-Islamic" activity. Inappropriate chit-chat on cell phone text-messaging, women with any exposed skin, men not at work – all of these could invite the wrath of these stick-wielding officers' (http://www.atimes. com/atimes/Middle_East/EF03Ak03.html). This is a curiously culturally specific example of when a crime isn't a crime but actually a legitimate tool of enforcement, and it corresponds alarmingly to all the exclusion clauses in the UK 'Protection From Harassment Act 1997 whereby under section 1 (3): 'Subsection (1) does not apply to a course of conduct if the person who pursued it shows (a) that it was pursued for the purpose of preventing or detecting crime, (b) that it was pursued under any enactment or rule of law' (http://194.128.65.3/acts/acts1997/2).

Despite these global anomalies, in the UK, the new crime is now taken so seriously that the Metropolitan Police have issued a guide book for investigating officers (http://www.met.police.uk/stalking/stalking.pdf). In its 'advice section' the guide begins by referring to the stalking of celebrities and ends with warnings of the Internet. Yet in many other countries the same behaviour and experience that makes such concern necessary in the UK seems not to exist. Clearly something has shifted stalking, semantically, into the 'sex and violence' discourses favoured by the news, then reconstructed it as crime and therefore subject to the legislative agenda of western cultures.

Constructing crime: news value and 'new' stories

Critically considering the way in which stalking has become criminalised is in no way to diminish the real harm that occasions when stalking becomes 'physical' – in which case, of course, such acts are subject to prosecutions under other sections of the criminal law. Nor is to deny that real distress and inhibition may seriously impact on victims' lives. Rather, it is simply to show that crimes are discursively constructed specific to cultures and historical contexts. That construction is often preceded by news accounts that assign new terms to existing behaviours that imply both newness and negativity. Mugging, for example, was a term imported from the US to the UK in the 1970s to explain street theft from a person. During this period racial tensions in British inner cities were frequently and inappropriately compared by journalists to US conflicts over Civil

Rights (Hartman and Husband, 1971). These accounts resorted to racist stereotypes from the time of slavery and empire and added a new one that linked black identity to crime perhaps for the first time (Hall et al., 1978):

> Mugging marked the introduction of a new racial stereotype, which added the potential of the exercise of containment of black people by law, to the freelance racism of the workplace, social community and housing market. (Wykes, 2001: 34)

In law there is not, nor has there ever been, a crime of mugging in the UK. In fact the term was unknown in Britain and the crime it describes is 'street robbery'. Its connotations with violence linked it to news values, making a previously not very reportable petty crime one laden with newsworthiness. Decades later, stalking with its connotations of stealth, violence, sex and celebrity turned the everyday nuisance of harassment into a potential front-page headline. Both terms are US imports via the mass media and say more about the media's values and representations than about real events. Both mugging and stalking are American embellishments of already existing British deviances. This process has been described as the export-import trade in social labels (Jenkins, 1992). Stalking is consistently used by the media, just as mugging was for street robbery, despite the existence of the perfectly comprehensible legal terms street robbery and harassment. Newsmakers of the 1970s reconstructed street robbery towards violence and race by means of mugging and now harassment is being reconstructed towards sex and violence, according to the demands of news values, into stalking and now cyberstalking.

News values have been thoroughly rehearsed, researched and written about for four decades (Galtung and Ruge, 1965; Chibnall, 1977; Fowler, 1991; Wykes, 2001; Jewkes, 2004) but remain vital to any proper investigation of the mass mediation of ideas or theorising of the role of the media. Briefly:

> The gathering of news immediately excludes all but a very few events that can be considered newsworthy. News is a selection of history made by journalists. The selection of stories is not arbitrary but highly systemised and conventionalised by conditions external to the story, as well as integral. External controls may include time, cost, access, expertise, publication space and news agenda. Potential news events have to be, practically, reportable but they also have to have particular internal features. Galtung and Ruge (1965) offered a model of news attributes and pointed out that these are mainly cultural not natural.

News attributes

frequency	(repetition/speed/quantity)
threshold	(importance/drama/level of action)
unambiguity	(simplicity/straightforwardness)
meaningfulness	(cultural fit/relevance to audience)
consonance	(expected/desired/anticipated)
unexpectedness	(rarity/suddenness)
continuity	(sustainability/durability)
composition	(fit with other news events/fit with news product)
elite nations	(superpowers/authoritative sources)
elite people	(stars/royalty/politicians)
personification	(individual causality/identification)
negativity	(damaging/deviant/sad)

(Wykes, 2001: 22–3)

These criteria clearly mark out crime, or events that can be reported as criminal, or deviant bordering criminal, as having great news value (Chibnall, 1977; Wykes, 2001). Yet, despite its constant featuring in the media, crime remains relatively rare for most people and extreme crime such as violence is extremely rare. Only 1.7 per cent of people are ever likely to be injured by violence in England and Wales (Povey et al., 2005). Nonetheless, it is violent crime, and particularly sexually violent crime, that particularly appeals to the rather prurient British public that continues to drag its Victorian morality around with it (Foucault, 1979). Sexually violent crime is not only rare (Dodd et al., 2004) but also has qualities of negativity, personifiability, cultural fit, drama and unambiguity. If it is possible to add eliteness to that mix by featuring a celebrity in the context of extreme crime, then the journalist's dream event has occurred because increasingly celebrity seems to determine the news values of real events (Wykes and Gunter, 2005). Celebrity via soap operas and news stories so often acts as a motif for what matters to us as human: 'Stars very often role-play publicly and fictionally the embodiment of extremes of human emotion, passion, privacy, pain and pleasure and they do so in intense and contracted episodes' (Wykes and Gunter, 2005: 104).

The celebrification of news certainly seems relevant to the construction of the crime of stalking. The newsworthiness of 'stalked celebrity' was particularly evident in the case of British television presenter Jill Dando. Dando was shot on her doorstep by a man described as a stalker in the news, although there was no actual reason to believe the killer had in any way followed or harassed or been obsessed by the celebrity. News about her murder, in April 1999, not only alluded to stalking but also to the possible use of the Internet to enable the offence, again with no evidence that this had happened: 'The home address of murdered BBC television presenter Jill Dando was traced by a possible stalker using the Internet, police have revealed' (http://news.bbc.co.uk/1/hi/uk/608972.stm).

In the US, celebrity also rules and the media seek out celebrity stories, especially those involving sex and violence. John Lennon of the Beatles was murdered by a stalker in New York in 1980, which is perhaps the case that instigated the reconstruction of obsessional harassment as a crime (http://news.bbc.co.uk/1/hi/entertainment/478085.stm). More common victims (at least as far as the media are concerned) are young, successful, slender, famous, blonde, white, heterosexual, celebrity women:

> Actress Nicole Kidman acknowledged a friendly 'Hello' from a fan with a smile and a 'Hello' back. What she didn't realise was this fan had already had a previous restraining order granted to his last victim, Claudia Schiffer. (http://www.diskdetectives.com/stalking. htm)
>
> Both Kidman and Schiffer have websites for fans with their life stories and schedules readily available. Moreover, increasingly both celebrity and the medium of cyberspace seem to feature in cases of stalking creating two new sets of relationships that may also be connected with each other – celebrity-and-victim and cyber-and-crime.

Victimised celebrity

In relation to these newsworthy cases that appear to have transformed stalking from nuisance or illness to crime in western criminal justice and popular imagination, the key seems to be whether or not a celebrity has interpreted overenthusiastic fan worship as threatening or damaging. This complies with UK legislation where a victim must experience 'alarm or distress' for the crime of harassment to exist. This definition has projected the role of victim to centre stage in the construction/definition of crime and hence criminal justice. Celebrity is central to this process because publicity, image and elite status make celebrities news and are valuable for both star and media, while the value of their image also makes stars take strident steps to protect 'themselves', their image and related livelihood.[2] This may mean stars suing newspapers for publishing unsolicited, unpaid for and/or unflattering images or it may mean prosecuting anyone whose 'attention' may actually or potentially harm a celebrity or their reputation or image. Celebrities also have the kind of disposable income necessary for private individuals to resort to law.

It may also be that stalking is the first new crime to be defined not only because celebrity has drawn the activity into the public sphere, but also as a result of the emergence of victimology in academic and popular discourse. Victimology is arguably attributable to feminist work on harm in the private spheres of family and sexual relations, particularly the effect of crimes on women, including rape and sexual violence (Kelly, 1988), child abuse (Campbell, 1988) and domestic violence (Pahl, 1985). Victimology is now firmly on academic and political agendas, and increasingly calls arise for the views of 'the victim' to actively be taken into account in the criminal justice process, leading to concern about a climate of *victimism* (Sumner, 1994) that may not necessarily improve justice or prevent crime. Such a climate may divert attention from offenders, or be over-punitive to appease victims or their families, or support a culture of 'self-interested individuals' (Sykes, 1992). This last label certainly applies to celebrities who may well see value in the publicity gained by claiming a 'stalker'. Stalking is only criminal under the 1997 UK legislation if the subjective interpretation of the experience is as 'victimising'. In the West, that process has been linked over and over with celebrity. Although defining such behaviours as criminal has varied over historical periods and continues to vary widely cross-culturally, it is curious that legislative and perceptive change is coinciding with concern for the victim, the development of feminism, the extent to which cultures are celebrified and the growth of the new global medium that is the Internet.

Stalking links culture, change, communication, celebrity and crime. The celebrification of news has not only made celebrity stalking experiences more public but also has made celebrities themselves more likely to complain and seek redress should such behaviour threaten their lives or livelihoods. Simultaneously it is has made them even more desirable to, and desirous of, media exposure. The World Wide Web plays a significant role because of the web presence of most major conventional media celebrities' own websites. It also offers specific potential for changing and escalating deviant/criminal activity partly because of the nature of the technology itself and partly due to the WWW's continually expanding reach, the volume and range of material it supports, the ease of publication in cyberspace and the lack of regulation.

Talking cyberstalking

The impact of the World Wide Web is such that cyberspace and cyberculture have served to further complicate the construction of this 'crime' that was already difficult to define, detect or prosecute. As with real stalking, there is no one clear legal definition of cyberstalking. Broadly, it is the 'repeated use of the Internet, email or other related digital electronic communication devices to annoy, alarm or threaten a specific individual or group of individuals' (D'Ovidio and Doyle, 2003: 10) or the use of the 'Internet or other telecommunication technologies to harass or menace another person' (Joseph, 2003: 106). However, problems of definition are only the beginning of our difficulties in dealing with stalking in cyberspace for several reasons: not all jurisdictions have appropriate laws for stalking; law covering 'real' stalking may not work in relation to the cyber version; 'free speech' may become paramount when cyber harassment involves publication about the victim; cyberstalkers may hide behind anonymous or semi-anonymous remailers requiring sophisticated policing and prosecution processes; victim and stalker may be in different states or even countries so jurisdictional or boundary issues also arise; law enforcement may not take cyber harassment seriously if there is no physical aspect; and old models of harassment as nothing more than a nuisance linger, culturally inhibiting controls even where it is illegal (see more detail at http://www.cyber-stalking.net/legal.htm).

Yet there is probably greater potential for stranger stalking online because of the large and increasing amount of personal data stored in computers, including addresses. It is more likely to be carried out from a distance, anonymous, invisible, untraceable and undetectable than the use of letters, phone calls, long-range lenses or listening devices.[3] It may involve abusive, threatening or obscene communication from one person to another (Ellison and Akdeniz, 1998) or electronic sabotage in the form of thousands of junk email messages (spamming) or sending computer viruses. Cyberstalkers may even impersonate their victims online and send abusive emails or fraudulent spam in the victim's name.

From one perspective, then, cyberstalking is just stalking with modern technology.[4] For example, Petherick argues that cyberstalking is 'simply an extension of the physical form of stalking where the electronic mediums such as the Internet are used to pursue, harass or contact another in an unsolicited fashion'.[5] This suggests that the Internet is irrelevant to the construction of the crime of stalking as the conduct can involve but is not caused by its existence. In contrast, Bocij and McFarlane (2003) argue that cyberstalking should be seen as a unique form of deviant behaviour which is completely distinct to other forms of stalking. From whichever viewpoint, though, the new medium is implicated, and cyberstalking can spill over into physical space (Ogilvie, 2000).

Cyberstalking is certainly not necessarily just fictional fantasy in a cathartic separate space – it can and does have 'real' effects. For example, in Australia, a young man tracked down a girl after obtaining her social security number, licence plate number and place of employment via the Internet. He detailed plans to kill her on the web then drove to her place of work and shot her (Romei, 1999). In another notorious case in the US, Gary Dellapenta pretended to be the victim he was stalking and posted rape fantasies on various chatrooms inviting men to call and giving her real address. 'Men would come to her door in the middle of the night' (http://www.wired.com/news/politics/0%2C1283%2C17504%2C00.html).

Publicity about the most extreme results of these kinds of activities in cybercommunities has led to a massive surge of calls for control, especially as stalking and paedophile grooming are now being merged to further exacerbate the connotations of the crime (which is now a very long way from the harassment definitions in the legislation). The more extreme the apparent danger, the more likely the control – not just legislative, but also via surveillance online. 'Stalking the stalkers'; stings; vigilantism, with all the problems of slander and defamation; extradition; prosecutions of ISPs; online shaming and technological filters are all prevalent now. Yet, as in real life (and, indeed, in relation to other crimes such as paedophile activities), most cyberstalkers live nearby their victims and only 2 per cent use anonymous remailers (ibid.: 16). Nonetheless much news (http://www.timesonline.co.uk/article/0,,2-2149780,00.html) and policy (http://www.ceop.gov.uk/) now focuses on the extreme and rare cases of paedophile cyberstalkers. The effect is an elevation of the meaning of harassment to its most extreme potential: the dangerous, sexual violation of an innocent victim by a stranger. Further, cyberculture is implicated, making the Internet itself newsworthy. As ever, when a medium is attributed with causality for crime, calls for control and censorship proliferate.

Criminology, cyberculture and celebrity

For criminologists, cyberculture throws into sharp relief the culturally relative, constructed nature of crime (in that in a space unbounded by jurisdictional control or national boundaries the same activity can be at once unrecognised, a nuisance, a joke, perverted and criminal). Such differences not only problematise definition but also throw into question the practical and ethical role of the law (see Yar, this volume). Also, comparing those differences cross-culturally reveals the way in which specific cultural values and practices interact to change meaning and shows the extent to which the media, new and traditional, play a role in that process. Exploring 'cyber'stalking reveals the complexity of that process. Stalking is not even an 'old crime'; its change in status has paralleled the global acceleration rate of the new Net technologies. Celebrity has been the motif that has accelerated stalking's reconstruction as crime. Celebrities maintain websites and court publicity and all of this happens in cyberspace and mainstream media which are increasingly blending. Media news about celebrity has foregrounded the problem of stalking and academic feminist concern with ordinary harassment has enabled celebrities to act upon stalkers using the law. Further, the 'rights' of victims have emerged largely as a result of feminist intervention in criminology. So why have stalking, and subsequently cyberstalking, evolved as the crime of harassment and what does that process tell us about our crime and culture?

It is difficult to overestimate the power of celebrity in this construction of crime – or perhaps more accurately, the wealth and power that underwrites and depends on celebrity. Nor is it possible to overestimate the role of the media – not as causal of crime but as purveyors of ideas – quickly, repetitively, simply, widely and more or less unilaterally. Added to that the WWW has made a huge difference to that process of construction and dissemination. Cyberspace is now both a site and topic of news and cyberstalking connotes not just irritating harassment but sexual violation of innocent victims and potential real physical harm. This shift in meaning of harassment towards extreme crime emerges from the celebrification and digitisation of our culture.

In our contemporary western world the old totalising value systems of class, religion and nation continue to be rapidly transgressed as our identities and activities shift accordingly across a borderless world where family, work, education and leisure may all involve real or cyber 'travel', dispersing each of us into a diasporic existence of difference and atopia. Increasingly the one thing we share is 'knowing' global celebrities – from Britney to the Beckhams. Celebrity is a kind of common cultural currency or shared language. It binds us together in a borderless world. It is thus a commodity both in its own right and as a motif of value, not just economic currency but cultural currency. Culture *is* celebrity; it travels easily from large screen to fanzine, football field to TV, stage to catwalk, biography to magazine, and endlessly though cyberspace. Celebrity is the new elite and a very public one that merges media, cosmetics, diet, exercise and fashion – the 'beauty' industries of looks and lifestyle.

That industry depends on its icons and their selling power. It also depends on the media to disseminate both and, in turn, the media symbiotically depend on the commercial value of celebrity. Both industries sell us the stars, their relationships and their 'talent' directly but also other products indirectly by association: leisure, fashion, cars, films, lifestyle, music, media products and all manner of goods and services. The unestimable value of celebrity to the beauty and media industries may well help explain the changing status of stalking toward cyberstalking and crime. The shift certainly parallels the rise of the Internet and accompanying massive growth in digital communication since the early 1990s. To construct harassment as crime is to offer protection to cultural icons, for whom any threat to their beauty is a threat not just to their power, but to the interests of the industries they represent. The impact of 'cyber' has been to accelerate and accentuate. It is mass media publicity beyond the controls applicable to mainstream media. Moreover, because the stars maintain websites full of information it is much easier for stalkers to both follow them and contact them, even if only virtually.

(Cyber)stalking is arguably the price of publicity for the celebrity. This new cultural elite has no natural authority – it is constructed, electronically enhanced and literally made consistent in size and shape to serve the image, diet, exercise and even cosmetic surgery industries, who encourage us to emulate our icons' size, shape and smile. Then the perfect face and form is embellished with goods we too can buy to create this season's look to make ourselves beautiful and give ourselves pleasure because we are 'worth it'. It is an illusion of beauty, an illusion that actually serves and depends on the massive new economic industries of body, leisure and pleasure. The power of illusion depends on maintaining illusion.

Stalking in all its manifestations – from misinformed or mischievous attention right through to murder – is a problem to this new elite that courts publicity so long as it is in its own interests. Two cases that demonstrate the reduction in value to a star commodity that paparazzi 'stalking' can prompt are actress Catherine Zeta-Jones, illicitly photographed while not very elegantly eating chocolate cake at her wedding, and model Naomi Campbell, exiting a Narcotics Anonymous meeting.[6] Both went to court to claim damages on the grounds that representing them without their consent was threatening to their career because they didn't look their best. Stalking undermines the control of the product of celebrity and illustrates the use of crime and law discourses to restore that power.

Celebrities also use the increasing focus on the individual's right to feel 'violated' to challenge harassment. Victimisation passes the power to 'control' crime from the state to the individual but, more than anything, the concept of victimisation protects the privileged because of the costs involved in investigation and litigation. Quite simply, those who go to law about harassment are often those who can afford to because of their fame and wealth, perpetuating the illusion that celebrity is systematically stalked.

Construction of crime has always been according to power. Now beauty is power – the owning of it and means of producing it are sites of power. Celebrities are the visible elite apex of the new beauty 'servicing' industries. Whereas the discursive construction of mugging as crime in the British press served the interests of the race/class elite of the 1970s, at the turn of the millennium the construction of stalking as crime serves a new incarnation of power. Stalking is a crime constructed in a new paradigm of globally industrialised, celebritified aesthetics that is meta-mediated through cyberculture. It may be a new paradigm but it is also, arguably, simply a new metaphor for old power that remains resolutely underpinned by access to media, money and law.

Notes

1 He used the speech to blame the media for her death, calling her the 'most hunted person of the modern age' (http://news.bbc.co.uk/onthisdav/hi/date$/stories/september/6/newsid_2502000/2502307.stm, 26/10/2005).
2 Similarly, celebrities have resorted to the courts and called for the introduction of privacy legislation to prevent paparazzi photographers 'stalking' them and

selling sometimes unflattering images to the media, as recently occurred when Michael Douglas and Catherine Zeta-Jones successfully sued after the unauthorised photography of their wedding and subsequent publication of the images (http://www.leealdav.co.uk/lexnex/cmck/cmckl50503a.htm, 18/04/2005).

3 Thanks to the students on 'Net-crime LAW 378', 2006, University of Sheffield, particularly K. Hovington, L. Stubbs and R. Taylor for their ideas on cyber-stalking.

4 http://www.stalking-research.org.uk/pdfs/Bocij%20and%20McFarlane%20-%20Seven%20Fallacies.pdf

5 http://www.stalking-research.org.uk/Ddfs/Forensic%20UiMlateD CLP72.pdf

6 'Zeta Jones said she felt "violated" by the unflattering snaps' (online at: http://www.dailymail.co.uk/pages/live/articles/showbiz/showbiznews.html?in_article_id=366038&in_page_id=1773, 26/10/2005). In Naomi Campbell's case: 'The case centred on the publication in February 2001 of a report about her drug addiction, including a photograph of her leaving a Narcotics Anonymous meeting in Kings Road, Chelsea', obviously an image detrimental to her reputation – however true (online at: http://news.bbc.co.uk/nolpda/ukfs_news/hi/newsid_3689000/3689049.stm, 26/10/2005).

References

Australian Institute of Criminology – see online at: http://www.aic.gov.au/publications/tandi/til66.pdf

Barker, J. and Petley, J. (1997) *Ill Effects: The Media/Violence Debate*. London: Routledge.

Bindel, J. (2005) The life stealers, *Guardian*, 16 April.

Bocij, P. and McFarlane, L. (2003) 'Seven fallacies about cyber-stalking', *Prison Service Journal*, 149, September, pp. 37–42.

Brownmiller, S. (1975) *Against Our Will*. Harmondsworth: Penguin.

Budd, T. and Mattinson, J. (2000) *The Extent and Nature of Stalking: Findings from the 1998 British Crime Survey*, Home Office Research Study 210 (online at: http://www.homeoffice.gov.uk/rds/pdfs/hors210.pdf).

Campbell, B. (1988) *Unofficial Secrets*. London: Virago.

Carter, C. (1998) 'When the ordinary becomes extraordinary', in C. Carter, G. Branston and S. Allan (eds), *News, Crime and Gender*. London: Routledge.

Celebrity stalking – see online at: http://news.bbc.co.uk/2/hi/entertainment/478085.stm

Chibnall, S. (1977) *Law-and-Order News: An Analysis of Crime Reporting in the British Press*. London: Tavistock.

Cyberstalking – see online at: http://www.cyber-stalking.net/

D'Ovidio, R. and Doyle, J. (2003) 'A study on cyber-stalking: understanding investigative hurdles', *FBI Law Enforcement Bulletin*, 72 (3): 10–17.

Dodd, T., Nicholas, S., Povey, D. and Walker, A. (2004) *Crime in England and Wales*, Home Office Statistical Bulletin (online at: (http://www.homeoffice.gov.uk/rds/pdfs04/hosb1004.pdf).

Edwards, S. (1987) *Policing Domestic Violence*. New York: Sage.

Ellison, L. and Akdeniz, Y. (1998) 'Cyber-stalking: the regulation of harassment on the Internet', *Criminal Law Review*, December special edition: 'Criminal Justice and the Internet', pp. 29–48.

Foucault, M. (1979) *The History of Sexuality Vol. 1*. London: Penguin.

Fowler, R. (1991) *Language in the News*. London: Routledge.

Galtung, J. and Ruge, M. (1965) 'Structuring and selecting news', in S. Cohen and J. Young (eds) (1982 edn), *The Manufacture of news: deviance, social problems and the mass media*. London: Constable.

Gelsthorpe, L. (1989) *Sexism and the Female Offender*. Aldershot: Gower.

Hall, S., Critcher, C., Jefferson, T. and Clarke, J. (eds) (1978) *Policing the Crisis: Mugging, the State, Law and Order*. Basingstoke: Macmillan.

Hanmer, J., Radford, J. and Stanko, B. (1989) *Women, Policing and Male Violence*. London: Routledge.

Hartman, P. and Husband, C. (1971) 'The mass media and racial conflict', in S. Cohen and J. Young (eds) (1981 edn), *The Manufacture of News: Deviance, Social Problems and the Mass Media*. London: Constable.

Jenkins, P. (1992) *Intimate Enemies: Moral Panics in Contemporary Great Britain*. New York: Aldine de Gruyter.

Jewkes, Y. (2004) *Media and Crime*. London: Sage.

Joseph, J. (2003) 'Cyberstalking: an international perspective' in Y. Jewkes (ed.), *Dot.cons: Crime, Deviance, Identity and the Internet*. Cullompton: Willan.

Kelly, L. (1988) *Surviving Sexual Violence*. Cambridge: Polity.

Kelly, L. and Humphreys, C. (2000) 'Stalking and paedophilia: ironies and contradictions in the politics of naming and legal reform', in J. Radford, M. Friedberg and L. Harne (eds), *Women, Violence and Strategies for Action*. Buckingham: Open University Press.

Malsch, M. (2000) *Stalking in the Netherlands*. Paper presented at the Criminal Justice Responses Conference, Sydney, Australia (online at: http://www.aic.gov.au/conferences/stalking/Malsch.pdf).

Metropolitan Police (n.d.) Anti-stalking guide (online at: http://www.met.police.uk/stalking/stalking.pdf).

Miller, N. and Nugent, H. (2002) *Stalking Laws and Implementation Practices: A National Review for Policymakers and Practitioners*. Full report. http://www.vaw.umn.edu/documents/ilj_stalk/iljinalrpt.htm/1 id2635043.

Mullen, P. E., Pathe, M., Purcell, R. and Stuart, G. W. (1999) 'A study of stalkers', *American Journal of Psychiatry*, 156: 1244–9.

Ogilvie, E. (2000) *Cyberstalking: Trends and Issues in Crime and Criminal Justice*. Australian Institute of Criminology, No. 166.

Pahl, J. (1985) 'Refuges for battered women: ideology and action', *Feminist Review*, 19 March, pp. 25–43.

Povey, D., Upson, A. and Jannson, K. (2005) *Crime in England Wales: Quarterly Update to June 2005* (online at: http://www.homeoffice.gov.uk/rds/pdfs05/hosbl805.pdf).

Protection from Harassment Act 1997 – see online at: http://194.128.65.3/acts/acts1997/97040--a.htm#2

Romei, S. (1999) 'Net firms lead killer to victim', *The Australian*, 4–5 December, pp. 19–22.

Smart, C. (1976) *Women, Crime and Criminology*. London: Routledge.

Smart, C. (1989) *Feminism and the Power of Law*. London: Routledge.

Smart, C. (1995) *Law, Crime and Sexuality*. London: Sage.

Stalking resource – see online at: http://www.ncvc.org/src/

Sumner, C. (1994) *The Sociology of Deviance: An Obituary*. Buckingham: Open University Press.

Sykes, C. (1992) *A Nation of Victims: The Decay of the American Character*. New York: St. Martin's Press.

Tjaden, P. and Thoennes, N. (1998) *Stalking in America: Findings From the National Violence Against Women Survey, Research in Brief*. Washington, DC: US Department of Justice, National Institute of Justice, NCJ169592 (online at: http://www.ncirs.org/txtfilesl/nil/183781.txt).

Wykes, M. (2001) *News, Crime and Culture*. London: Pluto Press.

Wykes, M. and Gunter, B. (2005) *The Media and Body Image: Looks could Kill*. London: Sage.

Zona, M. A., Sharma, K. K. and Lane, J. C. (1993) 'A comparative study of erotomanic and obsessional subjects in a forensic sample', *Journal of Forensic Sciences*, 38 (4): 894–903.

Chapter 10

Digital undergrounds: alternative politics and civil society

Rinella Cere

Introduction

A rich literature is available on alternative and underground media, much of which demonstrates the existence of direct links between underground activities and eventual changes in the civil and political societies in which they have developed (Downing, 2001). Part of that history, however, shows an equally strong attempt on the part of the state to criminalise and censor alternative political activities and their media. This chapter seeks to extend what I will call the alternative politics-civil networks paradigm to computer-mediated communications (CMCs) and political activism. Inevitably this will lead to a short exploration of the nature of the 'network society' (Castells, 1996) in addition to some of the theoretical approaches to 'political actions' and the way Internet technologies and alternative political activism (or 'hacktivism') are integral to one another. I will ask whether 'underground' political activities on the Net can affect changes in the societies in which they operate in the same way as underground media did before the introduction of the web. The chapter will refer to two specific case studies and relevant, related websites to highlight the type of relationship that exists between CMCs and political activism. In addition, I will consider how the state has reacted to online alternative politics and look at whether the criminalisation of alternative political activities on the Net is conducted by the state in a parallel fashion to underground political activities of the past. The two case studies discussed are somewhat different in nature but they both fall within the category of Internet political activities.

The chapter is essentially concerned with two groups: Net-dedicated activists or 'hacktivists' and political *users* of the Net (Margolis and

Resnick, 2000). Although the two categories are fluid and share some features, I understand the former as people who 'from their individuality, their singularity ... build cultural and political places in cyberspace ... the land of empowerment of individuals' (Jordan, 1999: 96). The latter refers to people whose main concerns are in the 'real' community but are nonetheless aware of the way in which political battles can be enhanced and linked at a local and global level through the Internet. The first case study (on the riots in France) falls somewhere between the first and the latter definition, while the second case study (on Palestine) is a clear example of the second definition, with the added proviso that politics that affect the Net and political uses of the Net are not always clearly separable, especially in relation to questions of regulation and censorship and the criminalisation of alternative politics online and offline. It is also worth noting that alternative political struggles started making use of the Internet long before mainstream politics or established political parties (Coleman et al., 1999; Davis, 1999). This is hardly surprising given that many of the people involved in radical or alternative politics have grown up with computer technologies and are completely *au fait* with their possibilities and potential. Nonetheless, as we will see below in the second of our examples, the digital divide remains firmly in place.

The many faces of the Internet

The 'network paradigm' and 'network politics'

One of the central features of alternative political movements is their 'network-like' nature. This has increased and intensified through use of the Internet, a technology which itself has a 'network' structure. From the early days of Unix, Usenet and BBSs to the recent expansion of the World Wide Web (WWW) and contemporary open source systems, the Net has established its place as a socio-technological formation 'with technologically and culturally embedded properties of interactivity and individualisation' (Castells, 1996: 358). In the same way that a movement consists of 'diversified and autonomous units which devote a large part of their available resources to the construction and maintenance of internal solidarity' (Melucci, 1996: 113), a communication and exchange network 'keeps the separate, quasi-autonomous cells in contact with each other' (ibid.). This interpretation is a useful way of conceptualising the nature of the thousands of politically and socially orientated 'webforms' to be found in the Net Galaxy. As with many of the activities described in this volume, it is the global network structure of the Internet that serves contemporary alternative political movements so very well both in organisational and informational terms. 'Alternative' websites are the lifeblood of counter-information, in spite of the growing commercialisation of the WWW and the concomitant changes brought about by what has been described as the 'process of normalisation' (Margolis and Resnick, 2000). Certainly the Internet with its 'young', utopian and libertarian nature clearly appeals to radical politics, but that is only half the story of the Net's origins, which could equally be seen as rooted in the defence strategy of the US National Security Agency (Gillies and Cailliau, 2000; Slevin, 2000). Furthermore, if the Internet is not only a 'revolution about *real information*' but is at the same time also 'a revolution about *virtual disinformation*' (Virilio, 2000: 108), the importance of a global forum for counter-information, both real and virtual, has arguably never been so vital. In relation to the case study of Palestine discussed below, alternative websites seem all the more vital in the light of studies which indicate that mainstream news about the Palestinian struggle has not informed the public about the real situation on the ground (Philo and Berry, 2004).

Hacktivists and activists: politics and technology

Another aspect which cannot be ignored when discussing political activism and the use of the Net is the technological one of 'open source' software. This is as much a political issue as it is a technological one and it is 'organically' tied to the space and direction that alternative political activism may have in the future. This was no clearer than at the zeligConf in 2000 where the aim of the organisers centred on ways to advance, coordinate and bring to fruition the different 'spirits' of the participants/ speakers:

> It will be as much about conducting an inventory of fixtures in the experience of digital communication practises of NGOs, social movements, militant initiatives or activism, as about attempting to formalise hypotheses on a wide integration of the Internet, and on potentialities of free software in the development of alternative communication initiatives. (http://www.zeligconf/)

Free software and open source systems, such as Linux, Gnu/Linux and Freenet have long been considered allies of alternative circuits of distribution and access, in spite of the fact that 'free' does not usually mean cost-free (see Yar, this volume).[1] These kinds of ambiguities spell out the contradictions and problems at the heart of those alliances, all the more so recently with what are perceived as mounting commercial pressures on successful open source systems to compete against the Microsoft monopoly which has control of 95 per cent of operating systems. Whether the perception spelled out by Richard Stallman of the

Free Software Foundation – that free software today has enormous commercial value – is actually shared by groups which are trying to combat inequalities locally and globally is another matter, but I suspect not. Perhaps we should remember that all these 'radical programmers' and their allies are nonetheless part of 'the technopower elite ... somewhere between the institutional giants and the underground hackers' (Jordan, 1999: 140). The words 'freedom' and 'free' are inarguably abused and overused in most walks of life, but nowhere more so than in the 'cyberwalks' of life.

In the *Philosophy behind the Freenet Project* – 'an adaptive peer-to-peer network application that permits publication, replication, and retrieval of data while protecting the anonymity of its users' (http://www.freenet-project.org/) – Ian Clarke suggests that we really need unlimited freedom to access information and that there is no such thing as 'good censorship'. He brings a somewhat cryptic example to bear: 'There are already criticisms that the anti-racism censorship in many European countries is hampering legitimate historical analysis of events such as the Second World War.' What this legitimate historical analysis might be is not actually spelled out, but more worrying is the notion that somehow racist views need to be in the open and people need to be exposed to them in order to counteract them: 'Unfortunately, preventing people from being aware of the often sophisticated arguments used by racists, makes them vulnerable to those arguments when they do eventually encounter them' (ibid.). The assumption that racists use sophisticated arguments is dubious enough, but the logic of such a statement is truly alarming, i.e. that if people are not subjected to racist arguments than they will not be able to counter their force, a familiar empirical argument proven wrong time and time again. Put simply, it is akin to saying that human beings cannot understand or be critical about situations for which they do not have first-hand experience. Apart from the fact that this would probably lead to political inaction, web-based political activities and their real-world counterparts disprove that point once and for all.

Hackers' cultures

The other aspect I want to consider briefly is both closely tied to open source ideals and clearly overlaps with political activism online: hackers' cultures. There are as many different hacker 'types' and typologies as there are Net-based political activities. However, two forms of hacking which draw from, and contribute to, alternative politics have been described as follows: 'Hacking is an important form of watchdog counter-response to the use of surveillance technology and data-gathering by the state, and to the increasingly monolithic communications power of giant corporations' and: 'Hacking, as guerrilla know-how, is essential to the task of maintaining fronts of cultural resistance and stocks of oppositional knowledge as a hedge against a techno-fascist future' (cited in Taylor, 1999: 43).

There is not sufficient space here to mention the many terms currently used for different types of hackers which range from the benign to the more criminally-orientated element who are usually defined as 'crackers'. The latter may engage in a range of unlawful activities from trespassing to information warfare. The literature on hackers is certainly proliferating to the point where hacking is being seen as a veritable 'ethic' of our age (Himanen, 2001). However, it is worth noting that alliances between 'benign' hackers and political activists hardly extend to women in the way that one might expect if one considers the intense Internet activities of feminists, as well as the women's struggles being publicised online around the world. I visited about a hundred women's/feminist websites for the purposes of researching this chapter and found that the hacker's world is still, with very few exceptions, a very masculine environment (cf. Cere, 2003; Taylor, 2003).

Their gender composition aside, hackers have undergone much change in recent years, to the point of professionalising their activities (Taylor, 1999). This trend is going some way to counteract the processes of demonisation and stigmatisation to which hackers have been subjected since the inception of CMCs. Prominent hackers have even become part of Internet governance, as in the case of the (short-lived as it turned out) election to ICANN (Internet Corporation for Assigned Numbers and Names) of the head of a German hacker group, the Chaos Computer Club, which had been established to challenge anti-corporatist values.

At the same time, however, criminalisation of political hackers has continued, not least in the efforts to equate their actions and motives with those of cyberterrorists. Electronic civil disobedience (ECD) with which most hackers are associated is as far removed from terrorist activities as it could be, yet increasingly the media and many commentators perpetuate the stereotype. One explanation for this is offered by Manion and Goodrum:

> It may be that describing hacktivists as criminals helps entrench a certain conception of, and control of intellectual property, and obscures the larger critique about the ownership of information, and the legal system's needs to protect the powerful economic interests of corporations attempting to dominate and completely commercialise the Internet. (Manion and Goodrum, 2001: 469; see also Yar, this volume)

It has become increasingly difficult to circumvent the machinations of 'digital capitalism' (Virilio, 2000: 110) as countries around the world have enacted computer laws and sought to restrain and block (not always successfully) any kind of electronic civil disobedience. As we will see below in the discussion of the case studies, this conflation has blurred the boundaries between genuine acts of political resistance and destructive acts without justification, and paved the way for government interference and/or excessive corporate power.

There are also other important considerations to apply when evaluating political hackers' activities, for example the political system in which they operate. In countries where governments control all information, hacktivists may well be justified in their acts even if these are of a destructive nature towards government departments and websites. In countries where democracy is in place it is felt that some hacktivist activities are less justified, yet as we will see in our two case studies, even in free countries not all is well with the treatment of certain groups of people, whether in terms of class, ethnic background or cultural and religious beliefs. Criminalisation undoubtedly serves two different purposes in different political systems; in authoritarian countries suppressing oppositional political activities online serves to prop up brutal regimes; in democratic countries the purpose is to prop up capital:

> One rationalisation for the vilification of hacktivism is the need for the power elite to rewrite property law in order to contain the effects of the new information technologies. As a result of the newly evolving intellectual property laws, information and knowledge can now be held as capital. (Manion and Goodrum (2001: 469)

Weblogs and resistance

Weblogs have been around since the late 1990s but have proliferated in the last few years following the introduction of free tools to build your own weblog. The original name – weblog – was coined by John Barger in 1997[2] and the shorter version happened somewhat by default when Peter Merholz introduced a play on words and called it wee-blog which ended up as blog.[3] Following the introduction of free easy-to-use tools and no prerequisite knowledge of html language, weblogs have undergone a transformation from thoughtful and critical sites with links (also called filter-style weblogs, because the editors ensured that these were not merely a repetition of mainstream news and events but a source of alternative viewpoints and criticism) to journal-style weblogs. The latter are much more fragmented in form, and have become a platform for individuals and micro-communities to discuss anything and everything under the sun.

The downside of these transformations is the overwhelming amount of blogs on the web and no amount of blog directories can help with sifting through them. In fact the directories themselves have become a barrier to searching the web: 'Weblogs, once filters of the Web, suddenly became so numerous they were as confusing as the Web itself' (Blood, 2002: 15). In addition to facilitating new forms of individualism, blogging is also used as a political tool. As new subcultures emerge, many possibilities for political change are explored in weblogs.

In the first case study I will look at the way in which the Internet in general, and blogs in particular, have been instrumental to the rebellious voices of young people from ethnic minorities in France. I will also look at the violent events which unfolded and the problems raised by a technologically determinist view of the role played by the Internet.

Case 1: 'Cyber-riots' on the 'streets' of France

In October 2005 a series of events in Paris sparked off one of the most prolonged and widespread periods of civil unrest in France, involving mainly members of ethnic communities. Two events in particular, very different in nature but nonetheless linked by deeply ingrained racist attitudes, were seen as 'the fuse that lit the powder' (Vidal, 2005: 1). The first was a throwaway, but deeply offensive, comment by the Home Office Minister, Sarkozy, when visiting one of the many deprived Parisian suburbs of Argenteuil. He stated that the area needed a clean-up with a 'power hose' and described some of the people living there as 'rabble'. A second, more serious event, was the death of two teenagers, Bouna Traore and Zyed Benna, electrocuted after climbing into an electrical sub-station in the Paris suburb of Clichy-sous-Bois, after being chased by the police.[4]

It was at Clichy-sous-Bois that the riots started, although they quickly spread to other areas of Paris and finally to at least 30 other French towns. The reasons for this kind of social disorder are very deep-rooted in France, as in other former colonial powers, and are tied to the continuing structural inequalities within French society among immigrant communities. In a detailed, 500-page report by the 'Cour des Comptes' the problem was described thus:

> The current crisis was not caused by immigration. It is the result of the way in which immigration has been handled . . . The situation that now confronts the authorities has developed over a number of decades. (cited in Vidal, 2005)

However, one of the notable differences between these events and similar disturbances that took place in 1961, again involving minorities in France (primarily Algerian immigrants), was the way in which the recent unrest was 'networked' electronically:

> It is the first time France has experienced a real crisis in the age of the Internet . . . And it's easy to see how the Internet can increase the momentum of the crisis. (Patino, quoted in Moore and Williams, 2005)

Blogging and hacking 'on the fire'

The media largely failed to highlight the underlying root causes of such massive violent civil unrest, a system of 'urban apartheid' that saw this part of one of the wealthiest cities in the world afflicted by high unemployment, under-achievement in education, and generalised poverty. Instead, discussions centred on youth culture (rap music was the first in line), followed by the Internet and the 'destructive' uses it was being put to:

> French police have opened an inquiry into two bloggers who urged French youths to riot and revolt against the police. The bloggers, a 16-year-old French teen and an 18-year-old with Ghanaian nationality, were detained on Monday in the Paris region, said the official. The bloggers face a charge of inciting harm to people and property over the Internet, with a penalty that carries a sentence of up to five years in prison and a $52,800 fine. (Blog Herald, 2005)

This was the first step in the criminalisation of the new technology alongside the people that used it. Many weblogs were blocked as they ran images of burning cars and police battles with young people and sought to act as forums of information and sympathy. Several websites and blogs carried images of the two adolescents who had died along with messages of condolences. Others carried irreverent cartoons about Sarkozy and the French government. Some websites detailed the events taking place and supplied a critical running commentary. Six months on messages are still coming and unsurprisingly they are increasingly politicised.

In parallel, other electronic activities relating to the unrest were singled out and criminalised, including an invasion of the websites of the Parisian suburb of Clichy-sous-Bois and the dispatch of thousands of fake emails announcing the mayor's resignation. Apart form the obvious 'entertainment' value of such protests, their status as 'criminal' acts is debatable, given the impossibility of proving a direct link between these kinds of activities and the 'real' events on the ground. As Wall has argued: 'many of the behaviours that have been identified as cybercrimes are not actually crimes as such but invoke civil remedies instead' (2001: 3). It also highlights the confusion surrounding any digital/electronically led activities, especially when related to civil disobedience and violence on the streets.

In the case of the French troubles, one of the main accusations directed at online activities among 'rioters' was that the Internet was used to coordinate activities in the different cities where violent attacks took place: 'Web monitors and sponsors said the greatest impact of the Internet has been as a forum conveying messages that incite further violence' (*Washington Post*, 10 November 2005). This kind of direct accusation about the Internet serving as a support network and organisational logistic to the violence on the streets is highly problematic (see Fafinski, this volume). As some commentators have argued, the Internet also served as a network to let people know the whereabouts of the police, who were also guilty in the eyes of some for their employment of heavy-handed tactics and excessive use of force (a law enforcement approach that was clearly legitimated by the comments of the Home Office Minister mentioned above). In addition, questions remained unanswered concerning the role the police had in the death of the two teenagers in Clichy-sous-Bois (which at the time of writing is still under investigation).

Singling out the Internet as an instrument for the incitement of violence clearly ignores the real causes of the violent outbursts. I would argue, as many other commentators have done in France and elsewhere, that the violence was directly connected to ongoing racist practices of the French state which left entire communities oppressed and disenfranchised:

> The concentration within the banlieus of all the evils that afflict the working classes epitomises the failure over 30 years of a succession of governments from both the right and – with a few exceptions – the left. (Vidal, 2005)

What is also evident is that hackers, bloggers, cybercrime, rioting on the streets and 'real' crime are all considered part of the same process. Many young people were arrested and detained and those without legalised status (*sans papier*) were immediately deported. The two bloggers referred to previously, and others investigated along with them, were considered cybercriminals and held responsible for actions hundreds of miles away. Computers and the Internet stood accused, yet arguably they simply served as a 'protected space' for the people of Clichy.

Social capital, digital divide and cyber-riots

Access or the lack of it has been one of the central issues debated in the rise of the Internet. To date there is a clear north–south, east–west divide in Internet access,[5] but even within high access countries such as France penetration stands at only 43 per cent, less than half of the population. There is a clear generational divide in most countries although other gaps – e.g. gender and ethnicity – are closing. One of the interesting paradoxes which emerges about Internet use and the riots in France is the way in which it challenges the conventional link between social capital and cultural competence (skills). By all accounts the people involved in the civil unrest in France had no access to the social capital which other groups of people take for granted (good jobs, education, decent housing, etc.) but they clearly have competence in the use of new technologies (computers, Internet, mobile phones) and this in turn has become their social capital. Throughout the period in which violent incidents took place, they used technology to share messages of solidarity, discuss their predicament, exchange information, underline their sense of alienation and, yes, escape the police. Independently of the accusations addressed towards these new technologies and their so called 'criminal role' in the unrest, they appear to have provided many young people with precisely the kind of 'community commitment'[6] which they had been accused of not possessing. This is not to assume another form of technological determinism where 'new media' have empowered otherwise disenfranchised people, but to acknowledge a material interaction between technologies, agency and historical contingency:

> it is less in new media practices ... than in the uncertainty of emerging and contested practices of communication that the struggle of groups to define and locate themselves is most easily observed. (Marvin, in Thrift, 1996: 1473)

By the time the unrest dissipated a new community had clearly emerged, and one which had common goals. A link had been made between 'underground' political activities, civic networks and potential future changes. Even the French state had to acknowledge the force of the discontent.[7] Although it could be argued that the Internet functioned as 'negative social capital', in the sense that some of the aims had clear negative consequences for others, the resulting process it generated clearly fitted into the findings of previous research[8] about the positive aspects of Internet use rather than with any negative effects (criminal activities) and/or loss of social capital.

Case 2: 'Terrorism' in cyberspace – Islam under attack

The criminalisation of Islam in the West has intensified since 11 September 2001 but Islamophobia has a long history reaching back to the Middle Ages:

> Insofar as Islam has always been seen as belonging to the Orient, its particular faith within the general structure of Orientalism has been to be looked at first of all as if it were one monolithic thing, and then with a very special hostility and fear. (Said, 1991: 205)

Following the attacks on the twin towers in New York this 'hostility and fear' has taken on new forms and one of these is that the word 'terrorism' has become quasi synonymous with 'Islamic', especially in the mainstream media. In the aftermath of 9/11, many 'Islamic' websites noted substantial increases in traffic, as people sought to understand Islam as a religion and the possible motivations for the attack (Bunt 2006). In the remainder of this chapter, however, I want to concentrate on Islamic political-related activities and look at two developments: first, at some of the organisations on the ground that have sought to use the Internet to further their struggle; and second, at the reasons for the conflation between their activism and terrorist activities generally. The following case study will consider the political struggle of the Palestinians for self-determination, their main websites and the problems that arise from their conflation with terrorism.

'Portals for sucide bombing'?

The problems raised in the first case study as to how to determine what constitutes real crime is also pertinent in relation to the following discussion about 'networking activities' by bodies considered to be terrorist organisations, in spite of the fact that in some cases they are legitimate. Palestinian organisations such as Hamas (which was recently democratically elected to lead the Palestinian people), Palestinian Islamic Jihad (PIJ), Fatah, the Popular Front for the Liberation of Palestine (PFLP) and Al-Aqsa Martyr's Brigade are all very different, but what they have in common is that they all have been under accusation of fostering terrorist activities, much of it via new technologies. Their acts of terror are said to be aimed principally against the Israeli state and its citizens, but also occasionally against Americans, as the USA is perceived as part of the problem in its uncritical support of the actions of successive Israeli governments. A basic search reveals that most entries on the WWW (which run into thousands) equate all these organisations with the word terrorism.

It is generally believed that Hamas has been using the Internet for some time to coordinate attacks against Israelis. In reality there is actually little independent evidence of this (that is, evidence that is not generated by Israeli secret services or other secret services around the world), and many accounts are based on anecdotes rather than reality. One such example is mentioned in Jihad Online (2002: 19–20) and is based on exchanges between three would-be assassins in a Hamas chat room. However, the discussion is more resonant of a gangster/horror movie than of serious military actions.

It is true that the Palestinian Information Centre (http://www.palestine-info.co.uk) website carries two Fatwas (April 2006), one supporting 'the legality of martyrs' operations in occupied Palestine' and one directed at leaders of Arab and Muslim nations stating: 'Normalising relations with Israel is a crime'. On the website there is also a link to a list of martyrs to the Palestinian cause (these links are not available in the English version) but these hardly constitute 'terrorism' and the website is also preoccupied with all the other aspects of Palestine's political, social and cultural life.

As for the armed wing of Hamas – the Qassam Brigades, one of the principal organisations believed to be responsible for tactics such as 'suicide bombing' – it is difficult to argue here that they use electronic networks for their activities as their website is presently inaccessible even in the Arabic version. Similarly the PIJ (Palestinian Islamic Jihad) and the two websites associated with it, Jihad Online and Quds Way, have also been blocked, having previously been hosted on American servers. Currently the site http://www.jihadonline.net/ takes the surfer to the 'World of Islam' portal, a rich website with many links which range from Islamic news to charity organisations to 'Muslim Bizz'.

Some of these Palestinian organisations have undoubtedly carried out attacks since the early 1990s but evidence of ICTs playing a major role in this is still largely unproven in spite of the 'netwar' concept being widely adopted:

> Networked structures are made feasible and effective by the informa-tion revolution, and have important implications for predicting and countering terrorist acts . . . terrorist groups will engage in informa-tion-age conflict or netwar, using information technology as an enabling factor. (Zanini, 1999: 247)

In addition, the figures for Internet access in Palestine are very low, around 160,000 or 5 per cent of a population of 3.8 million in 2004 (compared, for example, to Israel's access of 3.2 million on a population of 6.7 million, which is nearly 50 per cent).[9]

What becomes apparent in looking at the relevant websites is that many political activities taking place in cyberspace are not necessarily criminal activities and, contrary to widespread belief, they are not recruiting grounds for men and women to engage in suicide attacks against the Israeli military and settlers in the region. Instead, most websites are genuine attempts to connect up with the civil world of which they are part, and achieve a goal that they all share: that of ending Israeli occupation and establishing an independent Palestinian state. This clearly points to the 'political-civil network' paradigm mentioned at the begin-ning of this chapter, rather than to any criminal activity. As with the previous case study, it is difficult to pin real-life violence on website exchanges or other electronic networking activities, and it is equally problematic to 'blame' technology for direct action that takes place in response to oppressive state practices.

Terrorism undoubtedly has a presence in cyberspace. A recent study has identified eight different ways in which the Internet is used by terrorists, and unsurprisingly some of these potentially sinister activities are the same as many other organisations' mundane and everyday use of the Net, including networking, raising funds and distributing information. Of these eight categories, however, some are not so commonly used, such as: 'hiding instructions, manuals, and directions in coded messages or encrypted files' (Weimann, 2006). Such activities are clearly not widespread because of their very nature, and they are a far cry from the description of Islamic websites as 'portals of suicide terrorists' (which are clearly not encrypted) (Millard Burr and Collins, 2006). The reinforcement of homogenising views about Islam (which are perpetuated by the traditional and mainstream media) are clearly at odds with the plethora of Islamic views and contexts to be found on the web. Islamic-related activism on the Internet has created capillary information spaces about many different struggles around the world in Islamic countries, but it is not on the whole a 'recruitment ground' for terrorists.

Conclusion

As many chapters in this book have shown, the potential for criminal activities online are endless, but arguably no more so than the criminality that occurs offline. Time and again the Internet has been the focus of criticism for its purported role in the incitement of violence, fuelling debates about whether the medium of the Internet and the genres which have popularised it such as blogging help to preserve the fabric of society or fuel the strife which lies at the heart of most societies. Politically minded users of the Internet would argue that they have successfully employed the technology to circulate information about what is really happening and to inform each other and the rest of the world about ongoing political struggles and widespread iniquities. Equally they might argue that they have used the medium to organise successful protests in the face of an increasingly repressive and divisive economic world. The counter-argument to this view is that alternative politics online have served as a referent to many gatherings which also involved much violence, from one of the early protests against the World Economic Forum in Seattle right up to the events in France described above.[10] Alternative political activities online have increasingly been seen as a form of unlawful activity by states' national security forces and moves to criminalise them have proceeded apace. But the relationship between civil networks and political action on the Internet is now well established and no amount of government interference, short of total censorship, will be able to undermine it entirely. Other problems may well be on the horizon: Levine (2002) argues that the implications of civil society moving to the Internet is a 'worrying trend' rather than a positive process, and he outlines five main issues of concern: equity, weak social bonds, diminished public deliberation, rampant consumerism and the impact of eroding privacy on freedom of association.

There is no denying the increasing commercialisation of the Web on the one hand and the ongoing digital divide on the other. New technologies may well prove once again to be at the service of capitalism rather than social equality, but as alternative political movements grow in number and share information, knowledge and education, those in power are increasingly forced to reassess their views of minority and marginalised groups. In spite of attempts to criminalise many of their activities, the unrest in France and the ongoing Palestinian struggle have proved that it is possible to use the Net as a political and civic forum, and that the often vacuous virtual world has real material relations with mainstream society.

Notes

1 In an interview with *La Repubblica* both Richard Stallman and Richard Sterling have argued the case for free software: '. . . users should be free to study the workings of a program, modify it to their needs, distribute copies of it to other people and publish the improved copies. And if you are not programmers, you can charge somebody else for the task. This is what we mean when we talk about "free software": whether it is free in money terms doesn't influence its nature' (my translation). R. Staglianó, interview with Richard Stallman, 'Il Software deve essere tutto libero (Software must all be free), http://www.Repubblica.it, 8 April 2002.

2 John Barger is the creator of Robotwisdom, a website where he has posted comments and links from 1997 onwards (http://www.robotwisdom.com/).

3 See 'Play with your Words', posted on 17.5.2002 (http://www.peterme.com/archives/00000205.html).

4 For a chronology of the events from 25 October to 14 November see *BBC News Online*, 14 November 2005.

5 For current statistics about Internet access around the world see http://www.Internetworldstats.com/

6 A term introduced by Wellman et al. (2001: 1): 'Community Commitment: Social capital consists of more than going through the motions of interpersonal interaction and organisational involvement. When people have a strong attitude toward community – have a motivated, responsible sense of belonging – they will mobilise their social capital more willingly and effectively.'

7 'French President Jacques Chirac has vowed to create new opportunities for young people in an effort to prevent any resurgence of urban violence' in 'Chirac in new pledge to end riots', *BBC News Online*, 15 November 2005.

8 Wellman et al. (2001) note that heavy Internet use is associated with increased participation in voluntary organisations and politics. Further support for this effect is the positive association between offline and online participation in voluntary organisations and politics.

9 Statistics from the International Telecommunications Union (see online at: http://www.itu.int/home/).

10 The World Social Forum (WSF) was set up as a counter-movement to the World Economic Forum. One of its key initiatives is to challenge the global economic institutions which have failed to narrow the poverty gap. See Cere (2003: 157–159).

References

Blog Herald (2005) (online at: http://www.blogherald.com/2005/11/08/blogs-being-used-to-urge-french-riots/).

Blood, R. (2002) Introduction in Rodzilla, J. ed., *We've Got Blog. How Weblogs Are Changing Our Culture*. Cambridge, MA: Perseus Publishing.

Bunt, G. (2006) 'Towards an Islamic information revolution?', in E. Poole and J. E. Richardson (eds), *Muslims and the News Media*. London: IB Tauris.

Castells, M. (1996) *The Information Age: Economy, Society and Culture. The Rise of the Network Society*. Vol. 1. Oxford: Blackwell.

Cere, R. (2003) 'Digital counter-cultures and the nature of electronic social and political movements', in Y. Jewkes (ed.), *Dot.cons: Crime, Deviance and Identity on the Internet*. Cullompton: Willan.

Chadwick, A. (ed.) (2006) *Internet Politics: States, Citizens, and New Communications Technology*. Oxford: Oxford University Press.

Coleman, S., Taylor, J. and van De Donk, W. (1999) *Parliament in the Age of the Internet*. Oxford: Oxford University Press.

Davis, R. (1999) *The Web of Politics: The Internet's Impact on the American Political System*. Oxford: Oxford University Press.

Downing, J. D. H. (2001) *Radical Media: Rebellious Communication and Social Movements*. Thousand Oaks, CA: Sage.

Felouzis, G. and Perroton, J. (2005) 'The trouble with the schools', *Le Monde diplomatique*, December.

Gillies, J. and Cailliau, R. (2000) *How the Web Was Born: The History of the World Wide Web*. Oxford: Oxford University Press.

Himanen, P. (2001) *The Hacker Ethic and the Spirit of the Information Age*. London: Vintage.

Jihad Online: Anti-Defamation League (2002), Islamic Terrorists and the Internet.

Jordan, T. (1999) *Cyberpower: The Culture and Politics of Cyberspace and the Internet*. London: Routledge.

Levine, P. (2002) 'The Internet and civil society' (online at: http://www.imdp.org/artman/publish/cat_index_9.shtml.htm).

Levy, S. (1984) *Hackers: Heroes of the Computer Revolution*. Garden City, NY: Doubleday.

Manion, M. and Goodrum, A. (2001) 'Terrorism or civil disobedience: toward a hacktivist ethic', in R. H. Spinello and H. T. Tavani (eds), *Readings in CyberEthics*. Sudbury: Jones & Bartlett.

Margolis, M. and Resnick, D. (2000) *Politics as Usual: The Cyberspace Revolution*. Thousand Oaks, CA: Sage.

Millard Burr, J. and Collins, R. O. (2006) *Alms for Jihad: Charity and Terrorism in the Islamic World*. Cambridge: Cambridge University Press.

Moore, M. and Williams, D. (2005) 'France's youth battles also waged on the Web', *Washington Post*, 10 November.

Philo, G. and Berry, M. (2004) *Bad News from Israel*. London: Pluto.

Said, E. W. (1991; 1st edn 1978) *Orientalism: Western Conceptions of the Orient*. London: Penguin.

Schofield, H. (2005) 'French rappers' prophecies come true', *BBC News Online*, 16 November.

Slevin, J. (2000) *The Internet and Society*. Cambridge, Polity Press.

Taylor, P. A. (1999) *Hackers: Crime in the Digital Sublime*. London: Routledge.

Taylor, P. A. (2003) 'Maestros or misogynists? Gender and the social construction of hacking', in Y. Jewkes (ed.), *Dot.cons: Crime, Deviance and Identity on the Internet*. Cullompton: Willan.

Thrift, N. (1996) 'New urban eras and old technological fears: reconfiguring the goodwill of electronic things', *Urban Studies*, 33: 8, 1463–94.

Vidal, D. (2005) 'The fight against urban apartheid', *Le Monde diplomatique*, December (for the full report see: http://www.ccomptes.fr/Cour-des-comptes/publications/rapports/immigration/immigration.pdf).

Virilio, P. (2000) *The Information Bomb*. London: Verso.

Wall, D. (ed.) (2001) *Crime and the Internet*. London: Routledge.

Weiman, G. (2006) *Terror on the Internet: The New Arena, the New Challenges*. Washington, DC: United States Institute of Peace Press.

Wellman, B., Quan Haase, A., Witte, J. and Hampton, K. (2001) Does the Internet Increase, Decrease, or Supplement Social Capital? Social Networks, Participation and Community Commitment. Centre for Urban and Community Studies, Research Bulletin, No. 6, University of Toronto.

Zanini, M. (1999) 'Middle Eastern terrorism and Netwar', *Studies in Conflict and Terrorism*, 22: 247–56.

Websites

http://www.virtuallyislamic.com/
http://virtuallyislamic.blogspot.com/
http://www.palestine-info.co.uk/
http://www.palestine-info.cc/french/

Chapter 11

Beyond 'the desert of the real': crime control in a virtual(ised) reality

Katja Franko Aas[1]

Introduction

'Welcome to the desert of the real' was Morpheus' greeting to Neo in the iconic 1999 movie *The Matrix*. Neo, the main hero of the movie, realises that the 'reality' he was accustomed to is a virtual reality simulation created by a powerful artificial intelligence. Reality is fiction, a delusion piped into people's heads by machines in order to keep them in a perpetual state of slavery. Eventually awoken from the pre-programmed virtual world, Neo is met with a devastated landscape of Chicago in the aftermath of a global war. This is the 'desert of the real', resembling the images of war-stricken areas of Chechnya, Sarajevo or Falluja.

The *Matrix* trilogy has gained a considerable popular and academic following. The line 'welcome to the desert of the real', originally Baudrillard's (1994), was famously taken up by Žižek (2002) in his interpretation of the events of 11 September 2001. The fallen twin towers were seen as representing an abrupt influx of the real into the virtualised and insulated world of First World citizens. According to Žižek (2002), the collapse of the World Trade Center can be seen as a violent intrusion which managed to penetrate the 'phantasmic screen' separating the digitalised First World from the realities of the Third World. Ironically, this intrusion of the real itself resembles a spectacle. Drawing heavily on Baudrillard's (1994) work, Žižek describes western citizens as living in a de-materialised, artificial universe, resembling Hollywood movies and television commercials. '[T]he ultimate truth of the capitalist utilitarian

160

de-spiritualised universe is the de-materialisation of the "real life" itself, its reversal into a spectral show' (Žižek, 2002: 14).

This thought may no longer be particularly provocative, nor for that matter original. Simulation has by now taken its due place in cultural studies, philosophy and cultural theory. Nevertheless, criminological parallels to these developments are somewhat harder to find. While research on cyberspace has been experiencing a steady growth, there is still a clear boundary between the field of cybercrime and what might be termed 'terrestrial criminology', with the latter receiving the vast majority of criminological attention. Apart from sporadic discussions about whether, and to what extent, cybercrime differs from its terrestrial counterparts (Grabosky, 2001; Jewkes, 2003; Yar, 2005), online aspects of our sociality and social governance tend to be studied as a relatively separate realm, consigned to books and journals specifically dedicated to the topic. While these divisions of labour may be grounded in clear discontinuities between the offline and online realms, I would like to suggest that there is a need to explore possible meeting points between terrestrial criminology and the 'Internet galaxy', and between territorial and cyber governance. Challenging the perception of cyberspace as a separate sovereign world can, among other things, enhance our under-standing of the relevance of cyberstudies for criminological theory in general.

My objective in this chapter is therefore to explore the dynamics between offline and online aspects of social governance, particularly governance of crime. The fascination, sometimes resembling an obsession, that so many hold for *The Matrix* stems partly from the movie's intriguing ability to question the perceived 'reality' of the world we live in and the enslaving potential of virtuality.[2] The simulations we live in for part or most of our lives do have a 'real' impact. They are an essential aspect of social governance. The extraterritoriality of contemporary technologies calls into question a number of presuppositions about life and where it is lived. In the sociality mediated by the so-called space of information flows (Castells, 1996), physical reality may be just one of the 'windows' we have opened at a particular point in life while other windows may be open to our cyber lives or satellite-mediated realities (Turkle, 1995). The Net is therefore not a sphere situated at the outskirts of society, proverbially populated by nerds and deviants, but rather is woven into central aspects of contemporary social and economic life, including the discursive and practical aspects of crime and punishment.

An exploration of connections between online and offline social interaction would hopefully contribute to, on the one hand, a better understanding of how various forms and degrees of virtualisation are inscribed into 'real life' contexts and situations, and on the other hand the importance of 'multiple external contexts' (Kendall, 2002: 9) for the understanding of the life online. The objective is to look at the multiple meeting points, the blurring of boundaries and new hybridities created through the intertwining of the virtual and the real. The following discussion will therefore address the question of how the 'matrix' of our corporeal lives differs from the matrix of our cyber lives, if at all. What separates them and what brings them together? How are mediation and simulation present in the offline governance of crime and deviance, and what are the consequences for criminological theory?

The 'passion for the Real'

It may no longer be necessary to point out the extent to which information and communication technologies (ICTs) have become engrained into the fabric of our daily lives and have become a cornerstone of the new global economic order (Castells, 2001). According to some reports, the average Briton spends around 164 minutes online every day, compared with 148 minutes watching television (*Guardian*, 8 March 2006). This connectivity has inevitably been a source of vulnerability and insecurity, as pointed out by several contributions in this volume. My children's Internet use and my online eBay and Amazon.com accounts make me feel more vulnerable than if I simply forget to lock my home when leaving for work (see Brenner, this volume). Nevertheless, these risks and insecurities have been somewhat slow to penetrate the cannon of mainstream criminology.[3] In that respect criminology may be prone to, paraphrasing Žižek (2002), a certain 'passion for the Real', privileging 'real' life and experiences.

The relative reluctance of criminologists to incorporate the subject of cyber life into their research and writing may partly stem from some central theoretical dualisms and binary oppositions between beings and things, and technology and society, which define the conceptual apparatus of criminology. Brown argues that:

> Criminology has frequently been overly preoccupied with theoretical binary oppositions and this has resulted in a commitment to boundary maintenance strategies within criminological knowledge. The complexities of contemporary technological culture, however, demand precisely the dissolution of binary oppositions and, more particularly, human/technical splitting in the apprehension of the phenomenon of crime. (2006: 223)

This dualist approach, and its inherent tendency to essentialise the technological as instrumental properties of 'things', fails to recognise the transformative qualities of ICTs on the nature of our sociality and subjectivity. Maintaining clear boundaries between the social and the technical, and the 'real' and the virtual, is a strategy wrought with paradox in a world increasingly marked by global communication flows, mediation and simulation (Baudrillard, 1994; Shields, 2003). Nobody inhabits only cyberspace, and increasingly fewer people populate only the physical world as well (Kendall, 2002). However, the perception of life on the screen as an essentially separate realm of existence is not only endorsed by criminological 'realists' but also by many students and participants of cyber life who argue for its unique nature as a space of freedom. As Kendall (2002: 10) notes, 'much of the hype and hope of cyberspace reside in its sovereignty and separation from "real life" and its ability to correct the inequalities existing outside its boundaries'.

On the other hand, inspired by the so-called actor-network theory popularised by Latour and Callon, Brown (2006) proposes developing a 'criminology of hybrids' in order to account for the blurring lines between the technical and non-technical realms. Similarly, Barry (2001) tries to bridge the gap between the social and the technical by suggesting that we should focus instead on concrete arrangements of people and technical products in various forms and circumstances:

[I]nstead of drawing a line between the social and the technical, one might instead analyse *arrangements*: of artefacts, practices and techniques, instruments, language and bodies. These arrangements make up what we tend to think of as persons and institutions: states, markets, families and so on. They are collectivities which include technological components. In principle, the complexity of such arrangements is irreducible to their distinct 'social' and 'technical', 'natural' and 'cultural' elements. (Barry, 2001: 9, emphasis in original)

Consequently, Brown (2006) questions the view of cybercrime as a separate realm with its own rules of behaviour. While undoubtedly carrying much leverage, the perception of cybercrime as a *sui generis* category, distinct from 'embodied' crime, further emphasises the boundaries between the virtual and the 'real'. Brown (2006: 236) on the other hand suggests that 'crimes as network activities only contain varying degrees of virtual or embodied monads'. This approach therefore emphasises the blending of the virtual and the physical, and the creation of new hybrid forms of sociality. Similarly, the 'Virtual Society? Get Real!' appeal by Woolgar (2002) not only aptly covers the need to calm down the hype and hyperbole surrounding the alleged exceptionality of the virtual, but also serves as an encouragement to inscribe the virtual into the real-life contexts from which it emerges.

'Look past the flesh and see your enemy'

The previous discussion indicates that the meaning of the virtual is far from obvious. Shields (2003) points out that the term has a long history:

from various rituals and ritual spaces to *trompe-l'oeil* simulations in baroque architecture and beliefs in angels and ghosts. As such, the virtual represents 'a long held human capacity for imagination and a perceptual flair for filling in the gaps and flashing out visual images' (p. 71). Today, there is talk of the virtual office, virtual university, virtual relationships, virtual tours and even virtual warfare. Virtualisation is a vital part of the global capitalist economy (Castells, 2002; see Cere, this volume). The digital virtuality of the Internet and of computer games is therefore only one of several forms of virtuality present in contemporary life.

It is also not uncommon, (including in academic discussions) to find a phenomenon's importance – and hence 'reality' – illustrated by the number of 'hits' it gets on the Internet. Nor is it uncommon to 'Google' a person or subject to gain an impression of their nature. Therefore, rather than opposing the virtual with the real, Shields (2003) suggests that the virtual should be opposed to the actual and the concrete. Seen from this perspective, the virtual is real, but it is so only in essence and 'not actually so' (ibid.: 43). This view demands that we broaden our understanding of 'reality' and break it down 'into more fine-grained concepts' (ibid.: 20). It will be argued throughout this chapter that it is precisely an awareness of the hybridity of 'reality' that enables us to understand the various aspects and degrees of virtuality in many forms of contemporary crime and its control.

Teenagers playing online computer games may not inhabit the same physical space, yet they simultaneously interact in a *social* space, building teams and memories of youthful mastery, conquest and adventure which have as much an effect on their offline friendships as they do online. 'Real-life' embodied friendships are thus built through participation in online environments: 'Just as the virtual becomes more a part of everyday thought process, so everyday life is mixed up in the digitally virtual' (Shields, 2003: 114). Similarly, contemporary sex work and the sex trade in many ways retain their essentially embodied and abusive nature, while at the same time being facilitated and transformed by information and communication technologies such as the Internet and mobile phones (Altman, 2001; Sharp and Earle, 2003). The Internet offers prostitution guides to potential sex tourists and local customers in almost any corner of the world (Monzini, 2005). And while the famous 'electronic cloak' (DiMarco, 2003) enables netizens to experiment with their identity and to free themselves from the constraints of embodiment, some findings suggest that people's online personas often bear a considerable resemblance to their embodied counterparts, and that so-called virtual identities are often strongly connected to the 'real' selves (Kendall, 2002; Woolgar, 2002). Relationships of power, gender, race and global economic inequality are permeating cyber life, and are inscribed in cyber relations, just as they are in terrestrial life (Jewkes and Sharp, 2003; Cunneen and Stubbs, 2004). Kendall therefore argues that:

People who choose to enter online social spaces do not leave their offline world behind when they do so, but rather begin a process of weaving online communications and activities into their existing offline lives. (2002: 16)

This process of 'weaving' is precisely what I want to examine further in this chapter, the exceptional growth of blogging in recent years being one case in point. Life on the screen is not only a space of freedom from terrestrial constraints and governmental intervention but is gradually becoming an essential medium through which contemporary social mobilisations, including those related to crime and punishment, take place (see also Cere, this volume). Online communication has become 'an important site for the contestation of group values. Indeed, it is through this very contestation that new forms of collectivity are imagined and performed' (Valier, 2004: 93).

It is a telling example that the prime 'public enemies' of our time, Osama Bin Laden and his alleged network, are rendered 'real' primarily through various forms of virtually mediated reality such as videos and recorded messages posted on the Internet. Furthermore, abductions and executions of hostages in Iraq are frequently confirmed to global audiences by online videos. In that respect, 'look past the flesh and see your enemy', yet another *Matrix* line, captures the spirit. The Internet is therefore not only marked by its potential to obscure the face of the Other, but is also increasingly becoming a forum for creating images of the Other – not only criminal offenders, but also members of religious and ethnic groups, or, for that matter, supporters of opposing football teams (see also Fafinski, this volume). And as much as radical Muslim identities tend to be described as primitive and uncivilised by the various 'clash of civilisations' theses, they are sustained by distinctly global networks of communications such as the Internet, mobile phones and global television networks. Online connections are nurturing offline mobilisations by evoking a language adjusted to the cultural ethos of the MTV generation. Despite a pervasive digital divide in the Muslim world, Bunt (2003) points out that in the post 9/11 context, the Internet and cyber Islamic environments have played a major role in the development of various new forms of Muslim consciousness and activism (see Cere, this volume). Online environments are a part of the so-called global mediascapes and technoscapes (Appadurai, 1996) and are becoming essential forums for identity constitution. Taking a cue from these findings, I will proceed to explore some possible meeting points between online and offline sociality. An attempt will be made to re-examine the online/offline division, focusing primarily on the emerging hybrid notions of community, identity and governance.

Virtual or virtualised communities?

In his characteristically radical evaluation of the American condition, Baudrillard suggests that it is beyond the point to look for the 'real' behind the simulation, as simulation *is* social reality. Today, the question is no longer one of false representation of reality but 'of concealing the fact that the real is no longer real, and thus of saving the reality principle' (1994: 13). Baudrillard highlights Disneyland as the paradigmatic representation of the contemporary simulated existence. However, rather than describing Disneyland as exceptional, he claims that 'Disneyland exists in order to hide that it is the "real" country, all of America, that *is* Disneyland' (ibid.: 12). The theme has been taken up in recent years by a number of authors analysing simulated environments such as theme parks, tourist enclaves, shopping malls, restaurant and hotel chains, and the like, which have gradually become a prominent aspect of our daily lives (Cubitt, 2001). In his influential *Disneyisation of Society* Bryman (2004) argues that the contemporary world is increasingly converging towards the characteristics of the Disney theme parks.[4]

This literature raises the question of whether we can draw the line between the simulated and the 'authentic', including people's own experiences of their surroundings. In a recent documentary one resident of the celebrated Disney-created town Celebration recounted his experience: 'It was like coming home' (NRK, 2005). Home, however, was in this case a place that had previously never existed and was based on fictional representations. The point here is that staged reality may be experienced as 'authentic', perhaps in some cases even more authentic than the mundane and often dreary surroundings we otherwise inhabit.[5] One could clearly argue that the aforementioned academic perception of the contemporary (particularly American) condition as inauthentic and simulated is itself becoming somewhat of a cliché. Simulation theory is, as Cubitt (2001: 99) points out, open to the accusation that it plays 'a part in the processes through which the world loses its reality'. However, the theory's fundamental redrawing of the concept of 'real' and 'reality' is an important contribution which I want to draw further on in the remainder of this chapter.

Hayward (2004) points to the general criminological significance of consumer culture for the transformation of the contemporary urban experience. He raises the question of whether simulated urban spaces, exemplified by Ropongi, Tokyo, represent 'the future for urban spaces based around pleasure and entertainment':

> Groups of young people of differing nationalities staring into multi-sonorous screens, popping strobes and virtual reality headsets, each one obsessively re-playing looped games, prior to heading out into

the trance-like world of Ropongi's 'club scene' to experience yet another 'controlled loss of control', this time via a combination of digitally looped dance music and designer drugs. (2004: 193)

Contemporary web-based technologies therefore need to be understood within the broader social context of blurring boundaries between the virtual and the real, and of how simulation is inscribed into everyday life. California residents, for example, can obtain information about registered sex offenders in their community on a website operated by the Office of the Attorney General (http://www.meganslaw.ca.gov/). Information provided includes name, aliases, age, gender, race, physical description and photograph, as well as an individual's criminal convictions. Users can search the website by city, county, zip code or individual name. They can also type in the name of a park or school in a community to locate on a digital map sex offenders living in the vicinity. Importantly, the site provides home addresses of about 33,500 of the most serious offenders. Similar, more or less extensive registers are available in the majority of the US states. In this context, the virtually-mediated dangers can be experienced as more 'real' than individuals' actual and concrete experiences of these dangers, thus creating a separate world of hyper-real danger in the community (Shields, 2003).

The 'Megan's Law' mapping system described above can be seen as yet another example of the emerging surveillance society (Lyon, 2001). However, it also provides an insight into the changing notions of community and danger. The system represents by no means the kind of community that first comes to mind when we think of a virtual community. Nonetheless, it is an example of how the new punitive discourse about community safety – represented by the website's motto 'keeping children safe/parents informed' – is appropriating the surveillance potential of the latest technologies. And although the system can be seen as yet another example of the famous American exceptionalism, it needs to be pointed out that online mapping of offline dangers is a far more pervasive phenomenon. Geographic information systems (GIS) are gradually becoming a standard item of police equipment. Besides being a tool for facilitating efficiency and effectiveness of policing and allocation of resources, these systems also offer a simulated construction of community as an 'information hub'. Introducing the language of 'crime hotspots', 'criminogenic areas' and 'yob maps' (Coleman, 2004: 79), these systems provide and create images of low- and high-risk communities to the police and other agencies (Gundhus, 2005).

Graham (1998) points out that through the creation of 'spaces of surveillant simulation':

such simulations of the real world are then used to support new spatial practices based on the fine-grained allocation of goods and services, and intimate patterns of attempted social control, in real time, through the time-space fabric of material geographies. (1998: 483)

Through the use of geographically based statistical information about crime, demography and other aspects of their work, police and other agencies are able to enter various risk minimalisation strategies (Gundhus, 2005). Information sharing between the police and their partners, as well as the public, is a vital aspect of these strategies, as exemplified by the US Weed and Seed system where one can obtain information not only about crime-related matters, but also about the racial and ethnic composition of a community, demographic trends and income, education and housing levels of the local residents (http://www.weedandseed.info/). In this context deviance is not a normative concept but rather a question of collective community deviance defined through a departure from a digitally mapped statistical average. Crime mapping thus transforms the community from a concrete, local entity into an abstract simulation, aptly summarised in the motto of the West Midlands online system, modestly named COSMOS: 'The universe regarded as an orderly, harmonious whole' (http://www.cosmos-bcsp.com/mission.htm).[6]

As the examples of GIS and online sex offender registers indicate, the virtual is intricately woven into contemporary (actual and concrete) practices of social exclusion. Many aspects of community safety practices are shot through with virtualisation and 'surveillant simulation'. The question therefore arises: what is virtual and what is real? And what, after all, *is* a virtual community?

'We are all Danes now'

In contrast to the calculated risk management aspects outlined above, the Internet also represents a forum for more emotional, often hateful, discourses about deviance and crime control. In her analysis of online communication about crimes, trials and punishment, Valier (2004) shows how the Internet has become a site for various forms of 'technological populism' by encouraging popular participation in web polls and debates about crime and punishment, while framing the discussions in terms of 'tabloid justice':

The Internet plays an important part in the spread of tabloid justice. It permits anyone to act as reporter or publisher of images and information, to transmit material on any topic to a potentially global audience, as well as allowing people to participate in real-time conversations with distant others. (ibid.: 97)

Through online communication the 'new punitiveness' (Pratt et al., 2005) finds an additional forum, particularly as the Internet to a large extent transcends the restrictions imposed on print and television by legal and professional journalistic standards. The shift in the balance between populism and professionalism (Garland, 2001) therefore gains an additional dimension through the mushrooming of online forums.

Rather than seeing the Internet as an agent of social anomie and individualism or, alternatively, as an embodiment of the libertarian ideas of cyber tolerance and democracy, Valier (2004) points to emerging forms of online community and solidarity relating to issues of crime and punishment. Online communications 'bring new forms of imagined co-presence and connectedness, which question the Durkheimian association of the passion of punishment with locally or nationally based *communitas*' (p. 109). In highly publicised murder cases, such as that of James Bulger, these communications may obtain a global reach and form 'transnational vengeful networks' (p. 103) .What is important here is that the extraterritorial nature of online communication transforms the dynamics of public penal discourse and social belonging, which has been traditionally connected to bounded local and national communities.

The extraterritorial nature of new technologies opens up new and broader forms of solidarity. However, the idea of 'unbounded sociability' promoted by the early virtual community enthusiasts (Rheingold, 1993), clearly has some exclusionary undertones. 'We are all Danes now' was a message emerging on several websites in the aftermath of this year's heated discussions about Muhammad cartoons, first published in a Danish newspaper. The message was reminiscent of the one displayed on the cover of the French newspaper *Le Monde*, in the aftermath of the 11 September attacks, proclaiming that 'We are all Americans now'. Other than expressing global solidarity, the messages are a sign of the emerging 'world risk society', a society connected by its shared awareness and fear of 'de-bounded' global risks (Beck, 2002; Aas, 2006). The so far privileged position of the state and the national as the primary field of criminological reference seems to be increasingly overshadowed by various transnational and subnational configurations (Aas, 2006). Within the context of the network society and the space of flows, racial and religious hatred as well as fear and solidarity transcend national boundaries and increasingly gain transnational dimensions.

Emerging notions of online community need to be understood within the broader context of global transformations and the virtualisation of the transnational into a hybrid online/offline globality.[7] The world of global networks and flows introduces new notions of social ordering and exclusion, as well as challenging the prevailing conceptions of society, community, culture, and social belonging (Aas, 2006). Therefore, the virtual/real dichotomy runs parallel with the more frequently debated global/local division. Robertson's (1995) highly influential term 'glocalisation' may be a useful pointer here, denoting the immanent intertwining of the global and the local, as well as the online and offline hybridity. As Appadurai points out when it comes to the question of virtual neighbourhoods:

> These virtual neighbourhoods seem on the face of it to represent just that absence of face-to-face links, spatial contiguity, and multiplex social interaction that the idea of a neighbourhood seems centrally to imply. Yet we must not be too quick to oppose highly spatialised neighbourhoods to these virtual neighbourhoods of international electronic communication. The relationship between these two forms of neighbourhood is considerably more complex. (Appadurai, 1996: 195)

Appadurai points out that in the case of long-distance nationalism, virtual neighbourhoods have a considerable impact on locally lived neighbourhoods by mobilising ideas, opinions, money and social linkages. The perception of the Internet, and globalisation in general, as the antithesis of local community has shown to be a truth with many modifications. Even though the technical space of the Internet appears to be boundless, its social space and effects are not necessarily global, but rather depend on multiple local contexts and constraints.

Online social environments are not only media for almost unlimited self-expression and experimentation with identity, although this certainly is the case (Jewkes, 2003), but also spaces for shaping and maintaining typically 'terrestrial' social mobilisations, such as national(istic) and diasporic identities and discourses about crime and punishment. In addition to providing 'a locus for creative authorship of the self' (Jewkes and Sharp, 2003: 3), through blogs, chat groups and other fora, the Net also increasingly becomes a locus for constructing the face of our (global) Others, and thus becomes an integral part of contemporary strategies of social exclusion. Innumerable Internet marriage marketing sites, for example, offer First World men essentialised and racialised representations of Third World women as commodities. These virtually mediated male fantasies can often, as Cunneen and Stubbs (2004) show, end in a tragically violent reality. Similarly, the process of constructing and engaging with 'exotic others' through numerous sex tourism websites has made commercial sex an essential part of the contemporary tourist experience (Altman, 2001; O'Connell Davidson, 2005). These cyber subjectivities therefore precede physical encounters, often creating images of 'perfect partners' which are impossible to fulfil in reality (Cunneen and Stubbs, 2004). The virtual tourist and the virtual mail-order bride are marked by racial, economic and sexual relations whose online and offline dimensions are hard to untwine (Letherby and Marchbank, 2003).

Governance in a 'borderless' world

Links to a bloody new Flash videogame called Border Patrol, whose object is to kill as many illegal immigrants as possible, are making the rounds through email forwards. The game, which comes at a time when US leaders are working to revive a sweeping immigration bill in the Senate, encourages players to kill targets such as a 'Mexican nationalist', 'drug smuggler' and 'breeder' (a pregnant woman with two small children) 'at any cost' ... 'I certainly defend the game,' says self-described white supremacist Tom Metzger. 'I told a Mexican activist that he better be happy that we're just playing a game on a computer, because the temper of thousands ... is reaching boiling point'. (Newsweek, 2006a)

In Bordergames, freely available on the Web at bordergames.org, the player can take on the role of a young North African immigrant. Having entered Spain illegally and settled in Madrid, he must find work, avoid deportation, choose friends wisely and sidestep potential enemies. Social workers can help him integrate or find a job, but telling them his real name and hometown could lead to deportation. Drug dealers may be the wrong types to associate with, but they procure papers in order to find work ... (Newsweek, 2006b)

Terrestrial borders were for a long time seen as the antithesis of cyberlife. The prevailing image of the Internet was of a boundless economic frontier, a realm of freedom, often seen also as an almost complete absence of constraints, resembling a state of nature or the Wild West (Kendall, 2002). This perception of cyberspace as an idealised version of the liberal society – self-regulating, populated by free individuals engaged in communities of common interests – had a clear affinity with the laissez-faire ideology of the 1980s and 1990s and the prevailing ideal of minimal state and other regulatory intervention. In the heyday of neo-liberalism some observers also seemed to think that globalisation would eventually lead to a borderless world (Ohmae, 1990). This enchantment with the notion of a borderless world, however, was considerably longer-lived in the case of cyber-libertarians than it was in the case of terrestrial neo-liberal societies. Borders, and the protection of borders, have become an extremely salient and heated topic in the post-9/11 world (Aas, 2006), as the two computer games described above symbolically illustrate.

More important at this point is that the popular notion of cyberspace as a 'new frontier' and a space of unencumbered freedom has also gone through some fundamental revisions. One of the most salient criticisms came from Lawrence Lessig's *Code and Other Laws of Cyberspace* (1999). Refuting the popular perception that cyberspace 'cannot be governed', Lessig powerfully argues that the Net is evolving from 'an unregulable space to one that is highly regulable. The "nature" of the Net might once have been its unregulability; that "nature" is about to flip' (p. 25). Consequently, governance of the Internet is increasingly designed to fit the predominant features of the contemporary market societies:

[T]he invisble hand of cyberspace is building an architecture that is quite the opposite of what it was at cyberspace's birth. The invisible hand, through commerce, is constructing an architecture that perfects control – an architecture that makes possible highly efficient regulation. (Ibid.: 6)

Therefore, when it comes to online governance, the focus is gradually moving beyond the abstract debates between libertarians and proponents of state intervention, and acknowledging instead the specific varieties of technologies of governance that invariably develop in any kind of human interaction. We are witnessing not only the introduction of various types of private commercial barriers and surveillance efforts, but also a continuing salience of state surveillance and intervention, justified by a variety of online and offline concerns such as terrorism, pornography, spam, intellectual property rights and free speech (Luke, 1999; Lyon, 2003). Preston (2004) points out that, contrary to popular belief, state policies have been essential to the Internet's genesis, growth, direction and governance (security policy, content regulation and access), and that this political intervention in Internet governance and development can have a potentially positive role. This, of course, is still an intensely debated issue, and disagreements between cyber 'regulators' and 'libertarians' may at times seem as heated as ever, with the former, however, increasingly gaining ground when it comes to dictating practice.

In cyberlife, as in terrestrial life, the notion of freedom from regulation privileges a certain set of social values at the expense of others. Like our terrestrial selves, our cyber selves populate thoroughly regulated and commercialised environments, where democratically elected bodies lose out to private forms of regulation in the name of freedom. One of the major critiques mounted by Lessig is that the architecture of the Internet itself is not neutral and that we need to unveil the normative behind the seemingly 'natural' and technical. 'Code codifies values, and yet, oddly, most people speak as if code were just a question of engineering' (Lessig, 1999: 59). The code regulating cyberspace comes closer to natural laws, making breaches not only illegal but also impossible, just as architectural features of our physical environments enable certain behaviours while precluding others. The blurring lines between the normative and the technical are also gradually becoming a topic of criminological research due to the increasingly code-like language of 'terrestrial' penal governance (Deleuze, 1997; Lianos and Douglas, 2000; Jones, 2000; Aas, 2005).

Contemporary governance is adopting the language of computer-mediated technologies. And even though the buzz word of e-governance perhaps hasn't quite lived up to its hype, it is making an unmistakable impact on the ways we govern and relate to social institutions. Understanding the parameters of cyber governance may therefore open up more productive ways of examining and understanding the offline mechanisms of social governance (Jones, 2005).

Conclusion

Acknowledging the blurred lines of distinction between the 'virtual' and the 'real' carries a number of benefits for criminological enquiry. Issues of cybercrime and 'life on the screen' touch on some of the central themes and transformations within the field of criminological interests: from questions of impersonality and disembeddedness of social relations, transnational crime and the changing role of the state in a globalising world, to the issues of postmodernity, subjectivity, technology and control. The purpose of this chapter has been to reflect on the ability of cyberspace and ICTs in general to redefine and bring new dimensions to some central criminological concepts, from terms such as community, society, identity and danger, to the production of cultural values and mechanisms of social governance. The notion of pluralist governance (a lively topic of the present criminological discussions) and the diffusion of police and regulatory tasks has always been one of the trade marks of cyber governance (Jewkes, 2003). Furthermore, the constructed nature of space and identity, as well as crime and its victims, is accentuated in online environments. The question therefore arises as to whether there should be some lesson-drawing between 'terrestrial criminology' and its cyber counterpart?

The question of lesson-drawing becomes particularly relevant in the context of the increasingly transnationalising condition of criminological work and penal governance. The challenges posed by the extraterritorial nature of cyberspace clearly exemplify the changing parameters of penal governance, which is increasingly marked by its at-a-distance and geographically distributed nature (Aas, 2005). The extraterritoriality of the Internet and its (perceived and inherent) ingovernability challenge established notions of territorial penal governance. As Valier (2004: 92) observes:

> Penality has conventionally been thought in terms of the bounded entities of local community and nation-state. The penal practices of today however are shaped by the myriad ways in which global networks and flows, exemplified by the Internet, reconfigure the significance of the nation state.

173

While criminology in general is still in many ways deeply attached to the notion of the territorial nation state, the phenomena it seeks to understand increasingly seem to be global and transnational (Aas, 2006).

There is therefore a need to develop concepts and methods that are sensitive to the complexities of the global. However, a considerable part of criminological research appears in many ways to be guilty of what Beck (2002) terms 'methodological nationalism' – equating social boundaries with state boundaries, and having a nation-state outlook on society, law and justice. This may be partly due to the traditional connection between criminological knowledge and the nation-state apparatus. Consequently, criminology still is theoretically and methodologically badly equipped for understanding the relevance of the emerging space of flows (Aas, 2006). Here, cyber life with its (albeit mistaken) image of a boundless frontier may have much to offer, particularly as the old binary oppositions between the virtual and the 'real', global and local, and technological and social, become fluid and increasingly hard to discern.

Notes

1 Thanks to Heidi Mork Lomell and Richard Jones for their helpful comments, and to the Norwegian Research Council's KIM program for their generous financial support.
2 Even though *The Matrix* draws heavily on his work, Baudrillard himself describes the movie as a misunderstanding of his work due to the fact that it still envisages simulation as something that one can be freed of and step outside of. In that respect, Baudrillard argues, the movie's understanding of simulation comes closer to the concept of illusion (http://www.empyree.org/divers/Matrix-Baudrillard_english.htm l).
3 The words cyber and Internet do not appear in the prestigious *Oxford Handbook of Criminology* (Maguire et al., 2002), and these topics are only gradually attracting the attention of criminological textbooks.
4 One needs only to think of Dubai, one of the centres of the world economy and tourism, which is a city wrought through with simulation. One can ski in the middle of the desert, shop in immense shopping malls, play golf or tennis high above the sea and reside in gigantic hotels and on palm-shaped artificial islands.
5 Urry (2002: 9) points out that many tourist spaces are organised around 'staged authenticity' and a quest for experiences in other 'times' and other places away from everyday life.
6 As Gundhus (2005) points out, the level of abstraction embodied in GIS is by no means seen as unproblematic by police officers, who perceive statistical data as 'not nice to know' and contrast it with their own local knowledge and experiences from the streets.
7 I'm grateful to Richard Jones for bringing this to my attention.

References

Aas, K. F. (2005) *Sentencing in the Age of Information: From Faust to Macintosh*. London: GlassHouse Press.

Aas, K. F. (2006) 'Controlling a world in motion: global flows meet "criminology of the other"', *Theoretical Criminology*, 10 (forthcoming).

Altman, D. (2001) *Global Sex*. Chicago and London: University of Chicago Press.

Appadurai, A. (1996) *Modernity at Large: Cultural Dimensions of Globalization*. Minneapolis, MN: University of Minneapolis Press.

Barker, C. (1999) *Television, Globalization and Cultural Identities*. Buckingham: Open University Press.

Barry, A. (2001) *Political Machines: Governing a Technological Society*. London and New York: Athlone Press.

Baudrillard, J. (1994) *Simulacra and Simulation*. Ann Arbor, MI: University of Michigan Press.

Beck, U. (2002) 'The terrorist threat: world risk society revisited', *Theory, Culture & Society*, 19 (4): 39–55.

Beck, U. (2003) 'The analysis of global inequality: from national to cosmopolitan perspective', in M. Kaldor et al. (eds), *Global Civil Society*. London: Centre for the Study of Global Governance, Yearbook 2003.

Brown, S. (2006) 'The criminology of hybrids: rethinking crime and law and technosocial networks', *Theoretical Criminology*, 10 (2): 223–44.

Bryman, A. (2004) *The Disneyization of Society*. London: Sage.

Bunt, G. (2003) *Islam in the Digital Age: E-Jihad, Online Fatwas and Cyber Islamic Environments*. London and Sterling, VA: Pluto Press.

Castells, M. (1996) *The Rise of the Network Society*. Oxford: Blackwell.

Castells, M. (2002) *The Internet Galaxy: Reflections on the Internet, Business, and Society*. Oxford: Oxford University Press.

Coleman, R. (2004) *Reclaiming the Streets: Surveillance, Social Control and the City*. Cullompton: Willan.

Cubitt, S. (2001) *Simulation and Social Theory*. London: Sage.

Cunneen, C. and Stubbs, J. (2004) 'Cultural criminology and engagement with race, gender and post-colonial identities', in J. Ferrell et al. (eds), *Cultural Criminology Unleashed*. London: GlassHouse Press.

Deleuze, G. (1997) 'Postscript on the societies of control', in N. Leach (ed.), *Rethinking Architecture: A Reader in Cultural Theory*. London: Routledge.

DiMarco, H. (2003) 'The electronic cloak: secret sexual deviance in cybersociety', in Y. Jewkes (ed.) *Dot.cons: Crime, Deviance and Identity on the Internet*. Cullompton: Willan.

Garland, D. (2001) *The Culture of Control*. Oxford: Oxford University Press.

Grabosky, P. N. (2001) 'Virtual criminality: old wine in new bottles?', in *Social & Legal Studies*, 10 (2): 243–49.

Graham, S. (1998) 'Spaces of surveillant simulation: new technologies, digital representations, and material geographies', *Environment and Planning D: Society and Space*, 16: 483–504.

Guardian (2006) 'Britain turns off – and logs on' (online at: http://technology.guardian.co.uk/print/0,,329429230-117802,00.html).

Gundhus, H. (2005) '"Catching" and "Targeting": risk-based policing, local culture and gendered practices', *Journal of Scandinavian Studies in Criminology and Crime Prevention*, 6: 128–46.

Hayward, K. (2004) *City Limits: Crime, Consumer Culture and the Urban Experience*. London: GlassHouse Press.

Jewkes, Y. (ed.) (2003) *Dot.cons: Crime, Deviance and Identity on the Internet*. Cullompton: Willan.

Jewkes, Y. and Sharp, K. (2003) 'Crime, deviance and the disembodied self: transcending the dangers of corporeality', in Y. Jewkes, Y. (ed.), *Dot.cons: Crime, Deviance and Identity on the Internet*. Cullompton: Willan.

Jones, R. (2000) 'Digital rule: punishment, control and technology', *Punishment & Society*, 2 (1): 5–22.

Jones, R. (2005) 'Entertaining code: file sharing, digital rights management regimes, and criminological theories of compliance', *International Review of Law, Computers and Technology*, 19 (3): 287–303.

Kendall, L. (2002) *Hanging Out in the Virtual Pub: Masculinities and Relationships Online*. Berkeley, CA: University of California Press.

Lessig, L. (1999) *Code and Other Laws of Cyberspace*. New York: Basic Books.

Letherby, G. and Marchbank, J. (2003) 'Cyber-chattels: buying brides and babies on the Net' in Y. Jewkes (ed.), *Dot.cons: Crime, Deviance and Identity on the Internet*. Cullompton: Willan Publishing.

Lianos, M. with M. Douglas (2000) 'Dangerization and the end of deviance', in D. Garland and R. Sparks (eds), *Criminology and Social Theory*. Oxford: Oxford University Press.

Luke, T. W. (1999) 'Simulated sovereignty, telematic territoriality: the political economy of cyberspace', in M. Featherstone and S. Lash (eds), *Spaces of Culture: City – Nation – World*. London: Sage.

Lyon, D. (2001) *Surveillance Society: Monitoring Everyday Life*. Buckingham: Open University Press.

Lyon, D. (2003) *Surveillance After September 11*. Cambridge: Polity Press.

Maguire, M., Morgan, R. and Reiner, R. (eds) (2002) *The Oxford Handbook of Criminology*. Oxford: Oxford University Press.

Monzini, P. (2005) *Sex Traffic: Prostitution, Crime and Exploitation*. London and New York: Zed Books.

Newsweek (2006a) 'Games without frontiers', *Newsweek International*, 10 April, p. 12.

Newsweek (2006b) 'Over the (border) line' (online at: http://www.msnbc.msn.com/id/12554978/site/newsweek).

NRK (2005) *Celebration*. BBC Productions, 5 November.

O'Connell Davidson, J. (2005) *Children in the Global Sex Trade*. Cambridge: Polity.

Ohmae, K. (1990) *The Borderless World: Power and Strategy in the Interlinked Economy*. London: Collins.

Pratt, J., Brown, D., Brown, M., Hallworth, S. and Morrison, W. (eds) (2005) *The New Punitiveness: Trends, Theories, Perspectives*. Cullompton: Willan.

Preston, P. (2004) *The Meaning of Internet Governance*. Paper presented at the CMC Conference, Oslo, 3–4 November.

Rheingold, H. (1993) *The Virtual Community: Homesteading on the Electronic Frontier*. New York: Addison-Wesley.

Robertson, R. (1995) 'Glocalization: time – space and homogeneity – heterogeneity?', in M. Featherstone et al. (eds), *Global Modernities*. London: Sage.

Sharp, K. and Earle, S. (2003) 'Cyberpunters and cyberwhores: prostitution on the Internet', in Y. Jewkes (ed.), *Dot.cons: Crime, Deviance and Identity on the Internet*. Cullompton: Willan.

Shields, R. (2003) *The Virtual*. London and New York: Routledge.

Turkle, S. (1995) *Life on the Screen: Identity in the Age of the Internet*. London: Phoenix.

Urry, J. (2002) *The Tourist Gaze*, 2nd edn. London: Sage.

Valier, C. (2004) *Crime and Punishment in Contemporary Culture*. London and New York: Routledge.

Woolgar, S. (ed.) (2002) *Virtual Society? Technology, Cyberbole, Reality*. Oxford: Oxford University Press.

Yar, M. (2005) 'The novelty of "cybercrime": an assessment in light of routine activity theory', *European Journal of Criminology*, 2 (4): 407–27.

Žižek, S. (2002) *Welcome to the Desert of the Real! Five Essays on September 11 and Related Dates*. London and New York: Verso.

Index

Added to a page number 't' denotes a table.